AUSTRALIAN CITIES

OTHER MERIDIAN TITLES

Howard Bridgman, Robin Warner, and John Dodson, *Urban Biophysical Environments*

David Chapman, *Natural Hazards*, Second Edition

Arthur and Jeanette Conacher, *Rural Land Degradation in Australia*

Robert H. Fagan and Michael Webber, *Global Restructuring: The Australian Experience*, Second Edition

Dean Forbes, *Asian Metropolis: Urbanisation and the South-East Asian City*

Nick Harvey, *Environmental Impact Assessment: Procedures, Practice, and Prospects in Australia*

Nick Harvey and Brian Caton, *Coastal Management in Australia*

Iain Hay, *Communicating in Geography and the Environmental Sciences*

Iain Hay (ed.), *Qualitative Research Methods in Human Geography*

Louise Johnson, *Placebound: Australian Feminist Geographies*

Jamie Kirkpatrick, *A Continent Transformed: Human Impact on the Natural Vegetation of Australia*, Second Edition

Kevin O'Connor, Robert Stimson, and Maurice Daly, *Australia's Changing Economic Geography: A Society Dividing*

Elaine Stratford, *Australian Cultural Geographies*

AUSTRALIAN CITIES

CONTINUITY AND CHANGE

THIRD EDITION

CLIVE FORSTER

Series Editors
Deirdre Dragovich
Alaric Maude

OXFORD
UNIVERSITY PRESS

OXFORD
UNIVERSITY PRESS

253 Normanby Road, South Melbourne, Victoria 3205, Australia

Oxford University Press is a department of the University of Oxford.
It furthers the University's objective of excellence in research,
scholarship, and education by publishing worldwide in

Oxford New York

Auckland Bangkok Buenos Aires Cape Town Chennai
Dar es Salaam Delhi Hong Kong Istanbul Karachi Kolkata
Kuala Lumpur Madrid Melbourne Mexico City Mumbai Nairobi
São Paulo Shanghai Taipei Tokyo Toronto

OXFORD is a trade mark of Oxford University Press in the UK and
in certain other countries

National Library of Australia
Cataloguing-in-Publication data:

Forster,C. A. (Clive A.).
    Australian cities: continuity and change.

    3rd ed.
    Bibliography.
    Includes index.
    For tertiary students.
    ISBN 0 19 551734 2.

    1. Cities and towns—Australia—Growth. 2. Cities and
    towns—Australia—History. 3. City and town life—
    Australia. 4. City planning—Australia. 5. Urban policy—
    Australia. I. Title.

307.760994

Typeset by Cannon Typesetting
Printed by Bookpac Production Services, Singapore

Foreword

In recent years Australian geographers have produced some excellent textbooks that reflect the maturity of geographical research in this country. However, there is a continuing need for relatively short, low-cost books written for university students, books that fill the gap between chapter-length surveys and full-length texts and that explore the geographical issues and problems of Australia and its region, or present an Australian perspective on global geographical processes.

Meridian: Australian Geographical Perspectives is a series initiated by the Institute of Australian Geographers to fill this need. The term 'meridian' refers to a line of longitude linking points in a half-circle between the poles. In this series it symbolises the interconnections between places in the global environment and global economy, one of the key themes of contemporary geography.

The books in the series cover a variety of physical, environmental, economic, and social-geography topics, and are written for use in first- and second-year courses where existing texts and reference books lack a significant Australian perspective. To cope with the very varied content of geography courses taught in Australian universities, the books are not designed as comprehensive texts, but rather as modules on specific themes, to be used in a variety of courses. They are intended to be used either in one-semester courses, or in one-semester components of full-year courses.

Titles in the series cover a range of topics representing contemporary Australian teaching and research in geography—for example, economic restructuring, vegetation change, land degradation, cities, natural hazards, cultural geography, environmental impact assessment, and urban biophysical environments. Future topics include gender and geography, and coastal management. Although the emphasis in the series is on Australia, forthcoming publications in the series will include occasional titles on South-East Asia, drawing on the considerable expertise developed by Australian geographers in relation to this region.

In this third edition of *Australian Cities: Continuity and Change* Clive Forster examines Australian cities, the home and workplace of the majority of Australians, from the perspective of a geographer. The issues discussed are of continuing significance to debates about Australian society and economy, and have political relevance at state and federal levels. They include housing provision, urban planning for expanding cities, inequalities between suburbs, locational disadvantage, access to employment, urban consolidation, and the effects of economic restructuring. Differing ways of explaining what is happening in Australian cities, and differing viewpoints on what public policies, if any, are appropriate, are clearly and succinctly presented, and the competing pressures for economic efficiency, equity, and environmental sustainability are examined. While the book emphasises current changes in Australian cities, it is based on a clear account of how these cities have developed, for, as the author notes, 'we live, to a large extent, in yesterday's cities'.

Clive Forster has produced an exceptionally readable and balanced introduction to these issues, enlivened by his own brand of humour and ability to spot academic and bureaucratic pretensions. His book builds on thirty years of observing, researching, advising, and teaching on Australian cities, and draws on examples from all the major cities. It will be of interest to a wide variety of readers, including students of geography, urban planning, and urban sociology, and general readers interested in urban affairs.

DEIDRE DRAGOVICH,
University of Sydney

ALARIC MAUDE,
Flinders University

Contents

Figures

Tables

Acknowledgments

This book reflects thirty-five years spent teaching about and researching Australian cities. During those years my ideas about what is important have, like the cities themselves, undergone some fundamental restructurings. If students of today's cities find the outcome useful, much of the credit belongs to my colleagues in the School of Geography, Population and Environmental Management at Flinders University, and the students I have taught over the years. The former have provided a cooperative and stimulating teaching environment. The latter have endured my enthusiasms with forbearance (most of the time) and have constantly challenged me to reconsider content and strive for clarity.

Alaric Maude, series editor and colleague, first suggested that I write the book and has been an invaluable sounding board and source of ideas for the first and subsequent editions. Lucy McLoughlin and the other staff of Oxford University Press have been invariably patient and encouraging. Steve Fildes produced the maps and diagrams for the third edition with painstaking care. Anna, Rachel, John, David and Melanie have all in different ways provided support and inspiration, and kept me firmly in contact with the real world.

The following people and institutions kindly gave permission to reproduce or adapt material, and I gratefully acknowledge their assistance and cooperation: *Journal of the American Planning Association* for an extract from P. Gordon, H. W. Richardson, and M-J. Jun 1991, 'The Commuting Paradox: Evidence From the Top Twenty', © *American Planning Association Journal*, vol. 57, no. 4, and for a diagram based on one in S. Campbell, 'Green Cities, Growing Cities, Just Cities? Urban Planning and the Contradictions of Sustainable Development', © *Journal of the American Planning Association*, vol. 62, 1996; Commonwealth of Australia for an extract from *Atlas of the Australian People: South Australia*, AGPS, Canberra, 1989, © Commonwealth of Australia; Oxford University Press for an extract from R. H. Fagan and M. Webber 1997, *Global Restructuring: The Australian Experience*, Oxford

University Press, Melbourne, © Oxford University Press, www.oup.com.au; Taylor & Francis Ltd (http://www/tandf.co.uk/journals) for extracts from J. Yates 1997, 'Changing Directions in Australian Housing Policies: The End of Muddling Through?', *Housing Studies*, vol. 12, no. 2, pp. 265–77, M. T. Daly 1988, 'Australian Cities: The Challenge of the 1980s', *Australian Geographer*, vol. 19, no. 1, pp. 149–61; F. J. B. Stilwell 1989, 'Structural Change and Spatial Equity in Sydney', *Urban Policy and Research*, vol. 7, no. 1, pp. 3–14; D. Hayward 1997, 'The Privatised City: Urban Infrastructure Planning and Service Provision in the Era of Privatisation', *Urban Policy and Research*, vol. 15, no. 1, pp. 55–6; and for a map based on one in C. A. Maher 1993, 'Recent Trends in Australian Urban Development: Locational Change and the Policy Quandary', *Urban Studies*, vol. 30, nos. 4/5, pp. 797–825.

I dedicate this third edition to my grandson Jackson David McCall, in the hope that he and his generation grow up in Australian cities that retain their best traditional features, while winning the battle to improve environmental sustainability and social justice.

Introduction

Books about Australian cities tend to begin with 'gee-whiz' statistics. Six out of ten Australians—over eleven million people, they inform us breathlessly—live in our five largest cities; over seven million (four out of every ten) live in Sydney or Melbourne. These figures are true enough, but why the surprise? Since European settlement in Australia began, most immigrants have come to the cities. Most native-born Australians have grown up in them. It is in city environments that most of us make our homes, seek employment, enjoy recreation, interact with neighbours and friends, and get education, health care, and other services. Our cities determine how we live.

Our changing cities

Compared with city-dwellers almost anywhere else in the world, most urban Australians live in spacious housing, in healthy surroundings, and have good access to jobs, services, and facilities. Differences certainly exist between rich and poor suburbs, but the contrasts are less than in most countries. A survey by the international firm Mercer Human Resource Consulting in 2003 rated Sydney as having the fifth-highest quality of life of any major city in the world. Melbourne rated fifteenth, Perth twentieth, and Adelaide and Brisbane were joint thirty-first. In 1998 the International Real Estate Federation awarded Golden Grove in Adelaide the title of 'The World's Best Residential Address'. Depending where they live, readers of this book might produce much less favourable assessments of their urban environments. Residents of the same neighbourhood—even members of the same household—may see things very differently, depending on their income, age, gender, personal tastes, and so on. But most of us can regard ourselves as fortunate in the cities we live in. People living in smaller towns and country areas in Australia might also argue that city dwellers have very little to complain about, compared with the problems facing rural folk.

Yet it seems increasingly hard for young families in our cities to achieve the 'Great Australian Dream' of owning their own house and block of land. Homelessness has increased. Newspapers and TV programs report high levels of anxiety about crime and personal safety in big cities. Despite recent improvements in the unemployment rates, permanent full-time jobs are hard to find. Parents in particular worry about their children's safety, and their career and housing prospects.

Even people who tend not to worry too much about things cannot help noticing that our cities have changed. Old factory sites have been reborn as extravagantly titled business parks or arts centres. City centres have experienced frantic booms in the construction of tall office and apartment blocks. Docklands have become heritage precincts or upmarket residential developments. Warehouses have been transformed into studio apartments. Old working-class inner suburbs have become 'gentrified'. Local schools have closed while technology parks, theme parks, entertainment centres, and retail 'mega malls' have sprung up. Old public housing estates have been broken up and redeveloped. So-called 'McMansions' surround artificial lakes in new master-planned communities. In other parts of town, residents form Save our Suburbs groups to protest against Tuscan townhouses replacing old villas as part of government urban consolidation policies. Suburban mosques and Buddhist and Hindu temples signify changing ethnic patterns and an increasingly multicultural society.

We and our neighbours also seem to live differently. More married women work; more men retire early. More people have casual or part-time jobs—or no jobs at all. More marriages break down. There are more old people. If we live in one of the smaller capital cities we seem to have become less independent. National companies have taken over local banks. Our newspapers, TV, and radio are controlled from elsewhere and carry less locally produced material. On the other hand, we are less parochial, symbolised by the fact that local football, basketball, and netball teams now play in national leagues. Developments in information and communication technology have changed our everyday lives. Almost half the people in Australian cities now have a home computer and over 30 per cent access the Internet from home. Young people in particular cannot imagine life without a mobile phone. City government has also changed. Century-old local councils such as Collingwood in Melbourne or Thebarton in Adelaide have disappeared in the name of efficiency and rationalisation. Public transport, power, and water services have been contracted-out to private suppliers. Tollways have appeared in our biggest cities. Private schools flourish while the state education systems lose pupils. Meanwhile academics, journalists, and politicians conduct debates about globalisation, urban restructuring, and the nature of post-modern cities.

The changes have affected different cities—and different parts of cities—in different ways. Some areas and their residents seem to have been winners, others losers. Since the early 1990s the Australian economy has—as governments never tire of telling us—experienced a decade of almost unprecedented growth. Yet census data for Australian cities suggest rising levels of inequality between rich and poor suburbs, and opinion polls show that many Australians are pessimistic about their children's futures. While inner suburban 'trendies' prosper, people in battling outer suburban areas show their resentment at economic and cultural change that seems to exclude them by voting for One Nation or other protest parties. Planners express concern about the disadvantages faced by some households, particularly those on the fringes of the largest cities, because of their remoteness from jobs and services. Many urban Aborigines continue to live in very poor conditions. Are we, as recent writers have suggested (O'Connor et al. 2001), 'a society dividing'?

We have also become more aware of urban environmental issues. Our dependence on the automobile causes pollution and traffic congestion, as well as problems of isolation for those without cars. It also causes concern about dependence on non-renewable fossil fuels and the emission of greenhouse gases. As our large cities continue to spread, they threaten sensitive environments and productive agricultural land. Our houses are greedy consumers of energy for heating and cooling. Several states have introduced restrictions to combat the wasteful use of scarce water on suburban gardens. Planners increasingly question whether our current style of urban living is environmentally sustainable. We know that some city dwellers in Australia do not share in the overall good fortune when it comes to their urban environment. Is our luck generally running out?

About this book

This book explores the changing nature of Australian cities as human environments, examining how they have evolved and continue to develop in response to economic, social, and technological forces. But this theme of *change* needs to be balanced, as the subtitle suggests, by an awareness of *continuity*. We live, to a large extent, in yesterday's cities. Australia has a comparatively short history of urbanisation, but our urban environments are still a collection of selective survivals from past periods. Buildings, roads, railways, drainage systems, patterns of land ownership, patterns of social segregation, employment structures, the very locations of individual towns and cities, all long outlive the technological, social, and economic conditions that originally produced them. To understand Australian cities today, and to appreciate their unique character, we need to know their history. The book also pursues the currently unfashionable theme of *public policy*: the role past governments have played in shaping our cities, and the need—despite the current enthusiasm for allowing market forces to dictate things—for wise government policies now and in the future.

The study of cities is a multi-disciplinary exercise. The following chapters draw upon the work of planners, sociologists, economists, historians, and political theorists as well as geographers, and I hope the results will interest readers other than students of geography. Nonetheless the perspective is essentially geographical, based on the belief that the exercise of the 'geographical imagination' provides uniquely valuable insights. The geographical perspective focuses on how we have created and used space in Australian cities and how, in turn, the spatial structure of those cities shapes our everyday lives. The emphasis will be on urban environments and ways of life, not just as the passive outcomes of economic, social, and technological forces, but as significant factors in their own right and as important policy areas. The book does not adopt any one mode of explanation or theoretical point of view. The aim is to introduce readers to some of the main issues and debates concerning the geography of contemporary Australian cities.

The first edition of this book was published in 1995, followed by an expanded second edition in 1999. In the nine years since the original edition was written, major economic, social, technological, and political changes have continued to affect our cities. This extensively revised and expanded third edition concentrates on the impact of recent changes, using new material from the 2001 Census and other sources to analyse trends in population, housing, and employment. Throughout the book statistical material has been updated and the results of new research and thinking on urban issues incorporated wherever possible. The main changes in structure since the second edition are that the introductory historical chapter has been extended to cover the period up to 1990, a new chapter discusses the changing role of Australian cities in a globalising world, and the exploration of transport issues has been extended.

Chapter 1 discusses the history of urbanisation in Australia up to the end of the 1980s, and the ways in which internal and external forces shaped our cities during the previous two centuries. Chapter 2 examines in more detail the nature of Australian urbanisation since 1991, comparing trends in population growth and economic development in the different major cities and exploring their changing roles and fortunes both within the national settlement system and as part of a globalising world economy. The following chapters then deal with some of the transformations that are occurring *within* Australian cities as the result of recent economic, technological and demographic changes. Chapter 3 examines employment and labour force participation, and the implications of the changing relationships between 'work' and 'home'. Chapter 4 explores housing questions, particularly the changing nature of housing demand and supply and the future of the Great Australian Dream of suburban home ownership. Chapter 5 deals with population composition, segregation, and patterns of inequality. Chapter 6 discusses the changing nature of urban government in an era of privatisation and 'economic rationalism'. Chapter 7 examines the increasingly urgent debates about the environmental sustainability of our cities. Finally, because the most well-worn cliché about cities is that within them 'everything affects everything else', chapter 8 attempts to provide an integrated view of how Australian cities are changing, before reviewing planning options for the future and key policy debates.

Inevitably in such a short book the contents are selective. The topics for chapters 3 to 7 have been chosen because they encompass some major debates concerning urban Australia that have strong geographical dimensions, and to which geographers have made significant contributions. The book is largely confined—with apologies to those living in Canberra, Hobart, Darwin, and other smaller centres—to discussion of the five mainland state capital cities. When the term 'major cities' is used it means those cities, all of which now have populations of over one million.

Writing a book such as this involves a heavy debt to the many scholars who have addressed similar issues in the past. For the sake of clarity, references within the text have been kept to a minimum. The suggestions at the end of the book for further reading for each chapter also indicate and acknowledge the main sources that have been used, including Internet resources. Readers looking for more detailed information are strongly advised to consult these suggested sources. Because the book is primarily a teaching text, terms and concepts that may be unfamiliar to students are *italicised* and defined when they first appear.

The additions and changes incorporated in this third edition will, I hope, make the book more useful to readers, especially the undergraduate students for whom it is primarily written. But its aim remains unchanged. The latest edition, like the first, seeks to introduce the main issues and debates concerning the geography of contemporary Australian cities. It also emphasises the themes of continuity and change and the vital importance—even in a political climate favouring privatisation and free market approaches—of public policy in shaping our urban environments.

Foundations

It is impossible to understand what is going on in Australian cities today without an appreciation of their historical development. It is equally impossible to appreciate the evolving Australian urban scene without reference to world events and trends. We also need to clarify from the outset what we mean by terms such as city, urban, and urbanisation. This chapter begins with an outline of the process of urbanisation, then examines briefly the history of Australian urbanisation during the nineteenth and the first half of the twentieth centuries. We shall then look in rather more detail at urban development in Australia during the so-called long boom era between 1945 and 1970, and then during the time of economic, social, and political change that followed between about 1970 and 1990. Both periods played vital roles in shaping the urban environments we live in today.

Urbanisation

The sociologist Louis Wirth (1938) argued that urban settlements—towns or cities—differ from rural settlements in that they are characterised by *size*, *density*, and *heterogeneity*. Frost (1990, p. 7) put it more simply: 'A city...can be thought of as a dense cluster of people, engaged in a wide variety of non-agricultural occupations'. Cities have existed for thousands of years, but it is only during the past two centuries that they have become the dominant form of human settlement. Before that, cities consisted mainly of small urban islands set in a sea of rural settlement and agrarian activity. These *pre-industrial cities* certainly met Wirth's and Frost's criteria for urban status, and fulfilled important administrative, trading, and cultural functions. But they were not very large, only a small proportion of the population lived in them, and only a small proportion of total wealth was produced within them.

During the nineteenth century, following the economic, demographic, technological, and social upheavals of the industrial revolution in the United Kingdom and western Europe, things changed. The rise of industrial capitalism, which entailed manufacturing replacing agriculture as the main generator of wealth, was accompanied by a marked increase in the proportion of the population living in towns and cities. We refer to such an increase as *urbanisation* (as distinct from *urban growth,* which is simply a rise in the total number of people living in urban settlements).

The rapid urbanisation associated with the industrial revolution transformed the geography of the United Kingdom, parts of western Europe, and the eastern seaboard of the USA. For the first time in history, countries became predominantly urban. In England and Wales in 1801, only 25 per cent of the population lived in urban settlements of over 5000 people. By 1891 this figure—which is referred to as the *level of urbanisation*—had risen to almost 70 per cent. Large industrial and commercial cities had developed, with associated patterns of land use as well as contrasts in living conditions that clearly reflected the economic system and class structure of industrial capitalism. Those cities had centres dominated by offices and shops. They had factory districts surrounded by working-class housing. Residential suburbs evolved for the middle classes, served by public transport networks, and by reticulated water as well as power and sewerage systems. The foundations of modern urban life had been laid.

Australian cities in the nineteenth century

Urbanisation

It was during the period of industrial urbanisation in Europe that the British invaded and settled Australia. Cities developed rapidly here also, and by the end of the nineteenth century the level of urbanisation was among the highest in the world. In 1891, according to Frost (1990), 49 per cent of the country's population lived in urban settlements of over 2500 inhabitants (note that the threshold population above which a settlement is defined as urban tends to vary from country to country and from writer to writer—a perennial problem for students of cities).

The nature of Australian urbanisation and the character of the cities it produced differed significantly from the British experience in ways that continue to influence us today. Industrial urbanisation in the United Kingdom took place within a long-established framework of rural and pre-industrial urban settlement. It involved the movement of large numbers of people from the countryside into the cities as employment declined in agriculture and grew in manufacturing and commerce. Some industrial towns grew from nothing, but most involved the expansion of a pre-industrial town or city.

In Australia, things happened the other way round. European colonisation began with the first coastal cities and people moved out into the interior areas later, establishing a rural settlement pattern under the ruling influence of the colonial capitals. Australia's capital cities also resembled those in other New World areas such as North and South America, South Africa, and New Zealand, in that they were, from the outset, *commercial* or *mercantile* rather than industrial in character. Sydney, Hobart, and Brisbane, which were initially convict settlements, can perhaps be distinguished from Melbourne, Adelaide, and Perth, which were not. But all came to serve similar functions as administrative centres and as ports through which the produce of their rural hinterlands could be exported to Europe, and manufactured goods imported in return.

Metropolitan primacy

By the end of the nineteenth century, contemporary observers were commenting on the extraordinary degree to which the Australian population was concentrated not just in urban centres, but also in the capital cities. As A.F. Weber noted in 1899: 'The most remarkable concentration, or rather centralisation, of population occurs in that newest product of civilisation, Australia, where nearly one third of the entire population is settled in and about capital cities' (Weber 1963, p. 138). A New South Wales government statistician, T.A. Coghlan, viewed the phenomenon less dispassionately: 'The abnormal aggregation of the [Australian] population into their capital cities is a most unfortunate element in the progress of the colonies' (McCarty 1970, p. 112). Unfortunate or not, *metropolitan primacy*—the condition where the largest city in a country or province is many times larger than the second-largest—persisted as one of the most striking features of the Australian settlement pattern, particularly in Victoria, South Australia, and Western Australia.

The colonial capital cities maintained and increased their dominance as the result of several mutually reinforcing factors. As already noted, they were the first points of settlement and almost all trade passed through them. Each was the administrative centre of a separate colony, and was the natural location for public or private organisations providing services to the population. When settlers first opened up the rural hinterlands, it was for the production of wool: wool required little permanent rural labour and it generated more jobs in the cities than in the country areas, as it was exported through the cities. Later, when agriculture developed, it also employed relatively few people, because it was based on the typical New World pattern of large, mechanised, commercially run farms.

When the first railways were built from the mid nineteenth century onwards, the rail networks centred on the capital cities and reinforced their dominance. As a result, there was little basis in Australia for the development of smaller cities such as had existed in the Old World before the railway age, each able to dominate a local region because of the slow, primitive nature of long-distance transport. The main exceptions were in Queensland where a series of coastal cities developed, each serving its rural hinterland, and in Tasmania where Launceston served the north and Hobart the south. Mining settlements also sprung up and sometimes developed a large population rapidly, but usually the boom was short-lived. In any case, the head offices of the mining companies tended to locate in the capital cities and the miners spent much of their wealth back in the cities.

When significant manufacturing industry developed in Australia later in the nineteenth century (figure 1.1), much of it was also drawn naturally to the capital cities. As well as being the major points of transfer from sea to land transport, cities constituted the largest labour pools and the main domestic markets. And every manufacturing job reinforced the cities' attractiveness to new immigrants, who then created further needs for service employment. By this process of *cumulative causation*, the so-called *snowball effect* in which growth in turn generates more growth, the capital cities became ever more dominant from the 1870s onwards. By 1911, Sydney contained 47 per cent of the population of New South Wales, Melbourne contained 45 per cent of Victoria's population, and Adelaide and Perth were almost as prominent in their respective states (table 1.1).

Table 1.1   Capital city growth and urbanisation, 1851–1911

	Sydney			Melbourne			Adelaide		
	Pop	% Col	% Inc	Pop	% Col	% Inc	Pop	% Col	% Inc
1851	54	28		29	38		18	28	
1861	96	27	5.9	125	23	15.7	35	28	6.9
1871	138	27	3.7	191	26	4.3	51	27	3.9
1881	225	30	5.0	268	31	3.3	92	33	6.1
1891	400	35	5.9	473	41	5.8	117	37	2.4
1901	496	37	2.2	478	40	0.1	141	39	1.9
1911	648	47	2.7	593	45	2.2	169	41	1.8

	Brisbane			Perth			Hobart		
	Pop	% Col	% Inc	Pop	% Col	% Inc	Pop	% Col	% Inc
1851	3								
1861	6	20	7.2	5	33		25	28	
1871	15	13	9.6				26	25	0.4
1881	31	14	7.6	9	30	2.8	27	23	0.4
1891	94	24	11.7	16	32	5.9	33	22	2.0
1901	119	24	2.4	61	33	14.3	35	20	0.6
1911	141	23	1.7	107	38	5.8	40	21	1.3

Pop = total capital city population in thousands
% Col = capital city population as a percentage of total colony's population
% Inc = capital city average annual population increase in previous decade (%)

Source: McCarty 1970, pp. 119–21.

Figure 1.1 Industry on the banks of the Torrens River, Adelaide, *circa* 1870: wool scouring in the suburb of Thebarton

Source: Photograph courtesy of the State Library of South Australia, SLSA:B542

Growth cycles, booms, and busts

The capital cities did not grow at a regular pace during the second half of the nineteenth century. Boom decades alternated with periods of stagnation, and some cities grew while others stood still. Local causes were sometimes clearly apparent. Melbourne's massive growth during the 1850s, when the city's population increased fourfold in a mere ten years, arose directly from the discovery of gold in Victoria. The gold rushes in Western Australia towards the end of the century had a similar impact on Perth. Adelaide's rapid growth during the 1870s reflected the great period of northwards expansion of wheat farming in South Australia and a run of good seasons; the slow growth that followed during the 1890s reflected drought and depression just as clearly.

As well as these local events, there were more fundamental underlying cycles of growth and decline, reflecting the relationship between colonial Australia and the evolution of capitalism in the Western world. Berry (1984) argues that by the 1870s British investors had accumulated large amounts of surplus capital following several decades of strong industrial growth, but were faced with falling rates of return on investment in manufacturing. They therefore sought new investment opportunities, especially in South America and Australia, and poured capital into pastoralism, public utilities such as railways, and finally into urban residential development. British capital funded the high rates of growth in Sydney, Brisbane, and Melbourne during the 1880s, in particular the boom in 'Marvellous Melbourne', before the increasing amount of British and local speculative investment in real estate finally led to the inevitable market crash and the depression of the 1890s.

City life

When industrial urbanisation began in nineteenth-century Britain it produced conditions of great overcrowding, squalor, and ill-health. Industrial workers crowded into old pre-industrial courtyards and tenements within walking distance of their jobs in the factories, mines, or docks. Even in newly built workers' housing the conditions were little better, and city authorities did not begin to impose minimum standards of housing and sanitation until mid-century. Before then, the inadequate provision of fresh water and the lack of sewerage and drainage systems caused frequent outbreaks of diseases such as cholera and typhoid. The middle and upper classes had every incentive to escape these appalling conditions, and the development of urban public transport systems enabled them to do so. Horse omnibuses, trams, and railways allowed wealthier people to live some distance from the city, in spacious housing and healthy surroundings, yet within easy travelling time of the city centre. The residential suburb was born, as was the phenomenon of *residential segregation* as the different classes sorted themselves into distinct districts or quarters, mainly according to their ability to pay for housing. Friedrich Engels observed the results in Manchester in 1842. Immediately outside the central commercial area of the city, he wrote, were:

> unmixed working people's quarters, stretching like a girdle, averaging a mile and a half in breadth…Outside, beyond this girdle, lives the upper and middle bourgeoisie, the middle bourgeoisie in regularly laid out streets in the vicinity of working quarters…the upper bourgeoisie in remoter villas with gardens…in free, wholesome country air, in fine, comfortable homes, passed every half or quarter hour by omnibuses going into the city. (Engels 1962, p. 46)

How did the geography of nineteenth-century Australian cities compare with the British experience? There were some basic similarities. Here, too, one can recognise two distinct phases of development based on transport technology. Up to the 1870s the colonial capitals were compact *walking cities*, with working-class and middle-class housing alike clustered within walking distance of the commercial city centres, factories, and docksides. Then, with the establishment of tram and railway networks in the boom years of the 1870s and 1880s, our cities became true *public transport cities* (figure 1.2). As in the United Kingdom, the middle and upper classes—and some better-paid members of the working class—could aspire to a house and garden in residential suburbs served by train or tram lines radiating from the city centre.

As Cannon (1975) put it, 'a segregation of suburbs' developed. Different income levels were reproduced in bricks and mortar by variations in internal comfort and external display. But the pattern of segregation differed from Engels's Manchester of 1842. Instead of concentric rings of increasing affluence with distance from the city centre, Australian cities were characterised almost from the outset by *sectors* of different social status. Areas of working-class housing (figure 1.3) developed close to the factories and docks, often on flat unappealing land. On the other side of town, middle-class residential suburbs (figure 1.4) spread outwards along the public transport routes, in more attractive surroundings free from industrial pollution.

Melbourne during the boom period of the 1880s became a classic example of the relationship between public transport and suburban development (and, according to Cannon, of the equally close relationship between politicians and real estate speculators as the former approved the building of railway lines running through the land holdings of the latter). Old established industrial areas of the walking-city era such as Collingwood and Richmond were joined

Figure 1.2 The public transport city: trams in Unley Road, Adelaide, *circa* 1906

Source: Photograph courtesy of the State Library of South Australia, SLSA:B6314

Figure 1.3 Nineteenth-century workers' cottages in Fitzroy, Melbourne (photographed in 1970 shortly before their demolition)
Source: Clive Forster

Figure 1.4 An 1880s terrace in Albert Park, Melbourne (photographed in 1992)
Source: Clive Forster

on the west and north of the Yarra River by the new working-class suburbs of Brunswick, Northcote, and Footscray. On the other side of the river, leafy middle-class suburbs developed to the south and east in Kew, Hawthorn, Prahran, and Brighton. Similar patterns of residential segregation developed in cities throughout the Western world by the end of the nineteenth century, with the distinct middle-class and working-class sectors extending outwards as the cities expanded.

In spite of some general similarities, however, life in late nineteenth-century Australian cities differed from the British experience in several important respects. The most noticeable difference was that our cities covered very large areas compared with European cities of similar population. They were, as Jackson (1977 p. 102) writes, 'sprawling affairs' with typical population densities of 20–25 persons per hectare, compared with over 200 persons per hectare in parts of British cities. The reasons for this were complex. The younger cities in particular (Adelaide, Melbourne, and Perth) did not have a heritage of cramped pre-industrial housing. Land, compared with the United Kingdom, was abundant and cheap. Because Australian cities were commercial rather than industrial in nature there was a large middle-class, and incomes, even for manual workers, were relatively high. Many families could therefore aspire to own their own houses: approximately 50 per cent of Australians were owner-occupiers at the end of the nineteenth century, compared with only 10 per cent in the United Kingdom. Most Australian city growth also occurred during the public transport era, freeing people from the need to live close to their workplaces. In combination, these factors allowed large numbers of city-dwellers, most of them immigrants from the United Kingdom, to realise what Frost (1990, p. 44) has called 'the Anglo Saxon desire for the privacy of living in a suburban setting'.

Australian cities also did not generally contain the large areas of slum housing that Engels and others had noted in Britain, and had relatively low urban mortality and morbidity rates (although infant mortality was high). Again, these characteristics can be attributed to relatively high levels of per capita income, a commercial rather than industrial class structure, and a relatively small heritage of cramped housing from the walking-city period.

Frost (1990) adds a new dimension to the analysis, arguing that a significant distinction existed between, on the one hand, the old convict settlements of Sydney, Hobart, and Brisbane, and, on the other, what he terms the 'new urban frontier' cities of Adelaide, Melbourne, and Perth. He points out that the walking-city phase was more important in the older cities. Sydney in particular grew into a crowded, bustling, irregularly laid out city that, even in the 1880s, strongly reminded visitors of the Old World. The city had its slums and its epidemics, and its areas of high-density housing, although not to the extent of London or Liverpool. In contrast, Melbourne and the other 'new urban frontier' cities were, from the outset, more spacious and regular in layout. They experienced most of their growth as public transport cities, and tended rather more to exemplify the features that Jackson (1977) had identified.

Urban character

By Federation in 1901 Sydney and Melbourne had become cities of world importance, each with over half a million inhabitants. Adelaide, Brisbane, and Perth had populations of over 100 000; Hobart 35 000. The capitals of the newly constituted states were all complex, multi-faceted cities with a range of commercial, administrative, and industrial functions. In spite of the differences Frost identifies between them, their common characteristics were to have a vital influence upon Australian urban life in the future.

Already our cities were characterised by low-density residential suburbs, high levels of home ownership, and high general standards of well-being. Contemporary observers such as Richard Twopeny (1883) have left us vivid descriptions of how the so-called Great Australian Dream was taking shape. At the same time, significant differences had developed between living standards in low-income and high-income sectors, and this pattern of residential segregation was also to prove persistent.

High levels of urbanisation and metropolitan primacy had established themselves as the Australian norm. In the nineteenth century, as in the twentieth, the typical Australian was a city dweller, despite a literary tradition and popular culture based on the 'bush', much of which, according to McCarty (1970, p. 107), was created by writers who 'could be removed only forcibly from the Sydney bars they loved so well to the great outback about which they wrote so well'. And then, as now, fluctuations in the rates of immigration and capital investment from overseas left permanent legacies in the built environment, as the boom times and the intervening periods of stagnation were reflected in the urban landscape like the growth rings of a tree.

The first half of the twentieth century

Most writers on Australian cities have paid little attention to the early decades of the twentieth century. This period was certainly less spectacular than the booms of the 1870s and 1880s or, later, the 1950s and 1960s. Yet, especially during the 1920s, significant economic and technological changes affected our cities and another suburban building boom left its mark on the urban landscape, especially in Sydney.

Manufacturing and city growth

It was during the 1920s that manufacturing became a major economic force in Australia. It had an expanding domestic market to serve under the protection of the newly created federal tariff system, and generous amounts of capital investment from Britain. Apart from the steel industry, which concentrated near the coalfields in Newcastle and Wollongong, most of the new manufacturing jobs developed in the capital cities. Growth was particularly strong in Sydney and Melbourne, which formed (as always) the largest domestic markets and labour pools. However, Adelaide also experienced rapid industrialisation during the 1930s, with the vigorous encouragement of the South Australian government.

The domestic production of munitions during the Second World War caused further growth, and the 1947 Census showed that, for the first time, more Australians had manufacturing jobs (28 per cent of the workforce) than worked in primary production (18 per cent). The equivalent figures at Federation in 1901 had been 17 per cent and 33 per cent (Logan et al. 1981, p. 22). The capital cities had continued to capture most of this manufacturing growth. By 1946–47, Sydney, Melbourne, Adelaide, and Perth each held approximately 80 per cent of the factory jobs in their respective states (Berry 1984).

The rise of manufacturing therefore further reinforced the primacy of the capital cities. By 1947 Melbourne contained over 60 per cent of Victoria's population and Sydney, Adelaide, and Perth each held over half their states' inhabitants. Brisbane and Hobart were less dominant, but overall 51 per cent of Australia's total population of 7.6 million lived in the six state capitals. A further 18 per cent lived in other urban centres and 31 per cent were classified as rural. In contrast to both the nineteenth century and the forthcoming postwar period, immigration from overseas had played little part in city growth. Over 40 per cent resulted from natural increase—an excess of births over deaths in the relatively young city populations—but the majority (53 per cent) was the result of migration from rural areas as the mechanisation and rationalisation of agriculture caused farm sizes to rise and employment to fall.

Suburbia triumphant

By 1947 Sydney and Melbourne had each grown to well over 1 million inhabitants. The 'second division' cities—Adelaide, Brisbane, and Perth—each had populations of between 250 000 and 400 000. The geographical structure of the cities, and in many respects the lives of their inhabitants, still followed the patterns formed in the late nineteenth century. As the low-density suburbs extended like the arms of a starfish along the train and tram routes radiating from the city centres, they perpetuated the division of the city into established working-class and middle-class sectors.

The major technological change during the interwar period had been the electrification of some public transport systems and the widespread provision of domestic electric power. Besides speeding up the trams and trains, electrification reinforced suburbanisation and industrialisation by ushering in the age of domestic appliances. Australian women's magazines of the 1920s and 1930s began to follow the American model by portraying the ideal life as involving not only a house and garden, but a refrigerator and vacuum cleaner as well (Spearritt 1978). In the 1930s only a few people could afford such devices, or the motor cars and the garages that were appearing in house plans for the first time. But patterns were being set for the future.

The inter-war years also saw the beginnings of significant government involvement in housing provision and town planning. William Light's plan for the original City of Adelaide (1836) with its formal squares, wide streets, and belt of parkland, was a renowned example of nineteenth-century town planning. Central Melbourne also had its formal plan, designed by Robert Hoddle. But, during the rest of the nineteenth century, the growth of all the capital cities took place with very little planning or control, apart from the unambitious minimum standards imposed by local building regulations. The same was true of most new residential development in the first half of the twentieth century. However, during and after the First World War a handful of pioneer town planners and architects began to campaign for improved standards of urban design. Principal figures included Charles Reade in Adelaide, John Sulman in Sydney, and Walter Burley Griffin (Griffin won the competition to design the new national capital in 1912). What Freestone (1982) has called 'Garden City principles', imported largely from the United Kingdom, were applied to the design of a few model projects such as Colonel Light Gardens in Adelaide, Daceyville in Sydney, and Garden City in Port Melbourne, and they also helped lay the foundations of Australian town planning.

Life in the new suburbs—poorly designed or not—was much better than in the traditional working-class inner areas (figure 1.3), which had suffered severely from the unemployment and hardship of the Great Depression in the early 1930s. Campaigns by housing reform groups in the 1930s forced governments to set up inquiries into housing conditions in the inner suburbs. The inquiries led to the establishment of housing commissions in Victoria (1938) and New South Wales (1942), charged with the task of slum reclamation. The South Australian Housing Trust was also set up in 1936, though it was directed more towards the provision of inexpensive workers' housing as part of the state's industrialisation policy. Although some state banks had previously provided a small number of subsidised housing loans to low-income families, the founding of these housing authorities marked the real beginning of the public housing sector in Australia.

The long boom

At the end of the Second World War in 1945, Australia's major cities were poised to enter a remarkable period of rapid population growth, economic development, and physical expansion that was to last until the early 1970s. The sheer magnitude of urban growth during this so-called *long boom* was astonishing. It had taken well over a century for the population of Australia's five largest cities to grow to the 1947 total of four million. In a mere twenty-four years that total almost doubled. By 1971 Sydney and Melbourne were massive, sprawling metropolises with over 2.5 million inhabitants each, and the populations of Brisbane, Perth, and Adelaide all exceeded 700 000 (table 1.2). Metropolitan primacy also became even more marked. By 1971 Melbourne and Adelaide contained over 70 per cent of their respective state populations; Perth 68 per cent; and Sydney over 60 per cent. Overall, approximately 60 per cent of the country's total population lived in the major cities, compared with 54 per cent in 1947. (Note that the figures in table 1.2 are based on the boundaries of the cities in 1971. They therefore show a larger percentage of the 1947 population living in the major cities than that quoted earlier on p. 11 which is a figure based on the actual 1947 boundaries. The problem of how to compare city populations over time as their boundaries grow outwards is as persistent as the problem, discussed on p. 2, of how to define an urban settlement statistically.)

As well as growing very rapidly, the cities changed radically in structure. The basic character of Australian urban development may have been set during earlier periods; but the sprawling, decentralised, automobile-dependent,

Table 1.2 Major city growth and urbanisation, 1947–71

	1947			1971			1947–1971
	Pop ('000)	% State	% Aust	Pop ('000)	% State	% Aust	% Pop. Change
Sydney	1699	57	22	2808	61	22	65
Melbourne	1341	65	18	2503	72	20	87
Brisbane	402	36	5	868	48	7	116
Adelaide	383	59	5	843	72	7	120
Perth	273	54	4	703	68	6	158
Total	4098		54	7725		61	89

1971 data are for capital city Statistical Divisions;
1947 data are adjusted approximately to 1971 SD boundaries

Source: Burnley 1980, p. 70 and ABS 1971 Census.

ethnically diverse cities most of us live in today are mainly a legacy of the 1950s and 1960s. The period saw major economic, demographic, and technological changes. These changes will be discussed in turn, but it is vital to appreciate their essential interrelatedness. Economic growth, population increase, and a massive rise in automobile ownership interacted, together with government housing and planning policies, to fuel a seemingly unstoppable chain reaction of metropolitan expansion and suburbanisation.

Economic development

The long boom, as its name suggests, was a period of general economic growth, prosperity, and full employment. The growth came largely from the continued development of manufacturing industry, although mining became increasingly important in the later years. The boom in Australia was part of a general trend throughout the industrialised world following the end of the Second World War. It involved, as in earlier booms, the inflow of capital from overseas—this time particularly from the USA. Manufacturing of automobiles, whitegoods, chemicals, electronics, paper, and fertilisers expanded to meet sharply rising domestic demand. The industries enjoyed continued tariff protection and were enthusiastically encouraged by the various state governments, each eager to capture for itself as large a share as possible of the new investment and job opportunities.

The expansion of heavy industry caused Newcastle, Wollongong, Whyalla, and Geelong to grow rapidly during the postwar years. But, as in earlier periods, most of the new manufacturing jobs gravitated to the capital cities, particularly Melbourne, Sydney, and Adelaide. Their large domestic markets and labour pools, and the advantages new enterprises could gain by locating close to existing component suppliers and allied manufacturers, proved as attractive as ever. The state governments of New South Wales and Victoria even set up departments of decentralisation in attempts to woo industry away from the capital cities to country towns, but with little effect. The snowball process of cumulative causation still drew industrialists irresistibly to the rapidly expanding capitals. By 1971 manufacturing made up over 30 per cent of the jobs in Melbourne, almost 30 per cent in Sydney and Adelaide, and around 20 per cent in Brisbane and Perth.

Australian cities had entered a new phase of development, referred to by many writers as *corporate urbanisation* (to distinguish it from the *commercial* or *mercantile urbanisation* of the previous hundred years). Corporate cities, here and elsewhere in the world, were characterised by the dominant economic role of large transnational corporations such as Ford, General Motors, ICI, and Philips. Their inhabitants were drawn into what Daly (1988) has termed a *mass production–mass consumption* society, as more and more of them worked for large corporations and served as markets for their products.

Immigration and baby boom

Rapid population growth matched economic expansion. The postwar years saw what the National Population Inquiry (1975) later identified as a *marriage revolution*: couples got married at a younger age, fewer people remained unmarried, and the fertility rates of married women rose. The resulting baby boom, coupled with low mortality rates, produced high rates of natural population increase that accounted for between a third and a half of the total growth in capital city populations between 1947 and 1971 (table 1.3).

Internal migration played little part in capital city growth, except in Brisbane. In fact, Sydney and Melbourne suffered a small net population loss from this source. Table 1.3 shows that the main 'engine' of growth was undoubtedly immigration from overseas. Between 1947 and 1971 over half the population growth of Sydney, Melbourne, and Adelaide, almost half the growth of Perth, and one third of the growth of Brisbane and Hobart was due to net immigration. This was the direct result of federal government policy. There was a widespread belief, summed-up by the catchcry 'populate or perish', that the country's small population and vast land mass left Australia vulnerable to invasion from the north. The belief was strengthened (ironically, given the impending baby boom) by low birth rates during the 1930s and the wartime years. Postwar federal governments therefore supported a vigorous program of assisted immigration, and were encouraged to continue doing so by severe shortages of labour as the economy entered the long boom.

Most of the new immigrants flocked, as always, to the employment opportunities and social facilities in the capital cities. Once in the cities, they did not simply swell the population totals and meet the demand for labour. Together with the native-born families of the baby boom, they boosted the demand for housing and consumer goods. This in turn fuelled further industrial expansion

Table 1.3 Components of major city population growth, 1947–71 (%)

	Natural increase	Net internal migration	Net overseas migration	Total
Sydney	45.6	−1.8	56.1	100
Melbourne	43.8	−0.1	56.3	100
Brisbane	40.4	26.3	33.3	100
Adelaide	32.5	12.5	55.0	100
Perth	36.4	15.5	48.1	100

Source: Burnley 1974, pp. 58–9 and National Population Inquiry 1975, p. 164.

and growth in job opportunities, which provided the stimulus for further immigration.

Postwar immigration also transformed the ethnic character of our cities. To get the desired numbers of migrants, the government extended assistance programs for the first time to non-British settlers, initially targeting refugees from northern and eastern Europe, then concentrating on southern Europe and later the Middle East and Latin America. The ethnic composition of Australian capital cities became increasingly diverse, as successive waves of immigrants poured into them (table 1.4). Melbourne was most affected, followed by Sydney and Adelaide, though Adelaide (like Perth) mainly received British migrants. Immigration had much less impact on Brisbane and Hobart.

Distinct geographical patterns of ethnic residential segregation developed. The British mainly settled in the new outer suburbs, and migrants from

Table 1.4 Ethnic composition of major city populations, 1971

Birthplace	Sydney		Melbourne		Brisbane	
	Persons ('000)	%	Persons ('000)	%	Persons ('000)	%
Australia	2109	75.1	1816	72.6	728	83.9
UK and Ireland	254	9.0	214	8.5	77	8.9
Italy	64	2.3	107	4.3	8	0.9
Greece	48	1.7	76	3.0	3	0.3
Yugoslavia	39	1.4	42	1.7	3	0.3
Germany	25	0.9	30	1.2	6	0.7
Malta	21	0.7	24	1.0	1	0.1
Netherlands	18	0.6	24	1.0	6	0.7
Other*	230	8.3	170	6.7	36	4.2
Total	2808	100	2503	100	868	100

Birthplace	Perth		Adelaide	
	Persons ('000)	%	Persons ('000)	%
Australia	480	68.3	606	71.9
UK and Ireland	125	17.8	125	14.8
Italy	25	3.6	29	3.4
Greece	4	0.6	12	1.4
Yugoslavia	7	1.0	7	0.8
Germany	5	0.7	12	1.4
Malta	1	0.1	2	0.2
Netherlands	9	1.3	9	1.1
Other*	47	6.6	41	5.0
Total	703	100	843	100

Data are for Statistical Divisions
* Countries not comprising 1% of the population in any city

Source: ABS 1971 Census.

northern and eastern Europe tended to follow suit. Southern Europeans, in contrast, concentrated initially in the inner, older residential areas where they could buy housing cheaply. Distinct Greek, Italian, Yugoslavian, Maltese, and other enclaves developed, with their own shops, churches, and sporting clubs (particularly soccer) and social networks. *Chain migration* (people from specific regions, or even villages, in the countries of origin following one another to Australia) reinforced these inner-suburban concentrations. Later, as migrants became financially established, they tended to move outwards to more expensive housing in the middle and outer suburbs. Sectors formed, dominated by particular nationalities or groups of nationalities, for example the Italian-born in Melbourne's northern suburbs and Adelaide's eastern suburbs.

The automobile city

It was during the long boom that the private car became the main form of transport in Australian cities. In 1945 there were approximately 100 cars per 1000 persons in Australia as a whole, a ratio that had changed little since the early 1930s. Most people still used public transport. Then, from 1945 onwards, car ownership grew very rapidly, particularly following the removal of wartime petrol rationing in 1950. By the early 1970s there were almost 500 cars per 1000 persons. The 1971 Census revealed that 75 per cent of the households in Sydney and Melbourne owned at least one car and 25 per cent of households owned two or more. Ownership levels were even higher in the smaller capitals.

As cars, once a luxury, became commonplace the pattern of urban development responded accordingly. The star-shaped public transport city, with its 'arms' of residential development extending along the tram and train tracks radiating from a dominant city centre, was transformed and engulfed. Areas of previously inaccessible land between the public transport routes were eagerly developed for housing to meet the needs of the new migrant and baby-boom households. Some flats were built during the 1960s, especially in Sydney, but most new housing consisted of detached houses on large blocks. Our cities sprawled rapidly outwards (figure 1.5). The physical expansion of Adelaide between 1939 and 1965, for example, dwarfed the development of the previous 100 years. Sydney and Melbourne each grew to cover a larger area than London, a city with four times their population.

Manufacturing also expanded out into suburban areas, for a number of reasons. The development of efficient truck transport reduced the need to locate close to ports and railway yards; firms began instead to seek sites on the main interstate highways. Expanding companies moved from the inner suburbs in search of large, cheap sites for new factories. Particularly during times of labour shortage, there were advantages in being close to a suburbanising labour force. Whatever the precise combination of motives, manufacturing employment declined in the traditional inner-city locations and grew rapidly in the suburbs. Appropriately, automobile manufacturing itself typified the trend. The Holden—'Australia's Own Car'—was first produced in 1948, and massive automobile plants, surrounded by low-density housing for workers and their families, sprang up in outer suburban locations such as Broadmeadows in Melbourne and Elizabeth in Adelaide. These areas became perfect symbols of the so-called *Fordist* era of industrial organisation, named after the American car manufacturer Henry Ford who pioneered the production line. Fordism was characterised by mass-production technology, rigid job specialisation, strong blue-collar unions, and full male employment.

Retailing, too, chased its customers to the suburbs while undergoing its own technological revolution. As families acquired refrigerators and cars, they could shop less frequently and travel further to do so. Small shops on street corners and along tram routes gave way to supermarkets, which were more profitable because of their larger scale and lower labour costs. Large suburban regional shopping centres then developed, containing branches of major department stores and a wide range of speciality shops, surrounded by thousands of parking spaces. The first centre, Top Ryde, opened in Sydney in 1957. Melbourne's first opened in 1960 at Chadstone, and counterparts soon followed in all the mainland capital cities. Retail sales in central business districts declined, as customers shopping by car found the new suburban centres, with their air conditioning and easy parking, more convenient and attractive (figure 1.6).

More and more things, from drive-in cinemas and fast food outlets to the second generation of Australian universities, sought suburban, car-oriented locations. Used-car lots and service stations became dominant elements in the urban landscape. The whole structure of Australian cities changed. Star-shaped, relatively centralised *public transport cities* were replaced by sprawling, amorphous, decentralised, *automobile cities* (figure 1.7). Public transport lost customers and profits, could not attract investment, became outdated and inefficient, and lost even more customers in a self-reinforcing spiral of decline. Automobile ownership became not only commonplace but *essential*. Only cars could connect low-density suburban homes to jobs, schools, universities, health services, and entertainment venues that were themselves increasingly located in other suburban locations, served poorly—if at all—by public transport.

The role of government

The rise of the *corporate city* was accompanied throughout the Western world by a great expansion of the role governments played in shaping economic and urban development. Government intervention was very obvious in countries

Figure 1.5 Suburbia at the end of the long boom: western Sydney, 1971

Source: Clive Forster

Figure 1.6 The automobile city: Adelaide's first Kmart, 1971

Source: Clive Forster

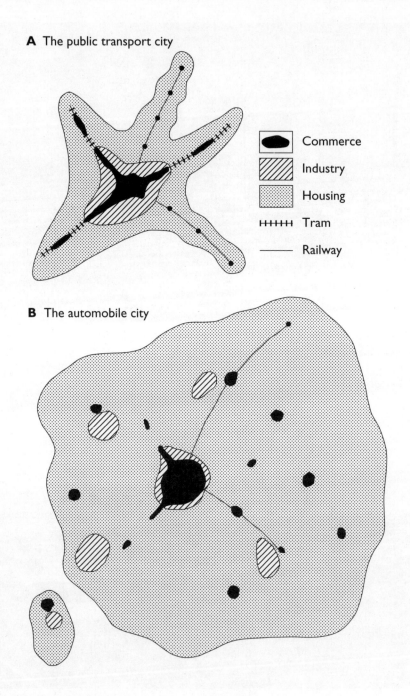

A The public transport city

B The automobile city

Commerce
Industry
Housing
⊦⊦⊦⊦ Tram
—— Railway

Figure 1.7 Transport technology and eras of urban form
Source: Clive Forster

such as the United Kingdom, where the postwar Labour government intro-duced ambitious policies to contain and shape the growth of the largest cities. With the emergence of the so-called 'welfare state', governments also took over major responsibility for education, health services, and transportation, and for the provision of low-income housing. These were not specifically 'urban' policies. However, government decisions on where to build housing estates, hospitals, schools, and roads became key factors in shaping the nature of urban development. Government policies encouraging people to buy their own homes also profoundly affected city growth. Even in the USA, where the public sector was much less prominent than in the United Kingdom, writers labelled the long boom the era of the *state-managed capitalist metropolis* (Soja et al. 1983). The rise of state management also went hand-in-hand with *modernism* in urban design. Modernism in city planning, as in architecture and art, was contemptuous of the past and emphasised efficiency, technology, functionalism, and the 'brave new world' of control and regulation (Freestone 1993, p. 18). During the long boom, city landscapes throughout the world became dominated by concrete and glass skyscrapers; slum-clearance schemes; high-rise public housing projects (figure 1.8) based on the ideas of the French architect Le Corbusier, who conceived of such buildings as 'machines for living'; freeway networks; and the rigid segregation of different land uses.

Australian cities are subject to three levels of government: federal, state, and local. At the beginning of the long boom the federal Department of Post-War Reconstruction introduced decentralisation policies in an attempt to steer urban growth away from the capital cities. It also generally showed an interest in city planning. But once the Liberal–Country Party coalition came to power in 1949, urban policy became—with the exception of Canberra—the concern of the states.

All the mainland state governments except Queensland (where the large Brisbane City Council looked after metropolitan planning) produced *master plans* for their capital cities. The New South Wales government established the Cumberland County Council in 1945, and approved its planning scheme for Sydney in 1951. The Melbourne and Metropolitan Board of Works was given town-planning responsibilities in 1949 and had its plan accepted in 1954. State governments adopted similar plans for Perth in 1963 and Adelaide in 1967. The Sydney plan was the most ambitious. It aimed to coordinate the suburbanisation and decentralisation of housing, manufacturing, and retail-ing, and the more equitable supply of services and facilities. It also sought to develop strong suburban regional centres and to restrict outwards sprawl by establishing a *green belt* of protected non-urban land.

The master plans, though not identical, were all essentially 'trend plans': they assumed that automobile-oriented suburbanisation would continue, and sought to tidy up the outcome. They relied largely on negative controls. Planning authorities were able to prohibit developments seen as inappropriate for a given location, but were powerless to create *desirable* developments. Their plans were even ignored in some cases by other state government departments. And local government authorities, which administered planning and building regulations in most cities, tended to favour local interests rather than the intentions of the metropolitan master plan (as well as often being accused of corruption).

An unkind commentator might therefore argue that, when it came to town planning policy, federal government was inactive, state governments were ineffective, and local government was negative and parochial. However, town planning was not the only influence shaping the character of Australian cities: other less specifically 'urban' policies were far more influential.

As we have seen, federal government policies encouraging immigration, and protecting manufacturing industry from overseas competition, certainly played a major role in the rapid growth of the capital cities. Federal and state governments also increased their influence on the nature of cities by taking over the provision of most education, health, and transport services. Housing policy, however, had the most impact. The public housing bodies that the states had set up during the 1930s expanded rapidly, following the recommendation by the federal Labor government's Department of Post-War Reconstruction that they be given federal funding. After the first Commonwealth–State Housing Agreement in 1947, housing commission or housing trust estates became familiar features of the suburban landscape. These estates were an important element in city growth during the long boom, especially in Adelaide where the South Australian Housing Trust was responsible for over 30 per cent of the new houses built during the 1950s and 1960s. Housing commission slum reclamation programs also transformed the inner suburbs of Melbourne and to a lesser extent Sydney. Large areas of nineteenth-century cottages were demolished and replaced—in classic modernist style—with the blocks of high-rise flats that still dominate the skyline (figure 1.8).

Public housing tends to be the first thing to spring to mind when considering the influence of government housing policy on our cities, but federal policies encouraging people to buy their own homes were actually far more important. The 1947 Census showed that the level of home ownership in Australian cities had changed little since the end of the nineteenth century, ranging from 40 per cent of dwellings in Sydney to 60 per cent in Brisbane. But by 1961 the percentage of households who owned or were buying their dwelling had risen to 68 in Sydney and 75 in Brisbane: some of the highest levels of home ownership in the world. This remarkable increase was no doubt related to economic prosperity, to the rising numbers of households with

Figure 1.8 Housing commission high-rise flats, Fitzroy, Melbourne, 1973

Source: Clive Forster

young children and to the privacy and security people associated with owning rather than renting a home. But federal government policies also played a crucial part. The taxation system treated owner-occupation very favourably. Many home purchasers could also get housing loans at subsidised low rates of interest from the savings banks and through special schemes for returned servicemen. Even the 'normal' interest rates were subject to tight controls. Overall, government policy made owner-occupation much more financially attractive than renting.

During the long boom, home-ownership was almost synonymous with new, detached housing. Many banks and building societies would lend on nothing else. The rise in owner-occupation therefore intensified the tendency towards suburban expansion in the capital cities, where most people were seeking to buy. The state governments also supported suburbanisation through their own public housing schemes and by building roads and other infrastructure. At the same time they allowed the inner suburbs to deteriorate and often threatened their inhabitants with slum clearance or freeway schemes. With specific government encouragement, owning one's own detached suburban home thus became—like owning a car—an expectation held by most Australian families. Arguably, it became *the* expectation: the essence of the Great Australian Dream.

The interests of capital

In the conventional view, the rapid development of low-density suburbs in Australian and other Western cities during the long boom was the result of a combination of technological, demographic, and behavioural factors, as well as the encouragement of governments. According to this view, the rise of car ownership and generous housing-finance policies allowed the young families that formed in the postwar years to exercise their preferences for low-density housing in suburbia. However, Marxist scholars such as Walker (1981) have suggested a different perspective, interpreting postwar suburbanisation in the USA as arising from the needs of capital.

The Marxist argument is that once the Second World War was over, the massive American manufacturing capacity that had developed to meet the needs of war suffered from a lack of demand. To stimulate demand, the owners of capital therefore switched their investments to housing, roads, and other infrastructure, with the assistance of the government. This obviously stimulated demand for building materials and equipment. More importantly, the development of low-density suburbs guaranteed demand for cars, refrigerators, washing machines, and other consumer durables, thereby restoring the profitability of manufacturing. According to the Marxist interpretation, government encouragement of suburbanisation through housing and service-provision policies was simply fulfilling the key role of the state in a capitalist society: seeking to restore and maintain conditions for the profitable circulation and accumulation of capital.

Badcock (1984) argues that this so-called *underconsumptionist* theory of suburbanisation fits postwar Australia less well than America. There was little evidence here of a lack of demand for manufactured goods, and much criticism of the *low* level of government investment in suburban infrastructure. However, state governments certainly aided the interests of large manufacturing companies by building public housing estates close to new suburban factories. The encouragement of home ownership by the federal government also acted, intentionally or not, to maintain high levels of demand for consumer goods. And the lack of public investment in the inner suburbs—other than in the form of freeway interchanges and flyovers—helped to make life in the outer suburbs seem preferable in comparison. Australian families may have chosen the suburban way of life freely, but it can be argued that they did so in circumstances, partly shaped by governments, that made any other choice difficult.

Divided cities?

Australian capital cities still had their individual characters at the end of the long boom, based on differences in physical site, historical development, economic base, and government policies. Journalists and essayists also claimed to recognise distinctive 'personalities': Sydney was dubbed the cosmopolitan, exciting, and frivolous 'Tinseltown'; Melbourne the solid, dull, earnestly radical 'St Petersburg' (Davidson 1986), and so on. But much more striking differences have always existed *within* our cities than *between* them; an upper-class suburb such as Toorak in Melbourne had a lot more in common with its Sydney counterpart, harbour views notwithstanding, than with working-class Richmond on the other side of the Yarra. And by the early 1970s many scholars, and even some politicians, believed that two decades of massive urban expansion had added a new dimension to patterns of residential segregation that had existed since the nineteenth century.

The new dimension was to do with the *scale* of segregation and the magnitude of differences in accessibility that had developed. As our cities expanded rapidly, so the sectors of contrasting social status and wealth dating from the nineteenth century became much larger. The western suburbs of Sydney and Melbourne, the northern and western suburbs of Adelaide, and similar areas in the other cities, came to consist of massive expanses of low-income housing, including most of the public rental stock, together with suburban concentrations of manufacturing employment. Hugh Stretton's (1989) influential book *Ideas for Australian Cities*, which was first published in 1970, pointed to the consequences of such patterns. Residents in low-income outer suburbs suffered because:

- Local councils had trouble raising rate revenue to pay for local services because of the low property values.
- The outer fringes were far removed from many state government services such as public hospitals (which tended to be located in city centres).
- Few doctors set up surgeries locally.
- Few of the teachers in the crowded and underfunded state schools lived locally.

On the other side of the city, comfortable middle-class suburbia had also perpetuated itself. Access to centrally located services was poor here too, but mattered less because there were more local doctors and better local shops, and because families could afford to own and run more cars. Local services were also better. The schools tended to have energetic, well-resourced parent bodies, and more teachers belonged to the local community. The local councils could raise ample rate revenue to provide better parks, swimming pools, and libraries. According to Stretton (1989, p. 321) our large, divided cities acted as 'both physical and psychological devices for quietly shifting resources from poorer to richer, and for excusing or concealing—with a baffled but complacent air— the increasing deprivation of the poor'. Labor Party leader Gough Whitlam's policy speech before the 1972 federal election contained perhaps the strongest—certainly the most often quoted—statement about urban inequality:

> Whatever benefits employees may secure through negotiation or arbitration will be immediately eroded by the costs of living in their cities; no amount of wealth redistribution through higher wages or lower taxes can really offset the inequalities imposed by the physical nature of the cities. Increasingly a citizen's real standard of living, the health of himself and his family, his children's opportunities for education and self-improvement, his access to employment opportunities, his ability to enjoy the nation's resources for recreation and culture, his ability to participate in the decisions and actions of the community are determined not by his income, nor by the hours he works, but by where he lives.

It was clearly somewhat far-fetched to argue that residential location determines a family's standard of living, independent of income. Income, after all, mainly determines where one can afford to live in the first place. But Stretton and other writers believed that by the end of the long boom, Australia's massive, sprawling, segregated cities significantly and unnecessarily *magnified* the differences in income. *Equity*—whether the nature of urban development was producing injustice for some groups in society—became a serious policy issue. Feminist writers also argued that life in low-density suburbs on the fringes of Australian cities had a particular impact on women, because poor access to facilities and job opportunities helped to trap them in the traditional domestic, child-rearing role. Suburbanisation was seen as reinforcing the patriarchal structure of society by heightening the distinction between the 'male' world of paid employment and production in factories and offices, and the 'female' world of unpaid domestic production, consumption, and repro-duction in the suburbs (Harman 1983). As more and more women sought to join the paid workforce, and as perceptions of the overall role of women in Australian society began to change, feminist writers increasingly questioned the image of the suburban 'good life', arguing that cities were built and planned by men, for men.

The dissatisfactions of suburban voters, particularly in the western suburbs of Sydney and Melbourne, forced urban issues back onto the federal political agenda for the first time since the 1940s. After the 1972 election the victorious Whitlam Labor government created a new federal Department of Urban and Regional Development (DURD). The new department immediately set up a program to reduce the growth of the capital cities by syphoning-off population to designated *new cities*. At the same time it sought to reduce inequality within the existing cities by providing funding directly to local councils in low-income areas. Australian cities in the early 1970s had experienced two decades of rapid expansion, and the transformation to a low-density, multi-centred structure in response to the rise of near-universal car ownership. There is no doubt that the standard of living of the average urban family had improved markedly during this time. But there was rising concern about whether our cities were becoming more unequal and less efficient, and about the environ-mental consequences of further suburban expansion. Writers from a wide range of perspectives—Marxist, conservative, 'small l liberal' reformist and feminist—were questioning the nature of city growth and seeking answers to the emerging policy issues.

Urban restructuring

The urban policy debates of the early 1970s were about issues that had arisen from city growth during a period of rapid population expansion and general economic prosperity. But even while these debates were going on, the long boom itself was ending. According to a later observer, the country was about to be 'plunged into a period of unprecedented social, cultural, political, economic and technological change in which the Australian way of life is being radically redefined' (Mackay 1993, p. 6). By the 1980s the most persistent theme in writings about our cities was *transition*. We had, it was argued, entered a new era of urban development in response to changes in society as a whole.

The term *economic restructuring* summarises the attempts by businesses and governments, following the end of the long boom, to restore profits and economic growth by changing patterns of investment, adopting new technology and changing the organisation of labour and production. The overall impact on our cities of this economic restructuring and associated demographic changes is often termed *urban restructuring*. A host of 'post' terms: *post-industrial, post-modern, post-suburban, post-Fordist*, and *post-welfare* were also imported from Europe and North America and applied to aspects of Australian cities and society. These terms, which we shall examine later, seem sometimes to have achieved what Pinch (1989, p. 905) calls 'a high level of use and a low level of meaning'. Nonetheless, our cities were undeniably affected during the 1970s and 1980s by some major and interrelated economic, technological, and demographic changes.

Economic restructuring

There were signs during the late 1960s that the long boom could not last for ever. Industries throughout the Western world experienced declining rates of profit as the impact of earlier technological innovations in manufacturing declined, as unions won increased levels of real wages for workers, and as the costs of the welfare state increased. Then in the early 1970s the international monetary system collapsed, as the US dollar crashed under the impact of the Vietnam war debt. Finally in 1973 the OPEC countries greatly increased the price of crude oil, severely damaging the economies of the Western manufacturing nations. Demand for goods fell, unemployment rose, and balance of payments crises deepened. At the same time, Japanese industrial production was achieving world dominance and the so-called newly industrialising countries (NICs) of east Asia and Latin America were emerging to capture traditional Western markets.

Transnational corporations had emerged during the 1960s: huge, diversified international companies with operations in many countries. In the 1970s the regulations that had previously controlled the movement of money between countries began to collapse, together with many tariffs and import controls that had protected domestic producers from foreign competition. Transnational corporations were then able to switch investment to whatever part of the globe offered the most profitable conditions for a given activity. They could, for example, respond to falling levels of profit by switching manufacturing operations to newly industrialising countries with low wages and low tax rates.

Australian manufacturing industries paid high wages and had developed to supply the domestic market, behind tariff barriers that protected them from overseas competition. In response to what has been called the *new international division of labour*, transnational companies with factories in Australia had every incentive to shift labour-intensive activities to countries where costs were lower, particularly after the federal government reduced the level of tariff protection. As a result, Australia lost several hundred thousand manufacturing jobs between 1971 and 1981. Employment in the service sector—particularly in business, finance, and community services—grew rapidly, as did part-time employment in the retail and wholesale trades. But unemployment rates still rose sharply and many workers suffered a loss in real income. The long boom was over.

All the major cities experienced significant changes in economic structure following the end of the long boom, as reflected in the changing nature of employment between 1971 and 1991 (table 1.5). Manufacturing jobs fell steeply in importance. The percentage of jobs in the construction, transport and storage, electricity, and communication categories also declined, though to a lesser degree. Wholesale and retail employment maintained its share of about 20 per cent of total jobs. In contrast, the finance and business, community services and entertainment (etc.) categories all rose in importance.

Table 1.5 Employment structure of major cities by industry, 1971–91 (%)

	Sydney		Melbourne		Brisbane		Adelaide		Perth	
Industry group	1971	1991	1971	1991	1971	1991	1971	1991	1971	1991
Agriculture, etc.	0.7	0.6	1.0	0.8	1.3	1.0	1.3	0.8	1.9	1.3
Mining	0.4	0.3	0.3	0.2	0.7	0.4	0.4	0.4	1.1	1.4
Manufacturing	28.3	14.0	31.4	17.8	20.8	12.8	27.5	15.3	18.8	11.2
Electricity	1.8	1.2	1.5	1.0	1.5	1.0	1.9	1.1	1.2	1.2
Construction	6.9	6.1	6.6	5.3	8.5	6.5	7.2	5.1	9.6	6.2
Wholesale and retail	19.5	19.4	19.3	19.8	22.8	20.9	21.4	19.1	22.7	20.4
Transport, storage	5.6	5.4	5.0	4.4	5.9	5.3	4.5	3.7	6.1	4.7
Communication	2.1	1.9	2.0	2.0	2.3	1.8	1.9	1.5	2.1	1.5
Finance, etc.	9.5	15.4	8.0	12.7	8.2	12.2	7.2	11.2	8.4	12.5
Public admin., defence	5.4	4.9	5.0	5.1	7.4	6.2	4.7	5.3	6.0	5.2
Community services	10.2	16.8	10.4	17.5	11.9	18.6	13.9	21.0	12.9	19.9
Entertainment, etc.	5.3	7.0	4.5	6.1	5.1	6.4	5.0	6.8	5.6	7.2
Other, not stated	4.5	7.0	5.0	7.4	3.7	6.8	3.0	8.5	3.7	7.6
Total employed	100	100	100	100	100	100	100	100	100	100
% of total Australian employment	23.9	22.0	20.5	18.6	6.6	8.1	6.6	6.2	5.5	6.7

Data are for major industry categories of the employed population of capital city Statistical Divisions, unadjusted for intercensal boundary changes

Source: ABS 1971 and 1991 censuses

New technology

Technological innovations accompanied structural economic change, and intensified its impact. Manufacturers who did not relocate to low-wage countries often sought instead to reduce costs by using computerised technology, leading to *deskilling* (skilled workers being replaced by cheaper unskilled operatives), and *jobless growth* (output rises but the number of workers remains the same or even falls). The same trends affected clerical employment in both the public and private sectors. At the same time many firms switched to *flexible production* styles of organisation, which involved replacing permanent, full-time workers, wherever possible, with casual, part-time employees or subcontractors who could be more easily hired or fired as demand rose or fell.

Advanced telecommunication and information-processing technology was also essential to the deregulated international financial system. Organisations could electronically transmit credit or debt, as well as huge amounts of complex information, almost instantaneously to any part of the world. The collection, processing, and exchange of information has been a major function of cities since ancient times, but the new technology transformed and intensified this role. Around the world, some cities emerged as information control centres in their national, or even the global economy. Others, in contrast, suffered a loss of influence and prosperity and had to seek fresh roles to play in the newly integrated national and international scenes.

Demographic change

The postwar population boom also ended during the 1970s. Fertility rates had been declining since 1961, and in 1976 finally fell below the 'replacement' or 'zero population growth' level of an average of 2.1 children born to each woman during her lifetime (Hugo 1986, pp. 44–5). At the same time, the new Whitlam federal Labor government had severely cut the intake of immigrants. All the major cities, but particularly Sydney and Melbourne, grew more slowly between 1971 and 1991 (table 1.6), reinforcing the impacts of economic and technological change by further reducing the demand for manufactured goods.

When the Fraser federal government turned the immigration 'tap' on again in the late 1970s, refugee programs brought many people to Australia from South East Asia—particularly Vietnam—and Latin America. The emphasis on family-reunion immigration during the 1980s further swelled these numbers. Many New Zealanders, who were a special category with free entry rights, also entered the country, as did people from the Middle East. The European countries that had been the main sources of migrants during the long boom—the UK, Italy, Greece, and Germany—declined in relative importance. In Sydney, Melbourne, and Adelaide the absolute numbers in these groups even

Table 1.6 Major city growth and urbanisation, 1971–91

	1971			1991			1971–1991
	Pop ('000)	% State	% Aust	Pop ('000)	% State	% Aust	% Pop change
Sydney	2808	61	22	3538	62	21	26
Melbourne	2503	72	20	3023	72	18	21
Brisbane	868	48	7	1334	45	8	54
Adelaide	843	72	7	1024	73	6	22
Perth	703	68	6	1143	72	7	63
Total	7725		61	10 062		60	30

Total population data are for capital city Statistical Divisions as defined at the 1971 and 1991 censuses and have not been adjusted for minor boundary changes

Source: ABS 1971 and 1991 censuses

fell, as deaths and return migrants outnumbered new arrivals. New Zealand, Vietnam, Lebanon, the Philippines, China, Malaysia, and other non-European countries became important countries of origin, and the populations of Sydney and Melbourne in particular became increasingly ethnically diverse. The 1991 Census revealed that in Sydney the two most common non-English languages spoken by people in their homes were Chinese and Arabic.

Family structures also changed significantly. Not only did the proportion of aged persons rise, but the young nuclear families that characterised Australian society during the long boom became a statistical minority, as households became smaller and more diverse. Single parent families became much more common, especially following the passing of the Family Law Act of 1974, which made divorce easier. Single parent families and the aged were the fastest growing low-income groups, and because females made up the majority in each group a *feminisation of poverty* occurred. Families supported by one male breadwinner also become a minority. Many more women stayed in the paid workforce after marriage, reflecting a combination of economic necessity, the changing role of women in society, and the changing nature of job opportunities. These demographic trends, as will be discussed in chapters 4 and 5, had major impacts on housing demand, the operation of housing markets, the population structure of residential areas in our cities, and demands for public services such as education and health care.

Post-modern cities?

The period of economic, technological, and demographic change following the long boom coincided with, and has been related to, the so-called post-modern period. Soja (1989) and other writers of the time discussed the emergence of the post-modern city. This term implies much more than a change in architecture. It is true that the functional concrete and glass boxes that characterised city centres and public housing projects alike during the modernist long boom gave way to an emphasis on external appearance, expressed in extravagant mixtures of shape, colour, and material, and in 'references' to past styles. But the post-modern city was also characterised generally by diversity, change, lack of order, the juxtapositioning of contrasting functions and buildings. We saw the 'creation' of urban landscapes: massive shopping malls, tourist theme parks, entertainment centres, and artificial marinas. Some of these things were clearly connected to economic restructuring: for example, the demise of functions associated with sea ports, warehousing and manufacturing, and the rise of tourism. Others seemed to relate to deeper cultural changes and, as Rabin (1974) suggested many years ago in his book *Soft City*, cannot be explained by 'hard' economic or demographic facts and figures. Perhaps the most striking developments were in the inner suburbs that had become so run-down and neglected during the long boom.

The gentrification of the inner suburbs

The term *gentrification* was first used in Britain in the 1960s to describe the invasion of run-down suburbs in inner London by middle- and upper-class people: the 'gentry'. Houses were renovated, property values rose, and working-class suburbs became transformed into 'trendy' residential areas. The same phenomenon, which also occurred in some North American cities, had emerged in Australia by the late 1960s. It began with the renovation of nineteenth-century terrace housing in areas such as Carlton in Melbourne and Paddington in Sydney (figure 1.9). Gentrification then spread rapidly to other inner suburbs occupied by low-income families, including many southern European migrants. Other types of residential development followed later, such as the conversion of warehouses and factories into apartments and the building of new townhouses on old industrial sites. All tend to be lumped together as gentrification, though a more general term such as *residential revitalisation* might be more accurate. In any case, significant concentrations of people with high incomes, university qualifications, and professional occupations developed in the inner suburbs of all five major cities, particularly Sydney, Melbourne, and Adelaide.

Gentrification provided a classic battleground for competing explanations of changing urban structure. Marxists argued that, as always, the circulation and accumulation of capital was the key (Smith & Williams 1986). The inner suburbs became run-down through disinvestment during the long boom, which eventually produced the conditions for profitable reinvestment as property became severely undercapitalised. Behaviourists stressed the changing

Figure 1.9 Gentrified nineteenth-century housing, inner Sydney, 1994
Source: Clive Forster

structure of households and shifts in housing preferences. The inner suburbs were close to the jobs, universities, and entertainment opportunities of the city centre and had 'character'. The young, childless, two-income couples that made up an increasing proportion of urban households began to find a smaller dwelling in the inner city more appealing than a new conventional house in the increasingly remote outer suburbs. Other writers pointed to the role of institutions, particularly the increasing willingness of banks and building societies to give loans to buy older property. Cultural geographers also pointed out the role played by gay and lesbian households in the revitalisation of some inner suburbs. Darlinghurst in Sydney is the best known example, but particular inner suburbs in all the major cities became preferred by some gay and lesbian people as more congenial and welcoming residential environments than outer suburbia dominated by 'straight' nuclear families.

Most recent explanations of the revitalisation of the inner suburbs, how-ever, have stressed the role of economic restructuring as the driving force behind gentrification. The nature of employment in the inner city changed markedly in the 1970s and 1980s, with the demise of manufacturing and the rise of advanced services jobs in finance and business. According to Ley (1986) it was this change that, 'produced the gentrifiers': young professionals with jobs in the inner city who set about colonising the nearby suburbs and shaping them to their needs. Gentrification does tend to conjure up images of 'yuppies', and 'trendies' in the financial world leading a lifestyle of conspicuous consumption.

Gentrification, broadly defined, undoubtedly had a major impact on our inner suburbs. Property values sky-rocketed. For example the value of residential property in Adelaide's inner suburbs doubled in real terms between 1970 and 1988. People who owned their dwellings were able to sell and realise a handsome capital gain. But many poor households in rented dwellings were displaced from suburbs that had traditionally provided cheap housing, good access to public transport and other services, and the support of close-knit communities. Overall, the proportion of owner-occupied dwellings rose and the supply of rental housing declined. But not all the poor left. The inner suburbs still contained many of the poorest people in the city—including the statistically invisible homeless—as well as the new 'gentry'. By the end of the 1980s, expensively renovated nineteenth- and early twentieth-century housing and shopping streets adjoined surviving working-class districts. Old factories and warehouses had become expensive studio apartments, cheek by jowl with new townhouses and the housing commission flats left over from the 1960s. Following the financial crash of the late 1980s, some office blocks in the heart of Melbourne's CBD were even converted to flats. The residential landscape of the inner city came to typify the economically polarised diversity and disorder of the post-modern era.

Continuity and change?

As noted earlier, writers have used a range of terms in addition to *post-modern* to imply transition to a distinctively different kind of urban life in the 1970s and 1980s in advanced capitalist societies such as Australia (Marcuse 1993). As early as 1973, Bell wrote of *post-industrial society*, denoting the decline of manufacturing industry as the dominant economic force, and the rise of the service and information economy. Later, *post-suburban* referred to the disappearance of the distinction between central commercial 'city' and surrounding largely residential 'suburbs', as employment becomes increasingly scattered within sprawling, multi-centred urban regions. *Post-Fordist* noted the adoption of flexible production systems of work organisation in place of Fordist mass production systems. *Post-welfare* referred to the changing and diminishing provision of public services, compared with the rapid growth of the welfare state during the long boom. By the 1980s, governments throughout the developed world were seeking to attract international capital by creating more profitable conditions for private investment. In attempting to do this, the Reagan administration in the United States of America and the Thatcher government in Britain led the way in reducing levels of public expenditure and indebtedness. By the mid 1980s, Australian governments of both political persuasions had followed suit.

During the 1970s and 1980s Australia's major cities might have grown more slowly than in the long boom. But, as the above list of *post*-terms implies, they still experienced significant changes, increasingly influenced by the economic, cultural, and political impacts of what we now refer to as *globalisation*. This phenomenon, which has dominated discussion about urban development and urban policy in recent years, is the subject of the next chapter. We should not get too carried away by notions of transition or transformation, however. There is nothing new about change. Cities throughout history have continually adapted to economic, social, and technological trends, but in ways that build upon their past history. We have seen that many of the characteristics of Australian cities today were already well established by the end of the nineteenth century: metropolitan primacy; low-density suburbs; high levels of home ownership; segregation by social class. The changes to Australian cities during the 1940s, 1950s, and 1960s—the further rise of home ownership, the transition from public transport to the automobile, the development of ethnic diversity through immigration, the growth of 'big government', the doubling of major city populations, and the suburbanisation of manufacturing and retailing—still play a tremendously important role in shaping urban life today. The 'urban problems' and policy debates of the early 1970s are still relevant to today's concerns about the economic and environmental consequences of continued low-density urban expansion, or about inequalities within cities in standards of living and access to jobs and services. And the economic restructuring of the 1980s set the scene for more recent trends.

Australia's major cities today are clearly undergoing some complex changes, with significant impacts on the lives of their inhabitants. The chapters that follow, in attempting to analyse and understand these changes, will stress the importance of recent economic, demographic, and technological trends. But we should never lose sight of the long-established and persistent character of Australian urban environments and culture, and the historical processes that have created them and will continue to influence their future.

2

Cities in a Globalising World

Australia and the other countries of the world have not simply operated since the mid-1970s in an environment of slower growth. They are also acting in an environment in which production, trade, and financial flows have been increasingly integrated across national boundaries in an emerging global economy. The process of globalisation has put firms in one country in direct competition with those in others, and appears to pit workers in different parts of the world against one another in competition for jobs, wages, and working conditions. (Fagan & Webber 1994, pp. 13–14)

Writers use the term *globalisation* to summarise the increasing degree to which our cities and our overall society are shaped by global flows of capital and ideas, and by the need to compete with the rest of the world. Stilwell (1997, p. 7) defines globalisation as 'the intensification of international economic connections' in the closely related areas of production, trade, investment, and finance. As Stilwell points out, and as should be clear from chapter 1, there is nothing new in Australian cities being influenced by international flows of capital, information, goods, and people. But during the past twenty-five years this influence has been intensified by the accelerated 'shrinking of space' brought about by developments in information technology and air transport, by the deregulation of the global financial system, and by government policies that aim to encourage freer international trade. The economic and social consequences of globalisation were already becoming apparent in the 1980s, as discussed in chapter 1, but the process gathered pace rapidly during the 1990s (O'Connor et al. 2001, pp. 18–30).

Economic change

Today's cities are open cities. Open to the influences of a deregulated international financial system. Open to the structural changes which have accompanied the growth of global manufacturing processes. Open to the implications of philosophies that argue for less rather than more government involvement. Open to the operational changes which the revolution in communication systems has produced. (Daly 1988, p. 150)

This quotation, now more than fifteen years old, comes from a paper titled *Australian Cities: the Challenge of the 1980s*. It summarised powerfully the impacts of globalisation on our cities, as seen at the time. Daly argued that the various major cities were seeking, or were having imposed upon them, different roles in the new national and international economic structure. During the long boom each city was still largely independent, the unquestioned economic and administrative leader of its semi-closed state economy. But since the 1970s, more than ever before, the cities have competed against one another— and against the rest of the world—as state governments strive, with few holds barred, to attract capital investment and employment.

Urban entrepreneurialism

Peter Hall, one of the world's best-known writers about cities, has gone so far as to claim that 'cities can increasingly determine their own future. It merely takes will and imagination' (Hall 1992, p. 7). Recent writers point to the success of cities such as Bilbao, an old industrial centre in the Basque region of Spain. Bilbao is becoming a major centre of cultural tourism following the construction of architect Frank Gehry's spectacular Guggenheim museum. Glasgow in Scotland, which suffered a catastrophic decline in its traditional manufacturing and shipbuilding industries, has also 're-made' itself as one of Europe's major arts, architecture, and design centres.

Hard-pressed Australian state governments at the end of 1980s, faced with economic recession and the loss of traditional industries, might well have objected to the term 'merely' in Hall's paper! But they all, led by the Kennett government in Victoria in the 1990s, became *urban entrepreneurs* desperately competing for investment and jobs. All tried to attract major capital investment projects—so called mega-projects—to their cities (figure 2.1). Most sponsored technology parks in the hope of capturing high-technology developments. All attempted to boost tourism. Each capital city now has its casino (Brisbane's, ironically, is located in the old State Treasury Building). The hosting of major sporting events came to be hotly contested. The Victorian government 'stole' the Australian Formula One Grand Prix from Adelaide in the early 1990s amid howls of protest. The success of Sydney's bid to host the 2000 Olympic Games was followed by Victorian allegations that Melbourne's bid for the 1996 Games was sabotaged by New South Wales interests. On the international stage, Adelaide losing to Kuala Lumpur in the contest to host the 1998 Commonwealth Games provided TV viewers with the spectacle of a tearful Lord Mayor and provoked local claims of political interference and unfair dealing.

Under the impact of globalisation the smaller capital cities in particular have become less inward-looking and parochial, and perhaps more exciting to live in. But has this been at the cost of local independence? Take the example of Adelaide. In the 1970s Adelaide had its own long-established trading bank. Its newspapers, radio, and TV stations, though not all locally owned, produced local material for local audiences. Major club-sport—notably Australian Rules football—was entirely played between teams from suburban Adelaide. Today, Adelaide's radio and TV stations are overwhelmingly controlled from beyond the state, more and more programs are networked nationally, and despite 'Australian content' rules we face an intense cultural bombardment of American and British programs (and advertisements). Only one local daily newspaper survives, and that duplicates increasing amounts of material from its national stablemate *The Australian*. Adelaide sporting clubs play against

Figure 2.1 Southbank, Melbourne, 2004: a residential, office, and entertainment mega-project built in the 1990s on old industrial land across the Yarra from the CBD. The building under construction is the 88 storey Eureka Tower, which will be the world's tallest residential building when completed. Note in the background the Melbourne Park tennis arenas, and the Melbourne Cricket Ground undergoing reconstruction in preparation for the 2006 Commonwealth Games.

Source: Clive Forster

clubs from other cities in national football, netball, soccer, basketball, baseball, hockey, and even ice-hockey competitions. In 1997 and 1998 'Crow mania' overwhelmed the city when the Adelaide Crows won two successive Australian (formerly Victorian) Football League premierships. Support for the local league, on the other hand, has declined and surveys suggest that young people increasingly identify with American basketball stars rather than home-grown sporting heroes. The Bank of Adelaide ceased to exist many years ago (though a new Adelaide Bank has arisen) and the State Bank of South Australia (now Bank SA) suffered from a disastrous foray into 'entrepreneurialism' in the late 1980s, aimed at boosting the state's ailing economy. Adelaide, like the other smaller capitals, has indeed become an *open city*, exposed to the pressures of a more uncertain and perilous world.

Like other cities, Adelaide has responded to changing circumstances by attempting to 'sell' itself to the world. An *Adelaide 21* strategy was adopted in the late 1990s, declaring Adelaide to be *The Contented Metropolis*, and attempting to promote the city centre in particular via five themes: *The Learning City, The City of Creative Imagination, The Gateway to South Australia, The Gathering Place*, and *The City of Light and Style*. In 2003, UK urban revitalisation expert Charles Landry was invited to Adelaide as part of the state government's Thinkers in Residence program, to advise on 'helping Adelaide unlock its creative potential'. It is too early to judge whether these measures will help—in Peter Hall's terms—to determine a new future for Adelaide. But the rest of this chapter highlights the urgency of the problems facing the city.

Structural change in city economies

Table 2.1 shows how the economic structure of the five major cities changed between 1991 and 2001, as measured by changes in the percentage of jobs in the main industry categories. The impact of globalisation and the accompanying economic restructuring has varied, partly because of the different industrial structures possessed by the cities in the 1980s and partly because of their differing degrees of success in attracting new economic development and population growth since then (O'Connor et al. 2001).

By 2001, finance, insurance, property, and business services had become the largest single employment category in Sydney, and was significantly more important than in the other cities, both in absolute numbers and as a proportion of total jobs. This reflects the degree to which Sydney has become Australia's key financial control centre, linking the country to the global financial system. Most of the country's top companies and financial institutions now have their headquarters in Sydney rather than in Melbourne, which had been dominant during the long boom. Sydney has therefore been particularly

Table 2.1 Employment structure of major cities by industry, 1991–2001

	Per cent employed in each industry group, 1991					Per cent employed in each industry group, 2001				
	Syd.	Melb.	Bris.	Per.	Adel.	Syd.	Melb.	Bris.	Per.	Adel.
Agriculture, forestry, fishing, and mining	1.0	1.0	1.6	2.9	1.3	0.8	1.0	1.5	3.0	1.6
Manufacturing	14.7	18.7	13.3	11.7	16.3	12.5	16.3	12.4	11.2	15.6
Electricity, gas, water supply, and construction	7.8	6.8	8.0	8.0	6.8	7.7	7.1	7.6	8.3	6.6
Wholesale and retail trade	21.1	21.7	22.9	22.3	21.3	19.9	21.1	21.0	21.5	20.3
Accommodation, cafes, and restaurants	4.1	3.3	3.6	4.0	3.8	4.9	4.2	4.5	4.5	4.5
Transport, storage, and communication services	7.8	7.0	7.6	6.6	5.7	7.5	6.3	7.1	5.8	5.7
Finance, insurance, property, and business services	17.3	14.5	13.8	14.2	13.1	21.1	18.1	16.0	16.3	14.7
Government admin. and defence	5.3	5.5	6.7	5.6	5.8	3.5	2.9	4.9	4.3	4.6
Education, health, and community services	15.1	16.1	16.9	18.2	19.8	15.7	16.6	18.5	18.3	20.0
Cultural, recreational, personal, and other services	5.7	5.4	5.7	6.4	6.2	6.5	6.2	6.5	6.8	6.5
Total employed	100	100	100	100	100	100	100	100	100	100
% of total Australian employment	22.0	18.6	8.1	6.8	6.2	21.9	18.6	8.9	7.3	5.6

	Number employed in each Industry group, 2001 ('000)				
	Syd.	Melb.	Bris.	Per.	Adel.
Agriculture, forestry, fishing, and mining	13.6	15.1	10.8	18.0	7.2
Manufacturing	226.4	252.4	92.1	68.0	72.9
Electricity, gas, water supply, and construction	139.8	110.0	56.4	50.5	30.6
Wholesale and retail trade	361.6	325.3	155.3	130.4	94.9
Accommodation, cafes, and restaurants	88.6	65.5	33.1	27.5	21.0
Transport, storage, and communication services	136.8	97.5	52.5	35.1	26.8
Finance, insurance, property, and business services	383.0	279.8	118.4	98.6	68.5
Government admin. and defence	63.3	45.4	36.3	26.1	21.3
Education, health, and community services	284.6	257.1	137.1	110.8	93.2
Cultural, recreational, personal, and other services	118.5	96.3	47.7	41.3	30.3
Total employed	1816.2	1544.3	739.8	606.4	466.8
% growth in employment 1991–2001	16.7	16.9	29.1	26.7	5.9

Data are for grouped major industry categories of the employed population of capital city Statistical Divisions, unadjusted for intercensal boundary changes. To improve comparability, 'not stated' and 'non-classifiable' categories in 1991 and 2001 have been allocated on a pro rata basis to the major industry groups.

Source: ABS 2001 Census, Time Series Community Profile.

successful in attracting jobs in *producer services* (services provided to other businesses), in contrast to *consumer services* such as health care, social welfare, education, and government administration where it lags behind the other capitals. Sydney also leads in the percentage of jobs that are associated with the hospitality and transport and communication industries. *Sydney: the Global City* (Searle 1996) has become a state government slogan, and hosting the 2000 Olympic Games further reinforced Sydney's status as Australia's main gateway to the world (Connell 2000).

Melbourne is still Australia's second most important financial centre, and strong economic growth in the 1990s resulted in finance, insurance, property, and business services employment growing strongly to 2001. Manufacturing has also remained more important in Melbourne than in the other cities. The Victorian government has attempted to make a virtue of this by promoting Melbourne as the core of the country's remaining manufacturing sector, though the city had suffered before 1991 by losing many manufacturing jobs without the compensating developments enjoyed by Sydney. The privatisation policies of the Kennett era also resulted in Melbourne having relatively less employment than the other cities in the main public-sector categories: government administration and defence, and education, health, and community services.

Perth and Brisbane have the smallest percentages of manufacturing employment, a reflection of their minor manufacturing role during the long boom. Despite recent growth, they also have smaller finance sectors than Sydney or Melbourne and are now clearly *service* economies, dominated by wholesaling and retailing, education, health, and community services, and entertainment. The economies of both Western Australia and Queensland depend heavily on agriculture and the exploitation of mineral resources, and Brisbane has also prospered through Queensland's boom in retirement migration and tourism, with heavy involvement of overseas capital. Table 2.1 also shows that Perth and Brisbane shared the highest rates of overall job growth between 1991 and 2001, with total employment increasing by almost 30 per cent compared with only 17 per cent in Sydney and Melbourne.

In Adelaide, the total number of jobs grew by only 6 per cent during the 1990s, and the structure of employment changed less than the other capitals—worrying signs for the state government. Manufacturing jobs were still relatively important in 2001, and education, health, and community services employed a higher percentage of people than in the other capitals. In contrast, Adelaide had the lowest percentage of jobs in the new key sector of finance, insurance, property, and business services.

In spite of these differences, the industrial structures of the five major cities in 2001 would probably still strike an observer from outside Australia as being essentially similar. Following the decline in manufacturing and the rise in finance and business, employment is spread more evenly over the major industry categories than it was in 1971 (table 1.5). In each city, manufacturing, wholesaling and retailing, finance and business, and community services are the only categories containing over 10 per cent of total jobs. No category contains more than 22 per cent. It is true that the importance of the categories varies from city to city. But even in Sydney, where the decline in manufacturing had been steepest, the category still employed 226 000 workers in 2001 and comprised 12.5 per cent of all jobs. In Adelaide, where the finance and business category was least important, it still made up 14.7 per cent of all jobs and employed almost 70 000 people. Our major cities may be developing different roles in the new 'open' global economy (Daly 1988), and some are certainly growing and prospering more than others. A feature in the *Australian* newspaper (Gunn 1998) claimed that Australia's cities were becoming 'more diverse and the myth of a nation of equality is being challenged'. But table 2.1 suggests that the contrasts in employment structure, though significant, are less marked than some commentators suggest. This is partly due to the cities' large size and their long-standing nature as diversified commercial and administrative centres rather than specialised manufacturing cities. The importance of consumer services is also a major stabilising factor; the cities each need approximately the same number of teachers, nurses, etc., per thousand residents.

Demographic change

Falling birth rates during the 1990s, coupled with the fact that people were living longer, continued to produce significant changes in the age structure of the major cities. Perth was the fastest-growing major city between 1991 and 2001 and Melbourne was one of the slowest. But figure 2.2 shows that they have experienced very similar reductions in the proportion of population aged below 35 and increases in the 45–59 age groups (the large baby boom generation whose progress towards retirement fills governments with such alarm) and the over 70 groups. In the other cities the general pattern is the same, as populations age and families with children make up a declining percentage of households.

The increasing intensity of connections between Australia and the rest of the world—a key part of globalisation—has complicated the impact of immigration on our cities. The federal government reduced annual quotas for permanent immigrants in the early 1990s, but intakes rose again in 1995–96. Since then the number of permanent settlers arriving each year has fluctuated between 80 000 and 100 000 (Australia, Department of Immigration and Multicultural and Indigenous Affairs 2003). The quota system has also changed to favour applicants with skills or economic resources, with smaller quotas in

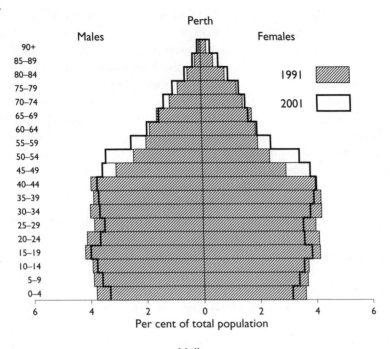

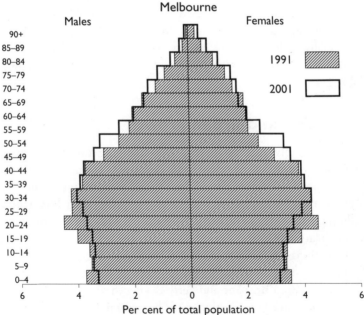

Figure 2.2 Age–sex structure of Perth and Melbourne, 1991–2001

Source: ABS 2001 Census, Time Series Community Profiles.

the humanitarian and family reunion categories. Of the 93 000 permanent settlers who arrived in 1999–2000, 35 per cent were in the skill category, compared with 22 per cent in the family category and 8 per cent in the humanitarian category. A further 34 per cent were New Zealand citizens, who have automatic right of entry to Australia. The origin of migrants has continued to diversify. New Zealand and the UK, the most important countries of origin, are now followed by China, South Africa, India, the Philippines, and Indonesia.

Another sign of the increasingly complex nature of migration is that in 1999–2000 the net population gain (arrivals minus departures) through permanent settlement was overtaken for the first time by net gain through long-term temporary migration (persons intending to stay in Australia for over a year but not settle permanently; Australia, Department of Immigration and Multicultural and Indigenous Affairs 2003). Since 1990 the number of long-term temporary migrants has almost doubled, to over 210 000 in 1999–2000. Most are either students, mainly from Indonesia, Korea, Malaysia, China, and India, or business people here for employment reasons, mainly from the UK, USA, Japan, China, and South Africa. Over the same period, the number of people leaving Australia on a long-term temporary basis has also risen, to almost 160 000.

Overall, Australia gained 107 000 people in 1999–2000 through net migration (permanent and long-term temporary arrivals minus permanent and long-term temporary departures). Most of these are located in the large cities, especially Sydney. Table 2.2 shows the cumulative impact of immigration on the major cities over the years, and makes an interesting comparison with table 1.4.

Urbanisation and urban growth

This book is mainly concerned with the changing internal geography of Australia's major cities, rather than with changes between them or with the changing nature of settlement patterns as a whole. But it is important to understand the general nature of trends at the between-city level. Sydney, with almost four million inhabitants in 2001, and Melbourne, with 3.4 million (table 2.3), are still much larger than the 'second division' cities. However Adelaide, which had been the third-largest city in 1966 following strong growth in manufacturing jobs and immigration during the long boom, is now firmly in fifth place and fell farther behind Brisbane and Perth during the 1990s.

Table 2.4 shows the contribution made by natural increase, internal migration, and migration from overseas to the growth of each mainland state's population (data for the capital cities themselves were not available at the time of writing, but their trends can be inferred from the state figures). Queensland

Table 2.2 Ethnic composition of major city populations, 2001

Birthplace	Sydney Persons ('000)	%	Melbourne Persons ('000)	%	Brisbane Persons ('000)	%	Perth Persons ('000)	%	Adelaide Persons ('000)	%
Australia	2454	66.6	2195	69.7	1200	78.0	843	66.8	769	75.3
United Kingdom	184	5.0	158	5.0	93	6.0	164	13.0	100	9.8
China (excluding Taiwan)	82	2.2	36	1.1	7	0.4	5	0.4	3	0.3
New Zealand	82	2.2	46	1.5	65	4.2	33	2.6	8	0.8
Viet Nam	61	1.7	56	1.8	11	0.7	10	0.8	10	1.0
Lebanon	52	1.4	14	0.4	1	0.1	1	0.1	1	0.1
Former Yugoslavia*	50	1.4	59	1.9	8	0.6	14	1.1	9	0.9
Italy	49	1.3	80	2.5	7	0.5	21	1.6	23	2.3
Philippines	47	1.3	20	0.6	8	0.5	4	0.3	4	0.4
Hong Kong	36	1.0	15	0.5	5	0.3	3	0.3	2	0.2
India	35	0.9	29	0.9	5	0.3	12	1.0	3	0.3
Greece	34	0.9	56	1.8	3	0.2	3	0.2	11	1.0
South Africa	25	0.7	14	0.5	9	0.6	14	1.1	3	0.3
Germany	20	0.5	22	0.7	9	0.6	8	0.6	10	1.0
Malaysia	19	0.5	24	0.8	5	0.4	17	1.3	4	0.4
Other**	458	12.4	325	10.3	103	6.7	110	8.7	60	5.8
Total***	3689	100	3149	100	1538	100	1261	100	1021	100

Data are for Statistical Divisions
   * Comprising Croatia, Macedonia, Serbia and Montenegro
  ** Countries not comprising 1% of the population in any city
*** Excluding not stated and overseas visitors
     = Six largest birthplace groups in each city

Source: ABS 2001 Census

Table 2.3 Major city growth and urbanisation, 1991–2001

	1991 Pop ('000)	% State	% Aust	2001 Pop ('000)	% State	% Aust	1991–2001 % Pop Change
Sydney	3538	62	21	3997	63	21	13
Melbourne	3023	72	18	3367	73	18	11
Brisbane	1334	45	8	1628	45	9	22
Adelaide	1024	73	6	1073	73	6	5
Perth	1143	72	7	1340	72	7	17
Total	10 062		60	11 404		60	13

Total population data are for capital city Statistical Divisions as defined at the 1991 and 2001 censuses and have not been adjusted for minor boundary changes

Source: ABS 1991 and 2001 censuses

and Western Australia were the only states to gain population by people moving from elsewhere in Australia. New South Wales suffered significant losses from internal migration, and depended for much of its growth on high levels of immigration from overseas to replace the people who had moved out, plus natural increase. Sydney is now clearly the main destination for new immigrants to Australia. Table 2.4 suggests that trends in Victoria were similar to New South Wales. But figures for the whole period 1991–2001 conceal the fact that by the late 1990s Melbourne was actually recording population gains through internal migration—an extraordinary tribute to the city's economic revival—and Sydney's losses had declined significantly (Hugo 2003, p.204). According to McDonald & Kippen (2002) much of this turnaround reflects the attractions of job opportunities in Sydney and Melbourne for young Australians from the smaller cities. Adelaide, which grew very slowly during the 1990s (table 2.3), depended almost entirely on natural increase and actually lost more people through internal migration than it gained from overseas.

When all Australian cities with populations over 100 000 are examined (table 2.5), it emerges that Adelaide grew more slowly than any of the other centres except Hobart between 1996 and 2001. The traditional industrial cities of Newcastle, Wollongong, and Geelong also languished. The most rapidly expanding major urban areas are now the resort/retirement centres of the Sunshine Coast and the Gold Coast, followed by Darwin, Townsville, and Brisbane. Canberra and Cairns—boom cities in the 1980s and early 1990s—grew much more slowly in the late 1990s.

Core-periphery or sunbelt-rustbelt?

Sydney and Melbourne still contained 39 per cent of the Australian population and 41 per cent of the country's jobs in 2001, compared with 42 per cent and 44 per cent respectively in 1971. That they remain so dominant, in spite of the more rapid growth of other centres such as Brisbane, Perth, and the Gold Coast, is a striking example of the power of *inertia*: the strong

Table 2.4 Components of population growth, mainland states, 1991–2001 (%)

	Natural increase	Net internal migration	Net overseas migration	Total
New South Wales	64.9	−21.5	56.6	100
Victoria	71.6	−23.4	51.8	100
Queensland	37.9	18.5	43.6	100
South Australia	103.5	−46.8	43.2	100
Western Australia	54.0	3.6	42.4	100

Source: ABS 2003c

influence of past development upon what happens in the future. Sydney and Melbourne are so big that, even if their rates of growth fall compared with smaller cities, their dominance will only decline very slowly. They continue to be by far the country's largest markets for goods and services, and the largest pools of labour. They continue to attract the majority of new immigrants and overseas visitors, and most capital investment. Almost all the country's largest companies and financial institutions have their headquarters in Sydney or Melbourne, and most research and development (R&D) activity is concentrated there. They remain the country's key gateways to the rest of the world, capturing approximately 70 per cent of international air passenger, air freight, and sea container traffic. Sydney is dominant in most of these measures but Melbourne, because of its sheer size, does not lag far behind except in air traffic and international immigrants and visitors (O'Connor et al. 2001, pp. 80–1). McDonald and Kippen (2002) also suggest that recent economic growth in Melbourne is complementary to Sydney's growth rather than in competition with the rival city, being based on Melbourne's different role as a manufacturing and goods transport centre.

It can therefore be argued that Australia still consists of a powerful economic and population *core* consisting of Victoria and New South Wales (and the Australian Capital Territory) and centred upon their capital cities, and a subservient *periphery* consisting of the other states and territories. Some

Table 2.5 Urban centres of over 100 000 population, 2001

	Population ('000)	% change 1991–96
Sydney*	3997	6.8
Melbourne*	3367	7.3
Brisbane*	1628	9.3
Perth*	1340	7.7
Adelaide*	1073	2.6
Newcastle**	471	4.6
Gold Coast–Tweed Heads**	444	18.1
Canberra–Queanbeyan**	353	5.4
Wollongong**	258	4.5
Sunshine Coast**	192	15.0
Hobart*	191	0.6
Geelong**	152	6.2
Townsville**	135	9.8
Cairns**	126	4.1
Darwin*	109	9.9

* Statistical Divisions
** Statistical Districts

Source: ABS 2001 Census

observers believe, however, that the recent shifts in the distribution of population, employment, and capital investment are producing fundamental
changes in the pattern of urban settlement. Much of the urban growth in
Queensland, Western Australia, and the Australian Capital Territory has been
based on people moving from the old 'industrial' states of New South Wales,
Victoria, and South Australia (table 2.4), either in search of job opportunities
or, especially in Queensland, to retire. This has been likened to the movement
of people and capital investment from the declining industrial *rustbelt* or
snowbelt cities in the north east of the USA, to the so-called *sunbelt* of the
south and the west coast. The term *sunbelt* tends to oversimplify a patchy and
complex process in both countries (*sunspots* has been suggested as more appropriate) but the population shift, especially to the coastal strip stretching from
north of Sydney to the Sunshine Coast, and with outliers as far north as
Cairns, is striking. Mullins (1993) has labelled much of the growth *tourism
urbanisation* '…based on the sale and consumption of fun'.

The core-periphery and sunbelt-rustbelt concepts are not mutually exclusive. The former emphasises continuity and the power of inertia; the latter
focuses on change. Both help to explain why Australia's settlement pattern is
increasingly dominated by almost continuous urban settlement along the
eastern and south-eastern coastline. Sydney is consolidating its position as
the major centre, but with the most rapid growth occurring to the north the
'centre of gravity' of the country's economic and population core is shifting
(figure 2.3). Population projections released by the ABS (2003d) suggest that
by the year 2051 Queensland's population will have overtaken that of Victoria,
with Brisbane's share of the total Australian population rising from 8.6 per
cent in 2001 to 11.4. Perth's share is also projected to rise from 7.1 per cent to
8.5. Sydney and Melbourne are expected to retain their current shares of about
21 per cent and 18 per cent respectively. In contrast, Adelaide's share is
projected to decline from its present 4.9 per cent to only 4.3.

Attempting to forecast populations fifty years into the future is obviously
very difficult, and the above figures are based on the middle of three sets
of assumptions about likely trends in fertility, immigration, and internal
migration—all of which may turn out to be wrong. But the direction of population shift within Australia's urban system seems clear, even if the magnitude
of change is less certain.

Mega-cities?

In the coastal belt of urban development, the distinction between city and
country is becoming increasingly blurred. Areas outside Sydney and Melbourne
that were once rural have experienced rapid population growth, made up of

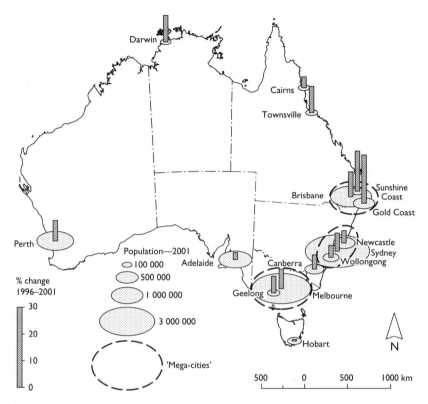

Figure 2.3 Australian major cities and other large urban areas, 2001

Source: adapted from Maher 1993, p. 800, and ABS 1996 and 2001 censuses

long distance commuters and people on retirement pensions or other welfare payments. As these fringe developments extend outwards, they have joined up with existing smaller centres. O'Connor (1993) contends that, as the result, *mega-cities* are evolving. Figure 2.3 shows O'Connor's suggested mega-cities, with populations updated from 2001 Census data. A Sydney mega-city of almost 5 million people now extends from Newcastle to Wollongong, rivalled further south by a Melbourne mega-city of 3.5 million, including Geelong. Significantly, a third, rapidly-growing mega-city is emerging in the Sunshine Coast–Greater Brisbane–Gold Coast region, which already has a total population of 2.3 million and is capable of overtaking the Melbourne region to become Australia's second-largest mega-city by the middle of the 21st century.

The three mega-cities are coming to resemble USA-style *conurbations*, formed when once separate cities begin to merge into massive, continuous, multi-centred urban regions. Perth and Adelaide remain as smaller, independent metropolitan regions with populations of over one million. Perth, which is remote from the traditional core but is part of the new sunbelt, has grown strongly through international and internal migration (although there was a slump in the early 1990s) and has strong economic links with nearby Asia. Adelaide, which is part of neither core nor sunbelt, faces an uncertain future. Perhaps the attempts, discussed on p. 39, to create its own future will succeed. Perhaps its 'liveability' will become increasingly attractive to businesses and households seeking to escape rising property prices, traffic congestion, pollution, and stress in the larger capitals. But population projections suggest that, if current trends continue, Adelaide might even experience an absolute fall in its population by the year 2051.

The recent economic, demographic, cultural, and technological changes associated with globalisation have had a strong impact on how Australia's large cities have grown and prospered—or not. The changes are also reshaping long-established patterns within our cities: patterns of housing, employment, transport, and residential segregation. The following chapters examine those changes, and their implications for urban governments and planning bodies as they pursue the elusive goals of environmental sustainability, social justice, and economic efficiency.

3

Employment and Urban Structure

Employment in Australian cities changed profoundly during the 1970s and 1980s as a result of the economic, technological, demographic, and social changes—the restructuring—discussed at the end of chapter 1. More recently, the forces of globalisation discussed in chapter 2 have continued to re-shape the nature of economic activity and jobs. Some changes have been obvious in the landscape: abandoned factory sites, gleaming new office towers in city centres, massive suburban shopping plazas, major office developments in the suburbs of Sydney and Melbourne, and recreation and leisure facilities of all kinds.

Other changes are less visible. Office blocks today contain fewer workers and a lot more electronic equipment than they did a few years ago. Shopping centres still employ plenty of people, but many of them are now juniors working on a part-time or casual basis. In the long boom, most suburban houses were occupied by a male worker in full-time employment and his dependent wife and children. The houses may look little different today but now 25 per cent of the families in Australia contain no one in paid employment, whereas almost 50 per cent have two or more workers in a variety of full-time and part-time jobs.

One person, usually the male breadwinner, used to leave each house to travel to a suburban factory or city-centre office in the morning 'rush hour', returning in the evening. Now there are often three or more people travelling to work at a range of times to different destinations, near and far, some with stops at a child-care centre en route. Or the only journey may be an unemployed person seeking work through the now privatised Job Network.

The location of jobs—the *geography* of employment—has also become more complex. Because travel to work is still a very important type of journey within our cities, producing the daily peaks of pressure on roads and public transport systems, this increased complexity is reflected in changing *urban structure*. By urban structure we mean the location of land uses and activities; the flows of people, goods, and information between different locations in the city; and the nature of the transport and communications systems that carry those flows. The social, economic, and environmental implications of changing urban structure are, in turn, of major concern to policy makers.

The changing nature of employment

Job opportunities

Chapter 2 examined the changing industrial structure of the major cities since 1991 (table 2.1). Table 3.1 shows what this has meant for job opportunities in major occupational groups. Occupation refers to the kind of job people do, rather than the industry they work in. Occupation and industry are obviously connected; the retail industry mainly employs salespersons, and manufacturing

Table 3.1 Employment structure of major cities by occupation, 2001 (%)

Males	Sydney	Melbourne	Brisbane	Perth	Adelaide
Managers & administrators	11.7	11.1	9.7	9.8	9.6
Professionals	19.1	18.5	16.8	17.1	16.6
Associate professionals	12.6	12.0	12.4	13.2	12.3
Tradespersons & related	18.2	19.3	19.7	20.9	19.8
Advanced clerical & service	1.0	0.8	0.8	0.8	0.9
Intermediate clerical, sales & service	9.7	9.4	10.0	9.0	9.4
Intermediate production & transport	11.5	12.1	12.5	12.1	12.8
Elementary clerical, sales & service	6.3	6.3	6.6	6.3	6.2
Labourers & related	7.8	8.3	9.5	8.8	10.3
Inadequately described	1.0	1.0	0.9	1.0	1.1
Not stated	1.2	1.2	1.1	0.9	0.9
Total	100	100	100	100	100
Females	Sydney	Melbourne	Brisbane	Perth	Adelaide
Managers & administrators	5.8	5.0	4.2	4.0	4.2
Professionals	23.7	23.3	21.3	20.8	21.3
Associate professionals	10.9	10.7	11.8	12.0	11.5
Tradespersons & related	2.6	2.8	2.7	3.0	3.1
Advanced clerical & service	8.8	7.6	7.1	8.0	6.5
Intermediate clerical, sales & service	26.3	25.8	28.3	27.4	27.9
Intermediate production & transport	2.4	2.9	2.4	2.3	2.4
Elementary clerical, sales & service	12.4	13.7	14.1	14.8	14.0
Labourers & related	5.2	6.2	6.5	6.2	7.6
Inadequately described	0.7	0.7	0.6	0.6	0.7
Not stated	1.2	1.3	1.1	1.0	1.0
Total	100	100	100	100	100

Data are for employed persons in Statistical Divisions

Source: ABS 2001 Census

mainly employs tradespersons and production workers. But people may be employed as clerks or managers, for example, in almost any industry category. The occupational structure of employment therefore gives the best picture of the mix of job opportunities available to people in a particular city, although industrial structure may be a better indicator of likely future economic growth or decline.

Table 3.1 reveals a consistent pattern in all the major cities in 2001. Almost a third of all males now work as professionals and associate professionals (technicians, nurses, police, and so on). Around 10 per cent work as managers and administrators. Approximately 20 per cent are skilled tradespersons and a further 20 per cent are semi-skilled and unskilled blue-collar workers. Only 16 to 17.5 per cent work in clerical, sales, and service jobs.

Jobs held by females are very different, and much less evenly spread across the occupational groups. In all the cities approximately half the female workers have clerical, sales, and service jobs, and over a third work as professionals or associate professionals. Only 5 per cent are managers and administrators, 3 per cent or less work as tradespersons, and 7.5 to 10 per cent do semi-skilled or unskilled blue-collar work.

Figure 3.1 shows that in all five cities between 1991 and 2001, professional and associate professional jobs grew far more strongly than other categories. Because of their higher rates of population growth, Brisbane and Perth experienced the highest rate of overall job growth, and even show an increase in trades, production, and transport employment. In contrast, Adelaide's low

A   Managers and administrators
B   Professionals and assoc. professionals
C   Clerical, sales, service workers
D   Trades, production, transport workers, labourers

Figure 3.1 Employment growth or decline by occupation, major cities, 1991–2001

Source: ABS 2001 Census, Time Series Community Profiles

rate of population growth led to a decline in clerical, sales, and service employment and weaker growth in professional and associate professional jobs.

All five cities are now clearly *post-industrial* in structure, dominated by service employment, particularly in professional and associate professional jobs demanding higher-level skills and qualifications. Blue-collar jobs continue to decline in relative importance, though they still make up a significant proportion of employment opportunities, especially for males. Table 3.1 also shows that there is still a strong, though not absolute, *gender division of labour.* Tradespersons, production and transport workers, managers, and administrators are predominantly male. Clerks, and sales and service workers are mainly female.

Workforce participation

Changes in the nature of jobs since the 1970s have been accompanied by even more marked changes in the way people participate—or don't participate—in paid work. To appreciate these changes it is important to understand how official statistics measure participation in work. The population aged 15 and over is divided into three categories:

a) persons in employment, part-time or full-time
b) persons not in employment but seeking work (the unemployed)
c) persons not in employment and not seeking work.

Categories a) and b) added together constitute the *workforce* or *labour force*. The *workforce participation rate* is calculated by expressing this workforce (a+b) as a percentage of the total population aged 15 and over (a+b+c). The *unemployment rate* is calculated by expressing the unemployed b) as a percentage of the workforce (a+b).

In all the major cities in 1971 approximately 80 per cent of males aged 15 and over were in the workforce, compared with only 36–40 per cent of females. By 1991 a transformation had occurred, with male participation rates falling towards 70 per cent while female rates rose to well over 50 per cent. The graphs of male and female age-specific participation rates, as figure 3.2 shows for the example of Sydney, had converged significantly. Male rates had fallen throughout the age range from 20 onwards, with more evidence of early retirement after the age of 50 (often associated with *hidden unemployment* where people give up looking for work—and therefore disappear from the unemployment figures—because they believe there is no chance of finding a job). Female rates, on the other hand, had risen significantly, even during the main child-bearing years.

Male participation rates have continued to fall since 1991, though the rise in early retirement has steadied. Changes in female participation in the workforce, however, have been more complex. Overall rates rose strongly, from

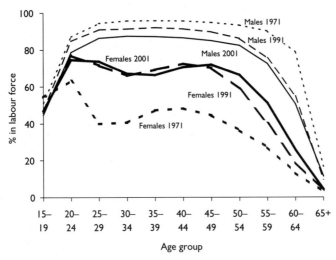

Figure 3.2 Age specific workforce participation, Sydney, 1971–2001

Source: ABS 1971, 1991, and 2001 censuses

52 to over 55 per cent, in Brisbane and Perth. Sydney and Melbourne experienced a smaller increase, from 53 to 54 per cent, whereas in Adelaide the rate fell slightly to 51.4 per cent. These differences reflect contrasts in age structure—Adelaide has a significantly older population than Brisbane and Perth—as well as the differing economic fortunes discussed in chapter 2.

The lines on figure 3.2 representing the age-specific female participation rates in Sydney for 1991 and 2001 show some more subtle trends. Rates continued to increase strongly in the ages above 49, as the baby boom generation that set the trend for rising female workforce participation moved into those age groups. Rates also increased slightly in the 25–34 age groups. But rates actually fell in the 35–44 age groups, probably as a result of women increasingly postponing child rearing until their thirties and forties. In Australia as a whole the average age at which women give birth to their first child is now 29 years. Cuts to government funding for pre-school child care during the 1990s may also have reduced the ability of women with young children to stay in the workforce. Age-specific rates for the other major cities show similar trends, though in Brisbane rates increased marginally rather than fell in the 35–44 age groups and in Adelaide rates fell in all age groups below 45.

Unemployment

Unemployment rates rose sharply following the end of the long boom, from 2 per cent or less in 1971—regarded by economists as the equivalent of full employment—to 10 per cent or more in 1991, representing a combined total of half a million people in the five major cities. Unemployment rates for young people aged 15–19 years were even higher, approaching 30 per cent, and a third of all unemployed people had been out of work for over a year. Unemployment rates have fallen in all the major cities since 1991 and at the 2001 Census ranged from 6.1 per cent in Sydney to 7.9 per cent in Adelaide. At the time of writing, the latest Australian Bureau of Statistics (ABS) Labour Force Survey (July 2003) showed that unemployment rates were continuing to fall, ranging from 5.1 per cent in Sydney to 6.1 per cent in Adelaide. These improved figures reflect the good economic growth trends of the 1990s, though they are also affected by changes in how unemployment is defined by the Federal government, with people in so-called *work for the dole* programs now regarded as employed. But unemployment rates for persons aged 15–19 still approach 20 per cent, and 25 per cent of all unemployed males have been without a job for over a year. Official unemployment figures also do not take account of the *underemployed* (part-time workers who would prefer to work longer hours) or the hidden unemployed. During the long boom there was work for all who wanted it. Today, despite the recent improvements, almost a third of a million people in our major cities are still officially classified as unemployed, plus perhaps another third of a million who either cannot get enough work or have given up the search altogether.

The growth of part-time work

The census data we have examined so far simply classify people as 'employed' or not, and take no account of the number of hours worked each week. As a result, they conceal some of the most important recent changes in the nature of work in Australian cities. As table 3.2 shows for the example of Adelaide, the number of full-time workers (defined as persons working 35 hours or more each week) actually declined slightly between 1991 and 2001. Part-time

Table 3.2 Persons employed full-time and part-time, Adelaide, 1991–2001

	Males			Females			Total		
	1991	2001	% Change	1991	2001	% Change	1991	2001	% Change
Part-time workers*	36541	55739	52.5	88345	108140	22.4	124886	163879	31.2
Full-time workers	195235	189164	–3.1	96112	101866	6.0	291347	291030	–0.1
(Hours worked not stated)	13132	6691		11384	5229		24516	11920	
Total	244908	251594	2.7	195841	215235	9.9	440749	466829	5.9

Data are for Adelaide Statistical Division
* 'Part-time' is defined as fewer than 35 hours per week

Source: ABS 2001 Census, Time Series Community Profile

employment, in contrast, grew by over 30 per cent. In all the other major cities, part-time jobs grew much more than full-time jobs. This growth of part-time and casual work has affected all industries and occupations to some extent but is particularly associated with sales and services. As noted in chapters 1 and 2, it is generally a symptom of the adoption of *flexible production* strategies and, in some industries, of the *deskilling* process. Table 3.2 also reveals the difference in employment growth trends for males and females since 1991, with the decline in the number of full-time male workers in Adelaide almost balanced by the growth in full-time female employment.

Other changes have occurred. Part-time employment may have increased greatly in importance, but at the other end of the spectrum the number of people—especially males—working very long hours is also rising sharply. In Sydney, for example, the 2001 Census showed that over 25 per cent of males and 10 per cent of females worked for more than 49 hours per week. Self-employment has also become more common, though a change in census categories prevents precise comparison through time. These trends, too, are related to flexible production. Employers find it more profitable to increase the hours worked by their existing core staff rather than hire more workers, and to hire self-employed consultants, cleaners, and caterers as required rather than have them on the permanent payroll. Rising self-employment may also be related to hidden unemployment, as people use redundancy packages to start small businesses in the absence of other job opportunities.

So the economic restructuring of our increasingly globalised cities has not simply meant the loss of jobs in manufacturing and construction and a spectacular growth in service jobs. Most of the increase in total employment has been in part-time jobs, and, as suggested by their increasing participation rates, females have taken most of those jobs. Many more residents of Australian cities (particularly females) are therefore having to combine paid employment with other activities such as education and caring for families. In addition, more people (usually males) are working very long hours, more people are self-employed, fewer people have complete job security, and many people still have no work at all. It is important to remember these points as we go on to consider changing patterns of job location, accessibility to job opportunities, and the journey to work.

The changing location of jobs

All the major cities experienced suburbanisation of employment, particularly in manufacturing and retailing, during the rapid urban growth of the long boom. By 1971 only 42 per cent of jobs in Melbourne, Sydney, and Adelaide were still located in the city centre (usually referred to as the central business district or CBD) and the surrounding inner suburbs (Maher 1982, p. 53). During the 1970s and 1980s, in spite of the slower growth of urban population and employment, jobs continued to suburbanise. In Melbourne, for example, the share of jobs located in the CBD and inner suburbs had fallen to 28 per cent by 1986 (O'Connor & Rapson 2003). Retailing and public services continued to chase their suburban customers and clients as new residential areas developed. Some office employment, particularly in the public sector, also began moving to major suburban centres such as Parramatta in western Sydney during the 1970s. Manufacturing and warehousing was still attracted to cheap land close to major interstate and suburban highways and near to a suburban labour supply.

Since the mid 1980s the suburbanisation of employment appears to have slowed, particularly in the slower-growing cities of Sydney, Melbourne, and Adelaide. The 2001 census suggests that the central regions may now be maintaining their share of total jobs, despite the continued outwards expansion of the metropolitan areas. What is happening?

Patterns of employment

Figure 3.3 shows the location of employment by Statistical Local Area (SLA) in Sydney and Melbourne in 2001. In both cities the CBD and adjacent areas of office development constitute by far the largest single concentration of job opportunities, and the focus of massive daily commuter flows (figures 3.4 and 3.5). Of the 1.7 million jobs in Sydney as a whole, 315 000 or 19 per cent are located in Sydney City (Inner), Sydney City (Remainder), and North Sydney. In Melbourne, of 1.44 million total jobs, 278 000 or 19 per cent are located in Melbourne City (Inner), Melbourne City (Remainder), and Southbank–Docklands. As figure 3.3 shows, well over half the jobs in these central concentrations are in the managerial, administrative, professional, or associate professional categories.

Significant employment is also located in the rest of the central regions, in inner suburbs adjacent to the CBDs. South Sydney and Leichhardt in Sydney contain 125 000 jobs. Port Phillip, Yarra, and Prahran in Melbourne contain 140 000. Here, too, professional and administrative employment now dominates and blue-collar jobs have declined in importance. In the case of Melbourne, O'Connor and Rapson (2003) argue that not only have the number of jobs in the central region increased significantly since 1991, but that the region is becoming almost a separate economy, closely associated with the city's global and national role. Hawthorn and Kew in the inner eastern suburbs might also be seen as part of this region. Similarly, in Sydney some writers have used the term 'Global Arc' to describe a region stretching from

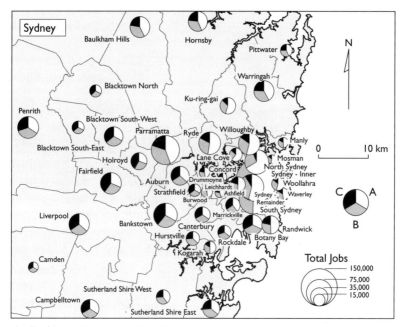

A   Professionals, associated professionals, managers, and administrators
B   Clerical, sales, and service workers
C   Tradespersons, production and transport workers, and labourers

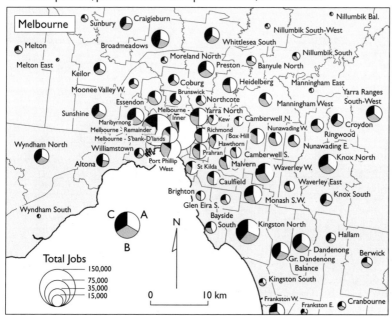

Figure 3.3 Employment location, Sydney and Melbourne, 2001

Source: ABS 2001 Census

Figure 3.4 Melbourne's CBD, 2004

Source: Clive Forster

Figure 3.5 Sydney's CBD and North Sydney, 2003. Note the commuter roads leading to the harbour bridge and tunnel.

Source: Clive Forster

South Sydney through the CBD and North Sydney to Willoughby (52 000 jobs), Lane Cove (19 000 jobs) and Ryde (52 000 jobs). This region includes the suburban office concentrations of Chatswood and St Leonards and the North Ryde (figure 3.6) high-technology industry precinct (Freestone 1996), as well as the CBD and environs. It is characterised by high percentages of professional and administrative employment (figure 3.3) and has reaped the main benefits from Sydney's growing role, as described in chapter 2, in the global and national economies.

Beyond these prosperous core regions and arcs, employment is scattered through the suburbs. In Sydney the largest numbers of jobs are in Parramatta (86 000), followed by Bankstown (61 000) and Penrith (50 000). Melbourne is divided into a larger number of smaller SLAs than Sydney, giving the impression in figure 3.3 that jobs are more scattered. But there are 83 000 jobs in Monash-Waverley as a whole, 70 000 in Dandenong, and 67 000 in Kingston. However the most striking feature of figure 3.3 is how widespread the suburbanisation of employment has become in both cities. Many other SLAs contain over 30 000 jobs, and only a handful of the smallest have fewer than 15 000.

Figure 3.6 North Ryde high-technology industry precinct, Sydney, 2003
Source: Clive Forster

Some of the suburban jobs are located in district centres such as Parramatta (figure 3.7) and Dandenong, which have developed with government encouragement as suburban 'mini-CBDs'. But recent research has confirmed that by far the fastest growth in jobs has occurred outside such centres as *dispersed employment*, scattered throughout the suburbs in innumerable small industrial sites, shops, schools, surgeries, petrol stations, and so on. Parolin and Kamara (2003) calculate that in Sydney the percentage of employment located in centres of all kinds, from the CBD downwards, fell from 48 to 42 between 1981 and 1996. Dispersed employment therefore increased from 52 to 58 per cent of the total.

Occupational structure (figure 3.3) varies from place to place, reflecting the economic history of different suburbs and variations in the impacts of economic restructuring. In Sydney's industrial western suburbs, from Marrickville and Canterbury in the inner west through Strathfield, Bankstown, and Auburn to Holroyd, Fairfield, Liverpool, and Blacktown in the outer suburbs, over a third of all jobs—and about half the jobs held by males—are in the blue-collar tradesperson, intermediate production and transport worker, and unskilled labourer categories. The traditional industrial suburbs in Melbourne's west (Maribyrnong, Sunshine, and Altona), north (Brunswick, Northcote, Coburg, Preston, Broadmeadows, and Whittlesea) and south east (Kingston

Figure 3.7 Suburban regional centre, Parramatta, Sydney, 2003
Source: Clive Forster

and Dandenong), have a similar employment structure. In contrast, middle-class residential suburbs in eastern and northern Sydney such as Waverley, Woolahra, Manly, Mosman, and Ku-ring-gai have few blue-collar jobs and more in the professional and administrative categories, as do suburbs in eastern Melbourne such as Malvern, Camberwell, and Box Hill.

The suburbanisation of jobs held by females is particularly striking. In the long boom, female employment was significantly more concentrated in the city core and inner suburbs than male employment, and job opportunities in the industrial outer suburbs were heavily male-oriented. But by 2001 there was little difference between the proportion of male and female jobs located in Sydney's core region (18.5 and 19.1 per cent respectively). As we have already noted, most of the employment growth since 1991 has been in jobs held by women, albeit many of them part-time (table 3.2). The suburbs have reflected this, but to varying degrees depending on their occupational structure. In most North Shore and Eastern Suburbs SLAs in 2001, women held over half the jobs. In contrast, women held less than 40 per cent of the jobs in Auburn, Holroyd, Fairfield, Bankstown, and a number of other western industrial suburbs. Areas dominated by manufacturing still provide fewer opportunities for women.

Economic restructuring within cities

What forces shape the distribution of employment within our cities? At one obvious level, the impact of economic restructuring has reflected an area's job composition. Suburbs dependent on vulnerable industries such as textiles, footwear, and clothing have been hardest hit by the overall decline in manufacturing employment. Areas characterised by high-technology manufacturing, such as Sydney's North Shore and the eastern suburbs of Melbourne, have experienced growth. The rapid rise in finance and business employment has had a major impact on the CBDs and nearby office centres such as North Sydney and South Melbourne. Overall, the decline of the most suburbanised employment sector (manufacturing) and the rise of the most centralised (producer services) might be expected to slow the rate of job suburbanisation.

However, the restructuring of production has, in some instances, reinforced suburbanisation and increased the range of jobs that have suburbanised. Firms seeking to rationalise production have closed older, less efficient plants and concentrated their activities at modern sites that tend to be located in outer suburbs. GMH, for example, closed down operations at their Woodville plant in Adelaide's middle western suburbs while putting major additional investment into Elizabeth in the outer north. And Searle (1993, p. 1) argues that 'the advent of a post-Fordist landscape of flexible accumulation has caused old production spaces and relationships to become obsolete in the face of new forms of productive relationships and accumulation possibilities'. In other words, the adoption of the flexible production methods discussed earlier has changed *where* people work as well as *how* they work. Searle found by analysing entries in the Sydney *Yellow Pages* telephone directory that the number of clothing making-up firms increased significantly between 1981 and 1991, even though the clothing industry was in decline, and that significant suburban concentrations of firms had emerged in Marrickville and Fairfield, which were centres of recent Vietnamese immigrant settlement. These changes appear to have been the result of established clothing firms reducing costs by subcontracting production to new, small companies which in turn employ women—often recent migrants—working at home for low wages. During the same period, management consultants (a rapidly expanding industry) tended to decentralise from the CBD to the prosperous North Shore suburbs and other high-status residential areas ranging from Paddington and Glebe to the northern beaches. Again, Searle suggests the increasing importance of small independent firms working from home, or from small offices close to home, in attractive locations.

Technological innovations during the past 25 years, particularly in telecommunications and computing, have helped to make these and other changes possible. We saw in chapter 2 that information technology has strengthened the dominance of financial control functions located in CBD head offices, particularly in Sydney. However, many of the changes associated with post-Fordism and flexible production also rely on this technology. Computerised machinery enables small firms to maintain a high standard of quality control, and to make rapid changes to their products. Thanks to fax machines, powerful personal computers, and the Internet, work that once required the facilities of a large company headquarters can now be done from any small office. Routine data processing can be done in a 'back office' anywhere in the suburbs, using local labour. Information technology, as well as boosting producer-services employment in CBDs, has therefore also helped to make possible the dispersal of many types of employment. More jobs can now locate in suburban office centres, in landscaped, campus-style technology precincts near suburban universities or CSIRO establishments, and even in people's homes.

Patterns of employment location in Sydney and Melbourne therefore reflect a period of economic restructuring, involving not only the impact of globalisation but also the rise of post-Fordist flexible production, a revolution in information technology and a continued change in how women participate in paid work. Patterns in Adelaide, Brisbane, and Perth reflect the same forces, operating on smaller cities with different growth rates and economic roles. In

Adelaide, for example, the city centre contained over 90 000 jobs in 2001, representing about 21 per cent of the metropolitan total, and had increased in both absolute numbers and in its relative importance since 1991. Despite having much more limited national and global roles than Sydney or Melbourne, the city centre and adjacent inner suburbs such as Unley and Norwood have job structures increasingly dominated by well-paid professional and administrative occupations, whereas in many western and northern suburbs over 40 per cent of all jobs are in the blue-collar categories. None of the smaller cities has suburban employment concentrations to rival Parramatta or Dandenong. Generally, suburban jobs are highly dispersed and dominated by retailing and manufacturing. Almost all middle and outer suburbs— particularly the latter—have experienced job growth. The nature of this growth has varied, though the transformation to a service economy, coupled with the changing nature of manufacturing, means that jobs in any suburb are now spread to some extent across a range of occupations. The proportion of employment taken up by women also varies, though in most suburbs they hold at least 40 per cent of the jobs.

In all five major cities the core areas are prospering, having restructured, as O'Connor and Rapson (2003) have suggested for Melbourne, to fulfil an increasingly specialised role in finance, business, tourism, and entertainment. Meanwhile the middle and outer suburbs are continuing to experience diverse employment growth, particularly in services, as they become increasingly independent of the city cores. In Sydney and Melbourne especially, researchers are suggesting that the distribution of different types of employment is reflecting a widening gap between the globally oriented economies of the city cores and associated high status suburbs, and more locally oriented and less prosperous suburban economies.

The journey to work

Even though the core areas of our cities are now maintaining their importance as job locations, the highly suburbanised nature of employment opportunities inevitably affects journey to work patterns. Even in Adelaide, where the CBD contains a higher percentage of total jobs than Sydney or Melbourne, only 22 per cent of workers in 1996 (the latest data available at the time of writing) travelled to work from the suburbs to the CBD. The great majority lived and worked in the suburbs. Almost 23 per cent lived and worked in the same Local Government Area (LGA). The rest—over half the workforce—lived in one suburban LGA and worked in another.

Patterns varied somewhat from area to area. People living in the inner suburbs were more likely to work in the CBD, as were residents of the higher status east and south east. In the working-class west and north, more people worked locally or in neighbouring LGAs. And in general 25 per cent of women travelled to the CBD to work, compared with only 18 per cent of males.

Mode of travel

Our cities were already *automobile cities* in 1971 (chapter 1). Most workers drove a private car to work, though females remained more dependent on public transport and were more likely than males to be car passengers. A significant proportion of CBD workers of either sex also used public transport, especially in Sydney and Melbourne. The continued suburbanisation of employment and housing since the 1970s has further reinforced dependence on the car. Jobs in the CBD and inner suburbs can usually be reached by public transport, and road congestion and parking problems discourage the use of cars. In contrast, jobs in the low-density middle and outer suburbs are often hard—if not impossible—to reach by public transport, while parking is usually easy and roads are relatively uncongested. This is particularly true of the increasing amount of dispersed employment, located outside suburban centres.

Not surprisingly, table 3.3 shows that the use of cars for the journey to work continued to rise between 1991 and 1996 in all the five major cities, while the already low percentages of trips by public transport and the so-called 'soft' transport modes of cycling and walking declined still further. But the 2001 data suggest that the increase in automobile dependence may finally have levelled out. In Sydney, Melbourne, and Brisbane the percentage of workers using cars (as drivers or passengers) has fallen slightly since 1996, and in Perth there was no increase. Public transport use increased in Sydney and Melbourne, and the use of two or more modes of travel (one of which is usually public transport) rose in all five cities. Several state public transport authorities have also reported increases in passenger numbers since the late 1990s. The census figures should be interpreted with caution. The changes are small, and the census classifications changed in 2001 to include 'truck' as a separate mode for the first time, whereas truck drivers in earlier censuses may have classified themselves as car drivers. This might account for the increase in the 'other' category, which in table 3.3 includes trucks. In any case, the levels of car dependence in 2001 were still higher than in 1991, and remain extremely high compared with cities anywhere else in the world except North America.

There are some contrasts between the cities. Sydney has a lower level of car-use and public transport is more important than in the other capitals, whereas the opposite is true of the smaller, less congested, and more suburbanised cities of Perth and Adelaide. However Perth has shown a steady increase since 1991 in the percentage of workers using two or more modes of transport. This is probably associated with improvements to the suburban rail system since the mid 1980s. Previously the state Liberal government had allowed the rail system to run down, and had closed the line from Perth to Fremantle. When Labor regained power in 1983 it reopened the Fremantle line, electrified the system and built the new Northern Suburbs Railway (Alexander & Houghton 1995). The new line runs from Perth to Joondalup, using the central reservation of the Mitchell Freeway which serves the fast-growing suburban area of Wannaroo. A series of transit interchanges link the line to cross-suburban bus services and the stations have large parking areas to encourage commuters to 'park and ride' (figure 3.8). The line is rightly held up as an excellent (though expensive to build) suburban rail service. But in spite of a threefold rise between 1991 and 2001 in the number of journeys taken wholly or partly by train in Perth as a whole, overall public transport use remains low in percentage terms and the city is still highly dependent on the car.

Table 3.3 Mode of travel to work in major cities, 1991–2001 (%)

Employed persons stating mode of travel

	Sydney			Melbourne			Brisbane		
	1991	1996	2001	1991	1996	2001	1991	1996	2001
Car driver only	58.0	60.1	58.8	67.8	70.7	70.5	64.4	67.0	66.8
Car passenger only	7.6	7.2	6.3	7.6	6.8	5.9	8.9	8.4	7.6
Public transport only	14.9	14.3	14.7	9.1	8.0	8.4	10.2	9.1	9.0
Walk or cycle only	5.6	4.8	4.9	4.6	3.8	3.7	4.8	4.0	3.9
Two or more modes	7.5	6.9	7.5	5.1	4.4	4.6	4.2	3.6	4.1
Other	2.2	2.3	3.1	1.7	1.8	2.4	3.0	3.0	3.7
Worked at home	4.2	4.5	4.6	4.2	4.5	4.5	4.5	4.9	4.9
Total	100	100	100	100	100	100	100	100	100

Employed persons stating mode of travel

	Perth			Adelaide		
	1991	1996	2001	1991	1996	2001
Car driver only	71.7	73.1	73.1	68.9	73.3	73.5
Car passenger only	8.1	7.6	6.6	8.8	7.7	6.8
Public transport only	7.0	5.8	5.5	8.6	7.0	6.8
Walk or cycle only	3.8	3.1	3.2	4.9	3.7	3.6
Two or more modes	2.7	3.4	4.2	2.9	2.3	2.8
Other	2.4	2.3	2.7	2.3	2.1	2.4
Worked at home	4.3	4.7	4.7	3.5	3.9	4.0
Total	100	100	100	100	100	100

Data are for Statistical Divisions

Source: ABS 1991, 1996, and 2001 censuses

Figure 3.8 'Park and ride' on Perth's Northern Suburbs Railway, 1998: an extensive parking area at an outer suburban station
Source: Clive Forster

Contrasts also still exist between the travel behaviour of males and females. As table 3.4 shows for Sydney—the least automobile-dependent of the cities— women remain more likely to use public transport or travel as car passengers, and less likely to drive their own cars. But these differences have become much less significant over the past 20 years, and continue to decline. As female and male workforce participation rates converge (figure 3.2), so too does travel behaviour. The proportion of women driving to work continues to rise while travelling as car passengers declines. As Lang (1992) points out, women often have to combine paid part-time work with child-raising and other responsibilities. They therefore need a form of transport that is reliable, quick, safe, and flexible, enabling them to make complex multi-purpose trips across the suburbs between home, work, schools, child-care centres, shops, etc. For many women with children the car is a vital 'management tool' (Dowling et al. 1999, pp. 107–8). Public transport is rarely adequate, and not surprisingly the rise in female workforce participation has therefore been accompanied by a further increase in the already high rates of motor-vehicle ownership.

In Adelaide – the most car-dependent of the major cities—the already low percentage of households without vehicles fell from 13.4 to 10.9 between 1991 and 2001, while the percentage with two or more vehicles continued to rise, from 42.5 to 44.8. Almost 12 per cent of households now have three vehicles or more. If we focus on households that consist of couples with children, 1996 data (equivalent information is not available for 2001) show that 74 per cent had two or more cars and 22 per cent had three or more, whereas less than 2 per cent had no car. Trends have been very similar in the other cities, though in Sydney only 40 per cent of total households now have two vehicles or more and 13 per cent have none, reflecting the greater use of public transport.

Gender and city-to-city contrasts aside, the main message from tables 3.3 and 3.4 is that dependence on the automobile for travel to work remains very high in all Australia's mainland capitals. In Sydney and Melbourne, when the number of people using cars for part of their journey to work is added to those driving all the way, almost a million cars in each city take to the road each day for that purpose alone. The consequences of this for economic efficiency, environmental sustainability, and equity will be discussed later in the book.

Job ratios and labour sheds

So most journeys to work—male and female—now take the form of car journeys criss-crossing the middle, outer, and fringe suburbs. What determines the pattern? Some areas have more jobs than workers and therefore must receive a net inflow of people each day. Other areas have fewer jobs than workers and experience an equally inevitable net outflow. Figure 3.9 shows the pattern of variation in job ratios (number of local jobs per resident worker) in Sydney in 2001. In the CBD and surrounding areas the number of jobs greatly

Table 3.4 Mode of travel to work by gender, Sydney, 1996–2001

	1996				2001			
Employed persons	*Male*		*Female*		*Male*		*Female*	
	no.	*%*	*no.*	*%*	*no.*	*%*	*no.*	*%*
Car driver only	551 592	65.1	338 546	53.3	566 165	62.5	379 506	54.0
Car passenger only	44 925	5.3	61 119	9.6	42 205	4.7	59 354	8.5
Public transport only	103 414	12.2	108 220	17.0	115 879	12.8	120 287	17.1
Walk or cycle only	39 279	4.6	31 729	5.0	42 521	4.7	35 800	5.1
Two or more modes	52 826	6.2	50 104	7.9	62 277	6.9	58 756	8.4
Other	27 939	3.3	5819	0.9	44 965	5.0	5538	0.8
Worked at home	26 712	3.2	39 630	6.2	31 680	3.5	43 002	6.1
Total stating mode	846 687	100	635 167	100	905 692	100	702 243	100
Did not go to work	64 434		101 084		70 151		107 115	
Not stated	14 109		13 980		16 201		14 823	
Total	925 230		750 231		992 044		824 181	

Source: ABS 1996 and 2001 censuses

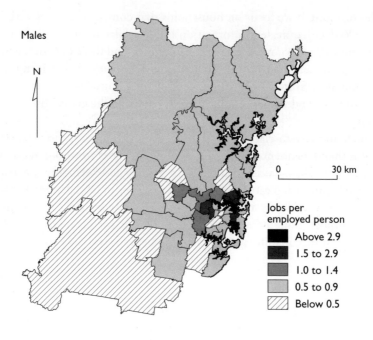

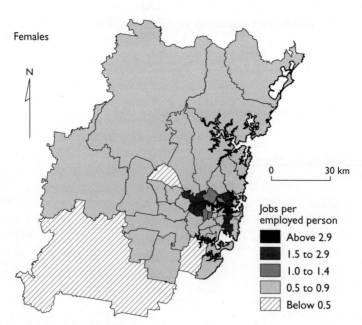

Figure 3.9 Job ratios, Sydney, 2001
Source: ABS 2001 Census

exceeds the number of resident workers. The situation in the inner and middle suburbs varies. Some LGAs have balanced numbers of jobs and workers. Others are dormitory suburbs with more resident workers than jobs. A few such as Auburn, Parramatta, Willoughby, and Botany have significant job surpluses. Throughout the outer and fringe suburbs there is a deficit of jobs.

In areas with job deficits (job ratios below 1 in figure 3.9), there is an inevitable outflow of workers each day. But we also know from earlier censuses that in areas with a reasonable overall balance between job opportunities and resident workers, or even with a surplus of jobs over workers, most local residents—particularly males—tend to travel to work elsewhere. This is because the composition of local job opportunities is highly unlikely to match exactly the skills of a local workforce, and even if it does there are many other reasons in a mobile, car-owning society why local jobs are not all filled by local people. Instead, each suburban concentration of employment will tend to draw its workers from quite a large surrounding *labour shed*. Most workers live locally and in neighbouring LGAs and the numbers then taper off with increasing distance. The majority of workers come from the same side of the city, though a few have very long journeys from the opposite edge of the urban area. Women tend to work closer to home than men, particularly in low-income areas.

Working at home: the electronic cottage?

Some workers do not have to travel to work. Traditionally this group has included retailers who 'live over the shop' and out-workers, mainly women, in the clothing industry. But developments in telecommunications and information-processing technology, especially the increasing power and falling cost of personal computers and the massive rise in Internet use, have led to predictions of a significant increase in working from home. Some of the more futuristic writers suggest massive reductions in energy consumption, pollution and traffic congestion as people become *telecommuters*, rather than having to travel physically to a separate workplace. They portray idyllic images of *electronic cottages*: a return to the less alienating way of life that allegedly existed before the industrial revolution and the factory system, with family members working at home and being able to juggle the time devoted to paid work, child-rearing, home maintenance, and leisure according to their individual needs and preferences.

There is no doubt that much work involving the processing of information, ranging from routine data-entry to highly specialised creative tasks, could now be done at home. The trend towards subcontracting, consulting, and self-employment might also be expected to encourage home-working. It is therefore not surprising that the percentage of employed persons working at home rose in all the capital cities between 1991 and 2001 (table 3.3). But the percentages are still small, ranging from 4 per cent in Adelaide to almost 5 per cent in Brisbane. Table 3.4 also shows that in Sydney more females work at home than males, probably reflecting the continuing dominance of traditional female activities such as out-working in the clothing and textiles industry (though out-working that occurs as part of the 'black economy' might not be picked up in the census). It is possible that we are on the threshold of a major change, but so far the electronic cottage has proved to be largely a myth. Most workers have jobs that still require physical presence, or have homes that are unsuitable as permanent workplaces. Even where home-working is technologically possible, most people value the personal interaction and comradeship of the workplace (a point we should also bear in mind when assessing the social as well as financial impact of unemployment) and find it hard psychologically to adjust to working entirely from home. Paid work has certainly become more flexible and complex in location and timing, but so far the main impact of personal computers, the Internet, and faxes has been to allow people to carry out some work at home (Newton & Wulff 1999), with the mobile phone even turning the car into a third workplace. There is no sign yet of a significant impact on the journey to work.

A new urban structure?

> The metropolis has recrystallised into a set of urban realms. Each realm has its own nucleus, few ties with the traditional core of the city, and virtually none with other realms. (Hart 1991, p. xii)

This quotation from the preface of an American book entitled *Our Changing Cities* expresses an increasingly common view about the structure of large Western cities. According to this view, the development of massive, low-density conurbations or 'mega-cities' has been accompanied by an internal breakdown. Traditional residential suburbs, subservient to the city core, are being supplanted by largely independent *urban realms* or 'cities-within-a-city' containing hundreds of thousands or even millions of people who reside, work, and socialise almost entirely within that particular part of the metropolitan area.

Kling et al. (1991) have described this 'new urban structure' as *post-suburban*, pointing to Orange County within the Los Angeles region as a classic example. Garreau's (1991) book *Edge City* popularised similar ideas, with particular emphasis on the suburban centres of office and high-technology employment that act as the cores of the urban realms. Castells (1989) had earlier coined the term *informational city*, to suggest the evolution of a new urban form based upon the ever-expanding importance of information technology in all types of work, and the associated changes in the forces that attract capital to particular locations.

How relevant are these concepts to Australia's major cities? Do we now live in post-suburban informational cities, recrystallising into largely independent *urban realms*, centred upon *edge cities*? Employment—including office and high-technology employment—has certainly suburbanised (figures 3.3 and 3.4), and information technology has been influential in this. Brotchie (1992) described Melbourne as being in transition to an *information economy*. Equally clearly, most journeys to work are now between suburban homes and suburban workplaces. Even before the end of the long boom, Logan (1968) argued that the decentralised *automobile city* discussed in chapter 1 (figure 1.7) was assuming a *polynuclear* structure, with significant suburban concentrations of employment rivalling the dominance of the CBD and drawing their workers from distinct suburban labour sheds.

It is true that many suburban areas now contain reasonably balanced numbers of jobs and workers (figure 3.9), and O'Connor and Rapson (2003) argue that suburban regions are becoming increasingly self-contained. But even in Sydney and Melbourne, where the decentralisation of jobs is most advanced, it does not seem warranted to talk of self-contained urban realms and edge cities. Journey to work data suggest that Sydney is probably still best pictured as a complex set of overlapping suburban labour sheds. In fact, each employment centre has several different labour sheds. Women work closer to home than men; part-timers work closer to home than full-time workers; blue-collar workers come from different suburbs than white-collar workers. This suburban pattern is then overlain by the labour sheds of the CBD which, despite its increasing distinctiveness, still draws workers from a wide area because of its central position, good public transport links, and large number of specialised jobs. Melbourne has a comparable structure, as described by Brotchie (1992). The other major cities are similar, but because of their smaller size and less decentralised pattern of employment, distinct suburban labour sheds are less well developed.

There are good reasons why our cities, though they have been subject to the same forces of global restructuring and technological change, should not conform to the pattern suggested by North American writers. There is the matter of scale. Orange County has a population of over two million, within a Greater Los Angeles region of over ten million, and the number of high-technology jobs is infinitely greater than in any Australian city. Our cities lack the extensive freeway networks with suburban intersections that have proved so attractive as locations for 'edge city' business concentrations in the United States of America. Our traditional CBDs and inner suburbs have also remained more attractive to businesses and residents than their American counterparts, where the city centre is often ringed by low-income Afro-American and Hispanic ghettos. In any case, changes in American cities may have not been quite so clear cut and revolutionary as suggested by terms such as 'recrystallised…urban realms' and 'edge cities' (Freestone & Murphy 1993). These terms and concepts provide a stimulating challenge to traditional ideas about cities structured around one dominant CBD. But, as later research on Sydney by Freestone and Murphy (1998) has confirmed, they should not tempt us to take an oversimplified view of what is happening.

Policy issues

In cities characterised by low-density residential suburbs, the suburbanisation of employment should theoretically lead to shorter average journeys to work than if all jobs remained in or near the city centre. Several writers (Brotchie 1992; Gordon et al. 1991) argue that the average time taken to travel to work in many large Australian and North American cities has fallen slightly, and attribute this to an increase in the proportion of short, cross-suburban journeys. Others (Mees 1994a) query the reliability of the data used to reach these conclusions. Any reductions in average travel times could, in any case, be partly attributable to a rise in the proportion of female workers and part-timers, who tend to work closer to home. But it does seem that average travel times are at least not increasing significantly, even though cities are continuing to expand.

The 'new urban structure' has therefore been hailed as economically efficient. Its supporters claim that it gives employers choice and flexibility as they seek to adapt to economic restructuring and new technology. Businesses can locate almost anywhere in the metropolitan area and still be accessible to their labour force. And households have the flexibility *they* need in times of changing workforce participation. From almost any suburb the various household members seeking part-time or full-time work will have access to a range of jobs within reasonable distance. If appropriate jobs cannot be found nearby it is possible to drive to more distant suburbs without crippling inconvenience. But the decentralised 'new urban structure', with its complex web of overlapping labour sheds, raises crucial issues of environmental sustainability and equity. Most cross-suburban journeys are difficult if not impossible to make by public transport. Shorter journey *times* have therefore only been achieved at the cost of increasing dependence on cars. Part of the reduction is simply the result of people switching from slower modes of travel—walking, cycling and public transport—to the faster automobile. Australian cities in the early twenty-first century may or may not be post-suburban or informational cities, but there is no doubt that they are automobile cities, even if car dependence has now possibly passed its peak (table 3.3). If people living in the suburbs wish to get a job, access to a car is almost essential. With a car, one can get to almost any job opportunity that may arise, at any time of day. Without a car the range of possible destinations is much more restricted, especially at night. No wonder the number of three-car households continues to rise!

Environmental sustainability

If we are not worried by this dependence on the automobile, a decentralised city structure certainly promises many advantages. But groups such as the Australian Conservation Foundation argue that such reliance on the car is a major problem. Cars are greedy consumers of fossil fuel, major producers of greenhouse gases, and the main cause of urban air pollution, which particularly affects vulnerable regions such as western Sydney. The new urban structure therefore raises serious questions of environmental sustainability, which we shall examine in detail in chapter 7.

Equity

Equity, in the sense of a fair deal for all members of society, is also an issue, because the decentralised city does not deliver its promises to everyone. Households without cars are obviously disadvantaged. So, potentially, are car-owning households where the number of workers exceeds the number of available vehicles. People on low incomes struggle financially to keep cars on the road and sometimes give up work—particularly part-time work—because the wage they earn is not worth the expense involved. A significant proportion of people also simply cannot drive because they are too young, too old, or have medical problems.

Even if access to cars is not a problem, some areas have more jobs—and a wider range of jobs—than others (Freestone & Murphy 1998). Suburban office and high-technology employment has mainly developed in areas such as Sydney's North Shore and eastern Melbourne, whose labour sheds take in the adjoining affluent middle and outer suburbs. Suburban job opportunities for women are also most plentiful in these areas. In the low-income suburbs of western and south-western Sydney, northern and western Melbourne, and northern Adelaide, the number of potential workers has grown more rapidly than the number of jobs, which also remain mainly concentrated in the manufacturing and retailing sectors. And women hold a below-average proportion of the jobs.

Working-class outer suburbs such as Fairfield in Sydney, Broadmeadows in Melbourne, Elizabeth in Adelaide, and Inala in Brisbane suffer from both limited local job opportunities and below-average levels of car ownership. The cost of running cars eats into low wages but workers without cars—many of whom tend to be women—are at the mercy of inadequate local job opportunities. Elizabeth had an unemployment rate of 21 per cent in 2001—four times higher than in Adelaide's affluent eastern suburbs—and a low female workforce-participation rate that suggests additional hidden unemployment. Fairfield, Broadmeadows, and Inala have similar characteristics. Such unemployment is not primarily caused by a shortage of local jobs. As will be discussed in chapter 5, the highest unemployment rates in Australian cities mainly occur in areas of low-cost housing, which are the only places people prone to unemployment can afford to live. People live there because they are poor, rather than being poor because they live there. But below-average accessibility to jobs then has a *compounding effect* that makes it more difficult for households to break out of the cycle of unemployment and poverty. The reality of life for many households in such areas is very different from the futuristic image of post-suburban informational cities. Their 'urban realm' represents marginalisation rather than convenience.

The future?

How can governments respond to these concerns about the 'new urban structure'? One view emanating from the United States of America is that they should simply keep out of the way:

> spontaneous relocation decisions by firms and households do a very nice job of achieving balance, and of keeping commuting times within tolerable limits without costly planning intervention. The appropriate role for planning agencies and jurisdictions should be to facilitate the decentralization of jobs by relaxing zoning restrictions that limit commercial land uses in residential communities, to help in land assembly, to provide economic infrastructure, and to discourage growth control initiatives—in other words, help the market to work rather than strangle it. (Gordon et al. 1991, p. 419)

This might seem remarkably uncritical in its enthusiasm for market forces but its influence was clearly recognisable in Australian planning strategies during the 1990s. For example *Sydney's Future* (NSW Dept of Planning 1993, pp. 48–9) specifically recognised the importance of dispersed suburban employment for 'the economic efficiency and competitiveness of the region' and advocated policies almost identical to those suggested by Gordon et al. The Sydney strategy conceded that most dispersed employment is highly dependent on the private car, but could only suggest car pools and express hopes for technological improvements in fuel efficiency and pollution control. Similarly the strategy recognised the equity implications of job shortages in Sydney's west, but simply hoped that some dispersed employment would be attracted there by large amounts of cheap land or the need to serve the local market.

The latest metropolitan strategic plans, for example *Melbourne 2030* (Victoria, Dept of Infrastructure 2002) place more emphasis on encouraging the concentration of employment into suburban district centres in order to tackle the environmental and equity issues posed by the dispersed suburbanisation of jobs and consequent car-dependence. But this involves finding a way to reverse current trends and O'Connor and Rapson (2003) argue that 'the planners are operating in a world of wishful thinking...remote from the real world priorities of employers and their employees'. In chapters 7 and 8 we shall return to these vitally important planning questions.

4

Housing Questions

Australia's major cities are, above all, residential environments. Most of their built-up areas consist of the houses, streets, and local facilities that constitute 'home' for 11 million people. The kind of housing people live in, whether it meets their needs, and what they have to pay for it largely determine their standard of living. The National Housing Strategy review, carried out by the federal government in the early 1990s, identified four key housing questions or issues: *affordability*, *appropriateness*, *equity*, and *environmental sustainability*. Affordability concerns the ability of people to get sound housing without paying too high a proportion of their income for it. Appropriateness refers to whether the nature of housing (size, location, style, and so on) matches the needs of households. Equity concerns whether the way housing is provided gives all types of household a fair deal. Environmental sustainability addresses whether our housing needs to change if we want to avoid long-term damage to the environment. The questions are obviously relevant to rural and urban Australia, but this chapter focuses on their particular significance for the major cities as we enter the twenty-first century. It begins by examining the nature of the urban housing stock before analysing the changing structure of urban households and discussing their housing needs and preferences. In conclusion this chapter considers policy issues and the changing role of government in housing provision. Issues of environmental sustainability and housing will be examined in chapter 7.

The urban housing stock

The housing stock in each major city consists of a diverse mixture of dwellings, varying in age, style, building materials, tenure, and cost. As discussed in chapter 1, these mixtures are historical legacies in bricks and mortar, inherited in particular from periods of rapid urban growth and strong demand for new housing. The housing booms of both the late nineteenth century and the

1920s left their mark on the inner suburbs, but the long boom of the 1950s and 1960s bequeathed the largest legacy. A vast number of houses were built between 1947 and 1971, more than doubling the number of dwellings in each city. Also, as discussed in chapter 1, home ownership levels rose sharply, public rental housing emerged, and private renting became much less important. The Australian housing system as we know it today took shape during this period. The suburban detached house also became firmly established as the norm. Separate houses reached their peak as a proportion of all dwellings in 1961, comprising from 83 per cent in Sydney to 93 per cent in Perth. A boom in flat-building then occurred during the 1960s, especially in Sydney, but in 1971 separate houses still predominated, ranging from 66 per cent of all dwellings in Sydney to 84 per cent in Brisbane.

The number of dwellings continued to grow quite rapidly during the 1970s and 1980s. The main factor affecting the amount of demand for housing is the rate at which new households form. Because small households consisting of couples or persons living alone were becoming increasingly common, the number of households increased much more rapidly than the number of people. Melbourne's population increased by only 21 per cent between 1971 and 1991 (table 1.6), whereas the number of households increased by 43 per cent. During the same period the population of Perth, the most rapidly growing major city, increased by 63 per cent but the number of households rose by 100 per cent. The demand for new housing, and the resulting growth of residential suburbs in the major cities, therefore far outstripped the simple rate of population increase.

Housing structure and density

Table 4.1 shows the nature of the housing stock in Australia's major cities in 2001 and how the stock has changed since 1991. The number of dwellings continues to grow at a greater rate than the cities' populations. In Perth and Brisbane, the fastest growing cities, the housing stock grew by around 30 per cent in the ten-year period. Sydney and Melbourne grew more slowly in percentage terms, but still over 200 000 dwellings were added to the stock in each city. Even in Adelaide, whose population grew by only 5 per cent, the housing stock grew by 14 per cent, representing almost 60 000 new dwellings.

At first glance, housing structure and density appear not to have changed very much since the end of the long boom. The separate house still predominates, though there are some differences between cities. Sydney's housing stock is significantly less dominated by separate houses, with flats—particularly those in blocks of 3 or more storeys—more common than elsewhere (though the Gold Coast actually contains the most notable concentration of high rise

Table 4.1 Structure and tenure of dwellings in major cities, 1991–2001

Structure of private	Per cent of total dwellings, 2001					Per cent change in number of dwellings, 1991–2001				
dwellings	Syd.	Melb.	Bris.	Per.	Adel.	Syd.	Melb.	Bris.	Per.	Adel.
Separate house	62.1	73.4	79.2	76.4	74.3	10.0	13.4	26.5	26.8	13.9
Semi-detached, townhouse, etc.	11.4	10.4	6.8	13.4	13.5	50.4	26.6	192.5	-0.7	-0.2
Flat, 3 or more storeys	17.7	5.3	5.6	4.2	1.4	35.7	38.5	67.5	16.5	35.0
Other flats	6.9	9.4	6.6	4.8	9.7	16.1	36.8	18.0	80.4	36.4
Other, not stated	1.9	1.5	1.8	1.2	1.1	-0.9	3.3	-8.6	11.5	-3.5
Total %	100	100	100	100	100	17.7	17.5	31.8	27.1	13.6
Total no. of dwellings ('000)	1546.7	1344.6	642.1	552.0	458.0					
Tenure of occupied private dwellings	Syd.	Melb.	Bris.	Per.	Adel.	Syd.	Melb.	Bris.	Per.	Adel.
Fully owned	39.0	41.9	35.0	35.8	38.7	18.3	24.3	18.6	22.9	12.9
Being purchased	23.7	28.1	29.6	34.1	30.2	5.6	9.8	33.7	32.0	15.6
Rented from housing authority	5.1	2.9	4.3	4.0	8.0	3.6	-0.8	21.9	-6.0	-17.1
Other rented	23.9	19.9	25.7	19.7	17.6	26.3	16.9	53.0	22.4	21.1
Other, not stated	8.3	7.2	5.4	6.4	5.5	49.4	39.8	35.5	77.4	54.1
Total %	100	100	100	100	100	17.9	18.5	31.6	26.7	13.4
Total no. of occupied dwellings ('000)	1438.4	1243.4	601.1	511.1	430.2					

Data are for Statistical Divisions
Source: ABS 2001 Census, Time Series Community Profiles

flats in the country). In Adelaide the large estates of semi-detached dwellings built by the South Australian Housing Trust during the long boom are still prominent. Brisbane still has the highest percentage of separate houses. But there are signs of change. The percentage change data in table 4.1 show that in Sydney, Melbourne, and Brisbane between 1991 and 2001 the number of medium-density dwellings (semi-detached, townhouses, terraces, etc.) and flats grew much more rapidly than the number of separate houses. In Perth and Adelaide also, the number of flats increased at a significantly faster rate than separate houses, but the number of semi-detached houses fell as public housing estates were demolished and redeveloped.

Higher-density housing now dominates new dwelling construction in Sydney (figure 4.1). Over the financial years 2001–02 and 2002–03, separate houses made up only 40 per cent of new residential construction. This

Figure 4.1 High-density living, Sydney, 2003: new residential developments adjacent to suburban railway stations; Strathfield (above) and Auburn (below)

Source: Clive Forster

compares with 68 per cent in Melbourne, 67 per cent in Brisbane, 85 per cent in Perth, and 77 per cent in Adelaide. In all the cities, there are signs that the 1990s was a significant watershed decade, during which the traditional low-density nature of new residential development began to change. But the overall nature of the housing stock remains strongly influenced by the building practices of past periods.

In all the cities, the structure and density of dwellings tend to vary with distance from the city centre and with age of development. Melbourne (figure 4.2) shows a particularly clear concentric pattern. In almost all the outer, recently developed suburbs, over 85 per cent of the housing stock consists of separate houses. In a broad belt of middle suburbs, separate houses still make up over 65 per cent of the stock. Pockets of higher-density dwellings occur in old villages, and where zoning regulations during the 1960s and 1970s allowed the building of flats, which were often along main roads, around suburban railway stations, and in beachside locations. In the inner, older suburbs less than half the housing stock consists of separate houses. The remainder is a complex mixture of original nineteenth-century terraces (figure 1.3) and higher-density redevelopment dating from the 1960s onwards: Victorian Housing Commission tower blocks (figure 1.8), private flats, townhouses, and units.

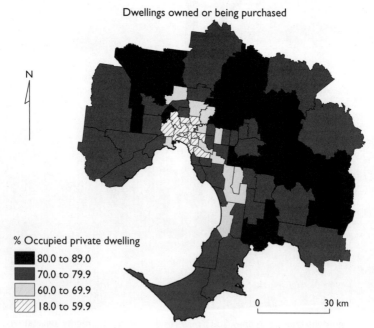

Figure 4.2 Spatial variations in the housing stock, Melbourne, 2001

Source: ABS 2001 Census

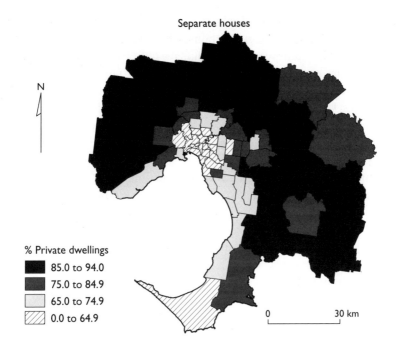

Separate houses

% Private dwellings
- 85.0 to 94.0
- 75.0 to 84.9
- 65.0 to 74.9
- 0.0 to 64.9

0   30 km

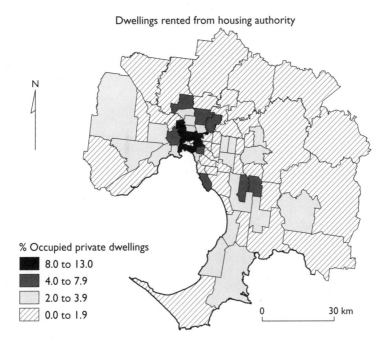

Dwellings rented from housing authority

% Occupied private dwellings
- 8.0 to 13.0
- 4.0 to 7.9
- 2.0 to 3.9
- 0.0 to 1.9

0   30 km

Figure 4.2 (cont.)

Most new housing on the fringes of all the cities still consists of conventional homes on separate blocks. But houses, blocks, and services to dwellings have all changed in recent years, in ways not always apparent from census data. During the long boom, there were few controls over how land at the urban fringe was subdivided for housing. Developers did not even have to provide basic services such as sealed roads and sewerage. The blocks were large, although not usually as large as the proverbial quarter acre. Zoning regulations, usually enforced by local councils, tended simply to prohibit the building of anything other than separate houses. Most councils also had by-laws enforcing minimum dimensions and standards of construction.

These days, although local councils continue to impose negative controls and minimum standards on new housing, their rules have become more flexible. Suburban allotments have become smaller on average, and more varied in size. Standard suburban blocks are now approximately 650 square metres in area, and 'courtyard' (450 m²) and 'villa' (300 m²) blocks have become increasingly common (figure 4.3). Dwellings on these courtyard and villa blocks are smaller than the traditional suburban home, but houses generally have become larger and better-appointed, with family rooms, rumpus rooms, and en-suite bathrooms. The average floor area of new separate houses

Figure 4.3 New 'villa' housing in Berwick, outer Melbourne, 1994. The compact dwellings on small blocks mimic the architectural style of the nineteenth-century inner suburbs

Source: Clive Forster

in Australia in 1999–2000 has been estimated as 222m² (ABS 2001), compared with 170 m² in 1985–86. The addition of extra rooms and even second storeys to older dwellings also became common from the 1980s onwards.

The development of new housing estates is now more controlled, and better coordinated with the extension of major state government services such as power, water supply, and sewerage. Developers are required to provide sealed roads and connections to sewer mains. Joint ventures between government departments and developers have also become common. These major projects, such as Golden Grove and Seaford Rise in Adelaide, and Wattle Grove in western Sydney, incorporate public and private housing together with the planned provision from the outset of both physical infrastructure (pipes and wires) and 'human' services such as schools. Overall, housing has become more expensive, though both houses and services have improved in standard. Dwellings are now more diverse in size and style than during the 1950s and 1960s, although the conventional separate house still predominates.

Tenure

The relative importance of the different housing tenures has also not changed radically since 1971 (table 4.1). Between 35 and 42 per cent of the households in each city own their dwellings outright and between 23 and 34 per cent are still paying off a housing loan. Between 20 and 26 per cent rent their dwelling from a private landlord. Only 3 to 5 per cent rent from a public housing authority, except in Adelaide where public rental housing is almost twice as important as elsewhere and the private rental sector is correspondingly smaller.

Structure and tenure are related, as figure 4.4 shows for the examples of Sydney and Adelaide. Over 80 per cent of owner-occupied dwellings are separate houses, whereas flats and other medium-density dwellings predominate in the private rental sector, particularly in Sydney. The public rental stock contains a mixture of structures, though semi-detached dwellings still predominate in Adelaide. The most striking single characteristic of the housing stock is that owner-occupied separate houses still make up approximately 60 per cent of all dwellings everywhere except Sydney. Slowly but surely, however, our urban housing stock is becoming more diverse.

Each city has its own distinctive geography of housing tenure. Figure 4.2 shows the basic pattern in Melbourne. Also, social atlases of each capital city, showing in great detail how the character of housing and population varies from suburb to suburb, have been published by the Australian Bureau of Statistics (ABS) based on the 2001 Census. The atlases use data for *collection districts*, which are small areas containing about 300 dwellings, and give a much more accurate picture of local variations than maps based on larger

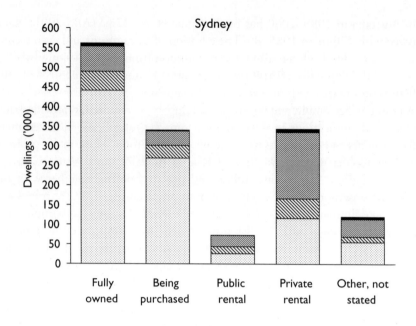

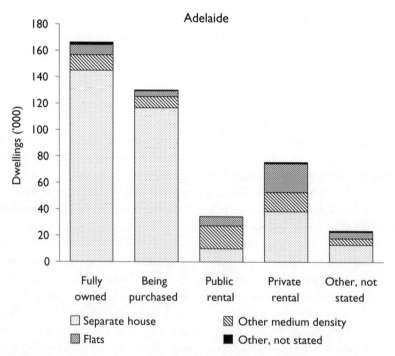

Figure 4.4 Dwelling structure by tenure, Sydney and Adelaide, 2001

Source: ABS 2001 Census

areas. The following paragraphs will profit from being read, if possible, in company with one or more of the 2001 social atlases.

Most suburbs contain a mixture of tenures, but owner-occupied housing tends to predominate. The proportion of outright owners as opposed to purchasers varies in an approximate concentric pattern, related to the period when areas were first settled. Purchasers are more common in the newer fringe suburbs—the 'mortgage belts' beloved of pollsters and political analysts—whereas the highest percentages of outright owners are found in the middle suburbs that were first settled in the interwar and long boom years.

Contrary to popular belief, dwellings rented from a private landlord are not totally concentrated in the inner suburbs, nor are they all old houses or flats. Even in low-density outer suburbs, one in ten of the houses at any given time is being rented privately. But it is true that only in the inner suburbs and in other pockets of older development (figure 4.2) do privately rented dwellings form a significant percentage of the total stock. Rental property in these areas, often in poor repair, has traditionally formed the main reservoir of low-cost private accommodation in Australian cities. The more detailed maps in the ABS social atlases also show that smaller concentrations of private rental dwellings occur in the middle suburbs where flats were built in the 1960s.

Public housing—dwellings rented from government housing authorities—is more highly concentrated than any of the other tenures, and is unique in being entirely absent from large areas of each city. (Note that the ABS social atlases show the distribution of all government-owned dwellings, and therefore include dwellings rented from the Defence Housing Authority by military personnel, as well as standard public housing.) The concentration is largely a heritage of the long boom when large public housing estates were built in what were then fringe suburbs close to suburban manufacturing (figure 4.5). Each city has well-known examples: Green Valley and Mt Druitt in Sydney; Inala in Brisbane; Broadmeadows in Melbourne; Elizabeth, Enfield, and Mitchell Park in Adelaide. In Melbourne (figures 1.8 and 4.2), and to a lesser extent Sydney, areas of publicly rented high-rise flats were also built in the inner suburbs.

Since the mid 1970s the housing authorities have generally tried to build smaller estates in a wider range of locations, and to build up stocks by 'spot purchase' of existing dwellings. New public housing has become more varied in size and type, with less emphasis on family housing. At the same time, some of the older suburban estates are being redeveloped and part of the stock sold off. Public housing has therefore become somewhat more diversified. And, as discussed later in the chapter, recent developments in federal government housing policy have drastically reduced the amount of new construction, and are producing radical changes in the whole public housing system. But because so much of the stock is still a legacy of the 1950s and 1960s, the old estates remain a distinctive element in the social geography of each major city.

Figure 4.5 Suburban public housing, Mitchell Park, Adelaide, 1990. These South Australian Housing Trust double units were built in the 1960s near a new car factory
Source: Clive Forster

The changing nature of urban households

Household size

Households have been getting smaller, which is why their numbers have grown more rapidly than the total population. In 1971 the average household contained 3.2 persons in Sydney and Adelaide and 3.3 in the other major cities. By 1991 the figure had fallen to 2.6 in Adelaide and 2.8 elsewhere. Household sizes continued to fall during the 1990s, and at the 2001 Census ranged from 2.7 in Sydney to only 2.4 in Adelaide. These long standing declines reflect a set of interrelated demographic, economic, and social trends. People are living longer, and the people who migrated to Australia as young adults during the postwar immigration boom have now reached retirement age. There has therefore been a rise in the proportion of older couples or lone persons. At the same time, young people have been leaving the parental home earlier (a trend that began during the 1960s), marrying later, and postponing child-bearing until later. As a result, more households now consist of young single persons living alone or couples. When couples do start a family, they are having fewer children than was common during the postwar baby boom, so nuclear families are smaller. More people are choosing not to live in conventional family households. Increased divorce rates since the 1970s have also played their part. Although most divorced people remarry, one household splits into two smaller ones for a while at least.

Household composition

Households, as well as declining in size, have become more diverse in demographic structure. The census distinguishes between *family households*, defined as two or more people living together and related by blood, marriage, or de facto relationship, and *non family households*, consisting of groups of unrelated people living together, or persons living alone. Table 4.2 shows that the composition of households is very similar in the five major cities. Two-parent families now make up only 31 to 38 per cent of total households; couples comprise between 23 and 26 per cent; and single-parent families, the fastest growing family type, about 11 per cent. People living alone have also increased rapidly in numbers and now make up about 23 per cent of all households. Adelaide differs a little from the other cities in having a lower proportion of two-parent families and more lone-person households, a reflection of its older age structure.

Households have also, as discussed in chapter 3, become much more diverse in workforce participation. Only 25 per cent of family households now have one breadwinner. Fifty per cent have two or more paid workers, and in the remaining 25 per cent no one at all is in paid employment.

Table 4.2 Household and family composition in major cities, 2001 (%)

Household type	Sydney	Melbourne	Brisbane	Perth	Adelaide
Family households					
1-parent families	10.9	10.7	11.7	11.0	11.3
2-parent families	37.6	36.8	33.9	33.9	30.5
Couples	23.2	23.5	25.0	24.9	25.6
Other	1.6	1.6	1.5	1.4	1.3
Group households	4.3	4.2	5.0	3.9	3.5
Lone person households	22.4	23.2	22.9	24.8	27.9
Total	100	100	100	100	100
% of persons					
In 2-parent families	54.7	54.7	51.5	52.4	48.8
In lone person households	8.9	9.4	9.5	10.4	12.3

Data are for Statistical Divisions

Source: ABS 2001 Census

The death of the traditional family?

Two-parent families—'traditional nuclear families'—are now a declining minority of households. Faced with this fact, the media and some political figures periodically assert that family life and values are threatened and the end of civilisation is at hand. Opposing groups, particularly during the International Year of the Family in 1994, replied that a diversity of living arrangements, including gay and lesbian relationships, are now as valid as the traditional nuclear family (the census recognised same-sex couples as a valid family type for the first time in 1996). However, the demise of the traditional family should not be exaggerated. Each two-parent family household contains, by definition, at least three people. As a result, approximately half the *population* of each major city currently lives in such households (table 4.2). This proportion is falling (though changes in census classifications make precise comparisons difficult), and there is no doubt that household structures have diversified. But in considering the nature of housing demand we need also to recognise that most people still spend most of their lives as members of two-parent families, first as children then later as parents.

Housing needs and preferences

The family life cycle

During the long boom, social scientists used a concept called the *family life cycle* to explain housing preferences (table 4.3). The 'typical' family was assumed to pass through a series of stages, from marriage to the death of the last surviving partner. Each stage was marked by particular housing needs, based on family size and composition. According to this concept, the postwar baby boom in countries such as the USA and Australia automatically led to the growth of low-density suburbia, as large numbers of families moved together into the

Table 4.3 The life cycle of the 'traditional' family

Stage	Begins	Importance of access to city centre	Importance of space
Pre-child	Leave parental home	High	Low
Child-bearing	Birth of first child	Falling	Rising
Child-rearing	Birth of last child	Low	High
Child-launching	First child leaves home	Low	High
Post-child	Last child leaves home	Low	Falling
Widowhood	Death of partner	Low	Low

Source: **Clive Forster**

child-bearing and *child-rearing* stages of the life cycle and demanded the appropriate housing.

According to this life cycle concept, housing needs and preferences in Australian cities should have become more diverse. Many more households are now in the *pre-child* and *post-child* stages of the life cycle. Many do not fit into the conventional life cycle at all, following higher rates of marriage breakdown and the emergence of non-traditional household types. As early as the mid 1970s, commentators in Australia began suggesting that a *mismatch* had developed between households' changing needs and a housing stock still dominated by conventional detached houses designed for nuclear families. Rising housing costs were seen as a further incentive for small households to economise by seeking smaller dwellings. Tables 4.1 and 4.2 suggest that the mismatch has worsened and, as already noted, the 1990 National Housing Strategy review identified housing *appropriateness* as one of its key issues. Yet surveys in the 1990s, including those carried out as part of the National Housing Strategy, suggest that households of all types still show a strong preference for owning their own conventional detached family house.

There are many good reasons why smaller households might still prefer a 'conventional' house. Small households do not necessarily need less space. Young couples may be intending to have children in the near future. Single-parent families do not take up fewer rooms than two-parent families. Couples whose children have left home (the 'empty nesters') want spare bedrooms for visitors or for conversion into studies and hobby rooms.

It is also important to recognise that housing does not just provide accommodation. For most families it is their only major financial investment. Many years ago, all the Australian states followed Queensland's lead in abolishing death duties, and federal capital gains tax does not apply to the family home. Many people therefore see owning the most expensive house they can afford as their best way of accumulating wealth and passing it on to their heirs, even if smaller, cheaper housing is available.

Finally, housing has symbolic significance. A conventional suburban house and garden epitomises the Great Australian Dream. People regard it as a genuine *home*, signifying independence and social status, and tend to view other types of dwellings as inferior, minority forms of accommodation. As Johnson (1993, p. 211) puts it: 'In order to understand more completely why Australians want new suburban housing…it is necessary to consider the house as a cultural artefact'.

Figure 4.6 shows, for the example of Sydney, that there is a clear relationship between household type, housing structure, and tenure. Most two-parent families own or are buying a home. Most group households are renting from a private landlord. A high percentage of single parents live in public rental

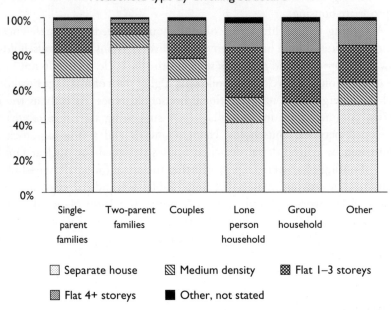

Household type by dwelling structure

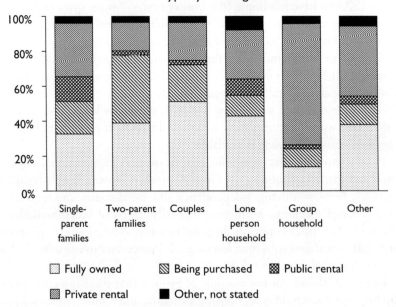

Household type by dwelling tenure

Figure 4.6 Household type by dwelling structure and tenure, Sydney, 2001
Source: ABS 2001 Census

housing. Almost all two-parent families live in separate houses, as do the majority of other family types. Higher proportions of group households and lone persons live in medium- or high-density housing. So, although separate houses predominate, significant numbers of households—especially in Sydney—do now live in other types of dwelling. The number is increasing, and might do so more rapidly if a wider choice of dwelling types was readily available, and if government tax policies did not encourage a preference for conventional housing. But it appears that the majority of households in Australian cities still aspire to own a low-density family house, whatever the financial difficulties involved and whatever views planners may hold about housing appropriateness.

Choice or constraint?

The concept of the family life cycle emphasises *choice*. It implies that housing supply responds to housing demand. In reality, people's housing preferences, and even more so their actual housing *options* and *outcomes*, are strongly shaped by the *constraints* of housing supply. For example, young people will be less able to leave their parents and form independent households if there is a shortage of cheap rental accommodation. And the decline in housing afford-ability during the 1970s no doubt also caused some married women to stay in the paid workforce longer that they would have chosen, and to use the newly available contraceptive pill to postpone child bearing until they had saved a housing deposit.

Housing supply can therefore shape life cycles, as well as vice versa. Recog-nising this, Kendig and Paris (1987) suggested the concept of the *housing ladder* (figure 4.7). Each rung of the ladder represents an improvement in housing circumstances, leading to the goal of outright ownership of a dwelling. Households attempt to climb the ladder with varying degrees of success. Some become trapped on the lower rungs in the private or public rental sectors. Economic or demographic events may cause others to fall down the ladder, having neared the top. Traditionally, the main factor in determining house-holds' housing conditions and economic well-being throughout their lifetime is their success or otherwise in reaching and staying on the home ownership rungs of the ladder. Success in climbing the housing ladder does not depend simply on income or household structure, but also on economic conditions at the time a household seeks to take its first steps. Some of the aged people in acute housing poverty in Australian cities today became trapped in the private rental sector during the 1930s Great Depression. Other families began their climb up the ladder during the easy years of the long boom and are now com-fortably off as outright home owners. And, as discussed later, young households

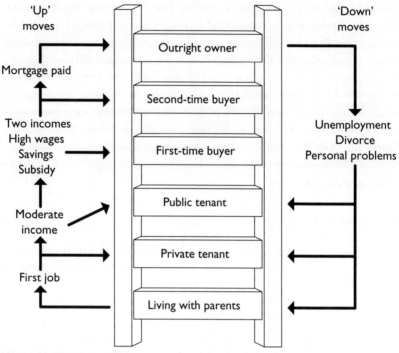

Figure 4.7 The 'housing ladder'
Source: adapted from Paris, 1993, p. 52

today are finding it increasingly hard get a foothold on the first home ownership rung of the ladder, particularly in Sydney.

Housing provision and the changing role of government

In spite of the relatively stable character of the housing stock, significant
changes have occurred in the nature of housing provision in Australian cities.
In a review of federal government housing policy, Yates (1997, p. 265) provides the following summary.

> From the post-war period through to the 1980s, Australia's housing system was
> dominated by tenure-based policies directed towards home ownership and the
> provision of public housing. Private tenants were virtually excluded from
> housing assistance of any form. The 1990s, however, have seen an apparent U-
> turn in housing policies with elimination of explicit home ownership policies,
> the withdrawal from direct involvement in public housing funding and a rapid

expansion of rental assistance for private tenants. Australia is about to follow its New Zealand neighbour in undertaking a wholesale shift away from direct intervention in the production of housing and movement towards consumer subsidies which rely on the effective operation of the private sector in meeting housing needs.

Home ownership and affordability

Home ownership was unusually affordable during the long boom. Rising real incomes coincided with the availability of low-interest housing loans and other government-sponsored incentives for first-home buyers. Saving the deposit for a house was still a struggle for the average family but, once people overcame that hurdle, it was possible, with overtime readily available in most industries, to meet housing loan repayments and live reasonably well from one wage packet.

Things were very different during the 1970s and 1980s. Housing standards certainly improved, but rising housing and land costs coupled with slower economic growth meant that house prices increased more rapidly than real incomes, particularly in Sydney and Melbourne. Interest rates on housing loans also rose sharply, particularly following the deregulation of the Australian financial system, to reach a peak of 18 per cent in the late 1980s. Between 1979 and 1990 the number of weeks of average earnings needed to secure a deposit on the average house in Sydney rose from 146 to 357 (Beer 1993, p. 170), and by 1986 it took 58 per cent of an average income to repay the loan on an average house (Daly 1988, p. 171).

Interest rates fell sharply during the early 1990s and at the time of writing are still low, at around 6 per cent. But average house prices have continued to rise more rapidly than average earnings. According to O'Neill & McGuirk (2002, p. 249), house prices tripled in Sydney between 1987 and 1999, whereas household real incomes increased by only 50 per cent. House prices then rose sharply in all the capital cities during the early 2000s. In July 2000 the federal government introduced the First Home Owners Scheme. This scheme gave people buying their first home a lump sum to compensate for the impact on building costs of the newly-introduced goods and services tax (GST), but probably contributed to rising house prices by stimulating demand (Berry 2003). According to a Commonwealth Bank study, housing affordability in mid-2003 was at its worst for 13 years.

Because of changing workforce-participation patterns, households have also become more diverse in their ability to afford housing, and particularly in their ability to begin buying their first house. Young couples with two incomes, especially if both are working in well-paid, white-collar jobs, may be well placed, perhaps accounting for the hint of resentment in terms like 'yuppies' (young urban professionals) and 'dinks' (double income, no kids). But for less affluent couples, buying a home has become a struggle even on two incomes. For households with only one income, especially with a breadwinner in a lower paid job, getting into home ownership is very hard indeed. The lack of job security, with the constant fear of unemployment or reduced income, also makes home ownership a risky venture.

At the bottom of the pile, buying a home is generally out of the question for households dependent on unemployment benefits, supporting-parent benefits, or other welfare payments. Retired people who did not attain home ownership earlier in life are in a similar position. Women have been particularly affected. Most single parents and most aged persons living alone are women, and females generally have lower incomes than males; many writers refer to the *feminisation of housing poverty*.

The current boom in house prices will no doubt—like all booms—come to an end. But it still seems unlikely that home ownership for the average household will ever become as attainable as it was in the 1960s. Young households will find it increasingly difficult to enter home ownership, especially in Sydney and Melbourne. And lower-income households who do manage to achieve that goal run the constant danger of overcommitting themselves and of being unable to maintain their mortgage payments, especially if interest rates rise.

In their book *Home Truths*, Badcock and Beer (2000) compare the very different circumstances of the baby boomer generation and the so-called Generation X that followed. The baby boomers were born between 1945 and 1960. They grew up and sought to enter the housing market from the late 1960s onwards at a time of low interest rates, general prosperity, and rising female participation in the labour force (with child-bearing postponed thanks to the arrival of the birth-control pill). While still aged in their twenties, couples found it relatively easy to establish their careers, build up savings and incomes, and begin to buy their first home. Many households then ascended the housing ladder as property markets boomed, and accumulated significant housing wealth—although significant numbers were affected by divorce and remarriage.

The following generation—Generation X—had a very different experience. Born between 1960 and the mid 1970s, and coming into adulthood in the 1980s and 1990s, they experienced the full impact of the global economic restructuring described in chapter 2. Compared with the baby boomers, Generation Xers took longer to get established in careers, were more likely to be in casual or part-time work (or be unemployed), entered into permanent relationships later, and postponed child-bearing until later. And they entered home ownership later, if at all. By 1994 only 55 per cent of Australians aged 30–34 years owned their own home, compared with 69 per cent in 1974 (Yates 2000). Some of this change was because of falling housing affordability, and increasing uncertainty about careers and families. But for some people in highly paid jobs it represented a choice about how to invest, especially if they wished to be mobile in their careers. The outcome is likely to be a fall in overall owner-occupation rates as the baby boomers die out, and increasing inequality in housing wealth that will have major implications for how people fare in their old age.

What of the future? Badcock and Beer (2000) describe the next generation, who entered the housing market in the late 1990s and the early years of the twenty-first century, as Keating's Children. The name refers to the federal treasurer and later prime minister who was mainly responsible for opening the Australian economy to the full force of global competition. This generation is being affected by all the forces of economic uncertainty experienced by Generation X, plus additional stresses such as having to repay Higher Education Contribution Scheme (HECS) debts while establishing careers and families. For them, the ability to enter home ownership seems likely to become even more unequal, depending not only on their household income and structure but also, of course, on where they live.

Public housing

As described in chapter 1, the public housing sector consists of dwellings rented from state housing commissions or trusts. It first became significant during the long boom, following the injection of federal government funds through the Commonwealth–State Housing Agreement (CSHA). Its role was to provide decent, affordable housing to working-class families who could not afford home ownership. Estates were often built close to new suburban factories and formed part of the state governments' industrial development policies, especially in Adelaide. Rents were lower than in the private sector because they were set to allow housing authorities simply to recover the costs of providing the housing, rather than make a profit.

The economic and demographic changes following the end of the long boom combined to produce a great rise in the demand for public housing from the unemployed, single parents and the aged, as well as from households depending on low-paid jobs. In addition, changing social attitudes resulted in physically and intellectually disabled people increasingly having to seek independent accommodation in the public sector, rather than being confined to institutions. Tenants already in public housing also proved particularly vulnerable to the loss of jobs and income. Households depending on pensions or benefits therefore came to dominate both the existing public housing stock and the ever-growing waiting lists. Even in 1977, only 57 per cent of applicants for South Australian Housing Trust accommodation were in paid employment. By 1991 the proportion had fallen to 29 per cent.

Simultaneously with the changes in demand, the Fraser Liberal–National Party Coalition government sought to target public housing more effectively to those in most need by imposing a *market rent* policy in the 1978 CSHA. Under this policy, housing authorities no longer set rents at a level that would cover their costs. Instead, households on average incomes or above paid rents supposedly similar to those in the private market, and low-income households were given rent rebates. The 1984 CSHA removed the compulsion to set market rents, but the system of means-tested rent rebates remained. Better-off households paid higher rents, and therefore had an incentive to find private housing. Rents for low-income households were rebated so that they did not exceed 25 per cent of their income. As a result of the combined changes in demand and supply, *public housing* became *welfare housing*. By the late 1980s, 85 per cent of the households living in areas of public rental housing were receiving rent rebates.

The level of federal financial support for public housing fluctuated, with peaks during the Whitlam years and in the early years of the Hawke Labor government in the mid 1980s, and a 'modest increase' at the 1989 CSHA (Paris 1993, p. 229). But the overall trend was a decline in funding, meaning that, despite increasing their stock of dwellings, the state housing authorities were not able to meet the growing demand from households in housing need.

The problem was not simply of inadequate numbers of dwellings. The households on the waiting lists were quite different from those housed during the long boom. There were more aged people, more small households and more people with disabilities. They needed different types of dwellings, in different locations. Since the 1970s all the housing authorities had attempted to build or buy a wider range of dwellings in a larger number of locations within the cities, but had been limited by a lack of funds. The authorities also faced a 'time bomb' in the form of the tens of thousands of public dwellings built during the 1950s and 1960s, increasingly inappropriate in design and location for many current housing applicants, and in increasing need of major expenditure or replacement.

In 1991 the percentage of households living in public rental housing ranged from 3.5 in Melbourne to 10.9 in Adelaide. These figures had changed very little since 1971. But table 4.1 shows that some major changes have occurred since. As with housing density and home ownership, we can now see that the 1990s was a watershed decade for public housing in Australia. Political support for public housing had generally weakened. Public housing thrived in most Western countries during the 'big government' era of the long boom, then came under attack subsequently as part of the general enthusiasm for privatisation. Critics argued that money would be better spent providing assistance to low-income households in owner-occupied and private rental housing, and encouraging the development of housing cooperatives and other forms of 'community housing', rather than building and managing a large, bureaucratic public housing sector. Debate about the role of public housing culminated in a federal government Industry Commission inquiry in 1993 whose report, while generally supporting the concept of public housing, recommended major changes to how rents were set and dwellings allocated to applicants.

Since the Howard Coalition government came to power in 1996, there has been a prolonged period of uncertainty about the future of public housing. Faced with declining financial support from the federal government, state housing authorities have been able to build few new dwellings. For example, only 700 new dwellings were approved for construction for the South Australian Housing Trust in Adelaide during 2001–02 and 2002–03, compared with over 14 000 approvals in the private sector. Elsewhere during that two-year period, public sector housing made up less than 2 per cent of approvals in Sydney, Melbourne, and Brisbane, and 4 per cent in Perth (ABS 2003a). Much energy has gone instead into redeveloping the old estates built in the 1950s and 1960s (Arthurson 1998). Westwood, in Adelaide's western suburbs, is Australia's largest public housing redevelopment project, a $340 million joint venture involving the SA Housing Trust, the development company Urban Pacific Ltd (a subsidiary of the Macquarie Bank), and the City of Port Adelaide–Enfield. Over a fifteen-year period, a five square kilometre area containing over 5000 dwellings will be completely redeveloped. Almost 2000 of the ageing Housing Trust rental dwellings will be demolished, almost 500 will be renovated, and 2400 new homes will be built (figure 4.8). The share of dwellings rented from the Housing Trust will fall from the current 60 per cent to about 22 per cent. The project also involves increasing residential densities and installing stormwater-detention basins and mini wetlands. Some of the dwellings will be put up for sale at attractive prices, with a special loan scheme to make them affordable to low-income households.

Schemes such as Westwood seem like a good idea on several grounds. Many old public housing estates were in poor repair and badly needed some form of redevelopment. Selling some of the old three-bedroom dwellings has provided the housing authorities with money to build new housing that better matches the needs of the smaller households on their waiting lists. Higher-density housing, smaller gardens, better handling of stormwater, and better integration with public transport also promises a more environmentally sustainable form of suburb. And introducing owner-occupiers into the estates

Figure 4.8 The redevelopment of public housing, Adelaide, 2003: double-unit rental dwellings in Westwood refurbished (above) or demolished and replaced by new compact dwellings (below)

Source: Clive Forster

helps, together with the new landscaping, a new name, and careful marketing, to combat the stigmatised, negative image of 'welfare housing'.

But there are significant problems with such 'urban renewal' schemes (Hoatson & Grace 2002). Old, established communities are broken up as existing tenants are relocated to make way for the redevelopment. The total amount of public rental housing also falls, because the profit when a refurbished dwelling is sold is not nearly enough to pay for building a new rental dwelling. The total number of dwellings rented by the South Australian Housing Trust has fallen every year since 1993, and at an increasing rate.

As the public housing stock shrinks, it not only disadvantages people on the waiting list. It also becomes more difficult to offer good alternative accommodation to tenants displaced from subsequent redevelopment schemes. In the early stages almost 30 per cent of displaced tenants were rehoused within the Westwood development and the rest within 5 kms in other Housing Trust estates. But this process becomes harder as time goes on. So redevelopment may make the old public housing estates better places to live, but some of their previous residents—and people waiting for public rental accommodation—are the losers (Arthurson 2002).

Table 4.1 shows the result of the redevelopment of old estates, coupled with low rates of new construction in the public sector. The number of public rental dwellings in Adelaide fell by 17 per cent between 1991 and 2001—a net loss of over 7000 dwellings—and now make up only 8 per cent of the total housing stock compared with 12 per cent in the 1980s. The number of public rental dwellings also fell in Perth and Melbourne, and even though numbers rose in Sydney and Brisbane they did so at a slower rate than total dwellings. Public rental housing therefore now makes up a smaller share of the housing stock in all the major cities than it did in 1991. And public housing estates are even more dominated by welfare-dependent households than they were in 1991. For example 92 per cent of the new tenants housed by the South Australian Housing Trust in 2001–02 were eligible for rent rebates, and 60 per cent were classified as *special needs* applicants: people who were homeless, had physical or intellectual disabilities, were escaping domestic violence, were indigenous or were from culturally and linguistically diverse backgrounds (South Australian Housing Trust 2002).

The future of public housing remains uncertain in an era of privatisation. Under the new Commonwealth–State Housing Agreement, negotiated in 1999–2000, state governments no longer receive significant funding from the Commonwealth to build new dwellings, and their own financial resources are limited. Australia now has a lower percentage of public rental housing than almost all the other OECD countries (Badcock & Beer 2000, p. 2). Yet waiting lists are still large and welfare lobby groups continue to defend public housing.

They point out that other forms of housing assistance or subsidies have yet to prove as effective in helping low-income households, particularly those with special needs, to find sound, secure, and affordable accommodation. Despite much publicity, community housing associations, cooperatives, and similar organisations provided only 33 500 dwellings throughout Australia in June 2001, representing 0.4 per cent of the total housing stock. Without the safety net of a properly funded public housing sector, many low-income households in our cities seem certain to be worse off in the struggle to find decent housing.

The private rental sector

The proportion of dwellings in the major cities rented from private landlords fell from almost half in 1947 to about 20 per cent in 1971, 'squeezed out' by government encouragement of home ownership on the one hand and the growth of public housing on the other. The sector then maintained its share between 1971 and 1991, partly because investors in rental property were treated kindly by the Australian taxation system. Since 1991, as table 4.1 shows, the proportion of dwellings rented privately (the 'other rented' category) has tended to increase, as both public renting and owner-occupation have declined. The private rental sector is not only an important and distinctive part of the housing stock in our major cities, but seems set to increase in significance in future.

Traditionally, private rental housing has fulfilled two quite different roles. It has provided immediately accessible, short-term accommodation for young households saving to buy a home, for mobile households who do not wish to settle down, and for others who need housing urgently, following marriage breakdown for example. For these people, renting privately has tended to be a convenient short-term rung on their housing ladder. But the private rental sector also houses many people on a long-term basis. Wulff (1997) estimates that 40 per cent of households in the private rental sector have been renting for over 10 years. Of these long-term renters, over a third rely for survival on pensions or benefits. They include many of the poorest households in Australian cities, people who will never be able to afford home ownership and who have not been able to get public rental housing. Private tenants miss out on both the financial advantages of home ownership and the subsidies received by public tenants, yet government attempts to ease hardship and improve housing conditions have met with limited success. Rent controls, as tried during wartime, discourage investment by landlords. The imposition of minimum housing standards, for example by the Housing Improvement Act in South Australia, can force landlords either to demolish property or to improve it and raise the rent. In either case the supply of low-rent housing gets smaller. In recent years the federal government has massively increased the amount of rental assistance paid directly to low income households in private rental housing. In 2002 almost a million clients received an average of just over $70 per fortnight. This provides welcome relief, but this is still much less than the average subsidy received by public tenants through rent rebates, and only people on welfare benefits or pensions are eligible for rental support in the private sector. The very existence of rent assistance may also enable private landlords to charge higher rents.

Private renting may therefore provide a vital degree of flexibility within the overall housing system, but it is also the source of some of the worst problems of poor housing conditions and housing-related poverty. The former role was particularly prominent during the 1960s, when the children of the baby boom were setting up independent households in large numbers, and is still important today; the populations of Australian cities are still relatively mobile and young. But the lower affordability of home ownership and reduced funding for public housing means that more households face the prospect of being trapped on the private rental rung of the housing ladder, often paying a high proportion of their incomes for low-quality accommodation. Inner suburbs such as St Kilda in Melbourne with high percentages of privately rented housing may be 'exciting' and cosmopolitan, but are also characterised by serious deprivation. And evidence is emerging that privatised ex-public housing in areas such as Elizabeth in Adelaide is being bought by private landlords and rented to low-income households, at higher rents and with fewer rights than they would have had as public tenants.

Urban housing issues in the twenty-first century

This brief review has omitted many topics. It has said nothing about caravans and mobile homes, or homelessness, or Aboriginal housing problems, or the rapid growth of retirement villages and other housing aimed at the aged. However, it is clear that for most people in Australian cities the immediate housing issues are *affordability* and *equity*: the problems arising, particularly for households on below average incomes, from the three interrelated trends that characterised the watershed decade of the 1990s are:

- the declining affordability of home ownership, coupled with falling job security for young households entering the housing market;
- the uncertain future of public rental housing at a time of declining government funding and falling supply;
- the poor conditions that exist in the private rental sector, made worse by increasing demand from households unable to get into either owner-occupied or public rental housing.

It seems likely that the gap in housing standards will widen between households that attained home ownership in easier times, and those trapped on the lower, rental, rungs of the housing ladder. These inequalities may also be passed on to the next generation. When those who bought housing during the boom in owner-occupation in the 1950s and 1960s die, they will bequeath their housing wealth, free of capital gains tax or death duties, to their children.

These issues are not intrinsically *urban*. By far the worst housing conditions in Australia are endured by Aborigines in rural areas. But housing costs and pressures tend to be higher in the larger cities, especially Sydney. Housing issues in the major cities also take on a particular character because of the sheer numbers of dwellings involved—over 1.5 million in Sydney and 1.3 million in Melbourne—the vast areas over which they extend, and their geographically differentiated nature.

Because the cities are so large, *relative location* makes a big difference to the desirability, and the cost, of housing. The cost of land has tended traditionally to fall with distance from the city centre, because more remote locations have poorer access to jobs and major services. A dwelling will therefore tend to cost more in an inner suburb than an identical one on the urban fringe. House prices also reflect the quality of local services and the perceived social status and desirability of a suburb. So a deterioration in housing affordability, as well as making it harder for lower income households to achieve home ownership, will tend to 'push' them into less desirable and accessible locations. The National Housing Strategy and other policy documents expressed particular concern about the *locational disadvantage* households may suffer if they can only obtain affordable and appropriate housing in fringe suburbs increasingly remote from the city centre.

We have also seen that certain types of housing tenure and structure are concentrated in particular parts of each major city. The changing role of public housing, for example, has therefore had major impacts on the areas where public rental housing makes up a significant proportion of the housing stock. The changes in housing provision that have arisen from economic restructuring in recent years, and the implications for affordability and equity, thus take on a particular geographical significance in large cities. Equity issues in particular are closely linked to the questions of residential segregation and differentiation that are discussed in the next chapter.

The debate about housing *appropriateness,* and Australian households' apparent strong preference for a detached house on its own block, also has particular significance in the large cities because it is the main 'engine' driving their continued expansion. The 1990s was again a decade of significant change, as medium- and high-density housing grew in importance. But most new dwellings are still separate houses, except in Sydney. Continued low-density suburban growth, as well as being likely to intensify the problems of locational disadvantage, raises two broad issues. The first is the cost to governments of providing physical and human services to new low-density suburbs. The second concerns *environmental sustainability*, as good agricultural land is lost to houses and gardens that use large amounts of energy and water. Of course low-density housing also combines with the decentralisation of employment discussed in chapter 3 to perpetuate our dependence on the automobile, with the attendant problems of atmospheric pollution and consumption of fossil fuels. Urban Australians have become used to a very high quality of housing by world standards but many observers believe that our preferences may no longer be compatible with the provision of affordable, appropriate, and environmentally sustainable housing in the future. Others believe just as passionately that attempts to increase housing densities will lower living standards and further disadvantage the poor, and may even increase pressure on the environment. This debate is revisited in chapters 7 and 8.

5

The Residential Mosaic

Each major Australian city consists of a patchwork—a residential mosaic—of districts and neighbourhoods inhabited by different types of households. Some areas are affluent, some are middle-income, and others are poor. Some are gaining population, others losing. Some are mainly occupied by young families with children. Others have high proportions of old people. Some areas have concentrations of particular ethnic groups. This phenomenon of *residential differentiation* is perhaps the most fundamental, and is certainly the most researched, aspect of the social geography of cities. As pointed out in chapter 1, some writers have argued that residential segregation significantly increases the inequality in living standards between rich and poor households. Even if one is not convinced about that, deliverers of public services such as health and education obviously need to know how population characteristics vary from suburb to suburb. So do people selling things—whether they are selling a detergent or a political party. Residential differentiation also has cultural significance, shaping people's day-to-day activities and experiences in the areas where they live.

Not surprisingly, geographers have spent much effort studying residential patterns, attempting to understand why they develop and change and whether it is possible, or desirable, to influence the degree of residential differentiation. Recently, interest has also focussed on the impacts of globalisation on the urban mosaic. Many researchers believe that our cities are becoming more differentiated and socially polarised as a result of the uneven impacts of economic restructuring, technological development, and social change. This chapter examines the general nature of residential differentiation and the competing explanations for it, before analysing in more detail how patterns are changing and what consequences these changes have for people living in different parts of Australian cities.

Traditional patterns of residential differentiation

Studies in the 1960s and 1970s found that the model shown in figure 5.1, initially developed by North American geographers and sociologists, described patterns of residential differentiation in Australian cities reasonably well. Each city had *sectors* of low and high socioeconomic status that had developed during the nineteenth century, as discussed in chapter 1, and then perpetuated themselves as the cities grew. Age structure and household composition, in contrast, tended to vary with distance from the city centre in a pattern of *concentric rings*. Families with young children dominated on the urban fringe and high percentages of old people lived in the inner suburbs. Such a pattern followed logically from the patterns of housing age, structure, and tenure described in chapter 4, and from the concept of the family life cycle and its influence on housing choice. Finally, distinct ethnic concentrations had emerged, particularly during the immigration boom of the 1950s and 1960s, to form a pattern of *patches*. Patterns in each city were obviously distorted by unique characteristics of historical development and physical layout, but still conformed broadly to the superimposed sectors, rings, and patches suggested by the model.

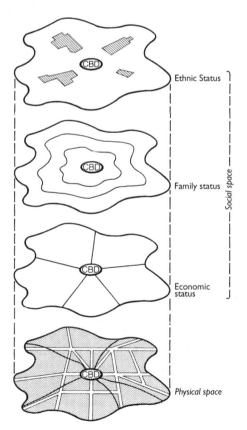

Figure 5.1 A model of residential segregation

Source: adapted from Murdie 1969, p. 9

Explanations

There was prolonged debate during the 1970s about how best to explain patterns of residential differentiation, along much the same lines as the debate about suburbanisation discussed in chapter 1. Supporters of *behavioural* explanations emphasised household preference and choice. They argued that patterns of segregation arose because households of similar income, life cycle stage, and ethnic character had similar housing needs and preferences, and therefore chose to live in similar areas. *Marxist* critics argued, as Engels had done in the nineteenth century, that many families, particularly those on low incomes, had little or no *choice* of where to live. Instead they were restricted to the areas 'appropriate' to their position within the capitalist class system: workers near the factories and docks, ethnic minorities in ghettos; while the bourgeoisie lived in pleasant residential suburbs on the other side of town. The *managerialist* view emphasised how the actions of officials—so called *urban gatekeepers*—in public housing authorities, building societies, banks, town planning departments, and the like, shaped the extent and nature of segregation.

In hindsight, all three approaches contributed to a full explanation. One could hardly ignore the importance of individual choice in cities where 70 per cent of households were owner-occupiers. Young families *did* tend to choose the spacious outer suburbs. People *did* tend, for both investment and status reasons, to choose housing within the 'best' sector they could afford. Migrants *were* attracted to areas where relatives were already living and their language was spoken.

However, bureaucracies *were* influential in limiting the range of choice people had. Building societies and banks decided which people they would lend to, and which houses they would allow them to buy. Many would only grant loans for new housing, effectively forcing first-home buyers to locate on the urban fringe. The maximum amount a bank would lend was rigidly tied to the income of the male breadwinner, restricting the range of housing that a family could afford. Institutions would not even take a wife's income into account, and very seldom granted loans to women in their own right. Public housing authorities decided what type of housing to build where, and which applicants to allocate to particular dwellings. By building large housing estates where land was cheapest, they reinforced the working-class character of particular sectors such as northern Adelaide and the western suburbs of Sydney. Town planners used zoning regulations to limit what could be built where. For example, they prohibited the building of flats in most new residential areas, leaving small households who did not want a conventional detached house a restricted choice of where to live.

But the economic and political structure of the parent society clearly limited the actions of both householders and officials. The amount of choice households had in where to live depended very much on income and wealth, which depended on their position within the class structure. Housing bureaucrats did not determine the total amount of money available for public housing, or for housing loans to owner-occupiers. The state of the national economy, and the financial and fiscal policies of the federal government dictated these things. As Gray (1975, p. 231) put it: 'individual households are actors (in a play designed and produced by capitalism) whose actions are constrained by a stage managed by the urban gatekeepers'.

The 'play', the 'actors', and the 'stage managers' have all changed significantly since the 1970s. Chapters 2 and 3 discussed how class structure has changed under the impact of global restructuring with the demise of manufacturing jobs, the growth of advanced services, and the increasing inequality between *work-rich* households with two or more members in good jobs and the *work-poor* getting by on insecure, poorly paid, part-time, or casual jobs, or on welfare payments of some sort. Gender relations in society have also changed with the rise in female participation in paid work and with the increasing number of female-headed single-parent families. Ethnic composition has changed markedly, as discussed in chapter 2. Chapter 4 described how households have changed in demographic structure and in their ability to afford housing (although not necessarily in their housing preferences). Housing authorities and other bureaucracies have become more flexible and liberal in their decision making, but have faced financial cutbacks and a political enthusiasm for privatisation and 'small government', and declining housing affordability, especially in the largest cities, as incomes have failed to keep up with rising property values.

The rest of this chapter will examine the impact of these changes on the residential mosaic, concentrating on the period 1991–2001. It will look in turn at the three dimensions of age and household structure, socioeconomic status, and ethnicity. The chapter will then consider the overall pattern and ask whether a distinctive new residential mosaic has emerged and, if so, what the implications are for people living in our cities. Maps have been included showing patterns in several of the major cities but, as with chapter 4, the reader should also if possible consult one or more of the 2001 social atlases published by the Australian Bureau of Statistics.

Changing patterns of age structure and household composition

Up to the mid 1980s, patterns of variation in age structure, population growth, and household composition in Australian cities still fitted quite well into the concentric rings suggested by figure 5.1. Despite the gentrification described in chapter 1, the inner suburbs were losing population as family households moved out and were replaced by 'dinks' or lone persons, and as old housing was demolished. Melbourne demonstrated the so-called *doughnut effect*—the emergence of a hollow urban centre—almost perfectly. The old inner suburbs lost over 10 per cent of their population between 1981 and 1986. The households that remained were a mix of old people and young adults, with very few families with children.

The middle suburbs, which had been the outer suburbs during the postwar long boom, had become areas of population stagnation or decline. They were fully built-up and many households had reached the 'empty nest' stage of their life cycle. Areas such as Enfield in Adelaide were classic examples of the *life cycle of the suburb*, where the young families who first settled the areas in the 1950s had passed in unison through the various stages of the family life cycle to reach the post-child stage together (figure 5.2). These suburbs had high

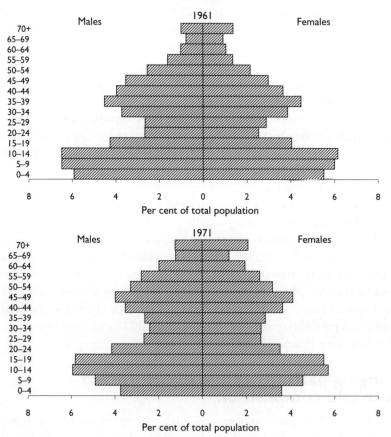

Figure 5.2 Age–sex structure of Enfield LGA, 1961–2001
Source: ABS 1961, 1971, 1981, 1991, and 2001 censuses

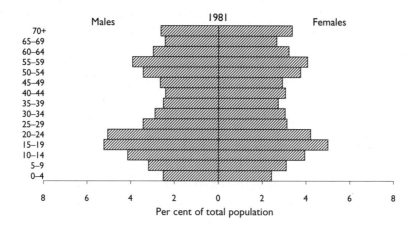

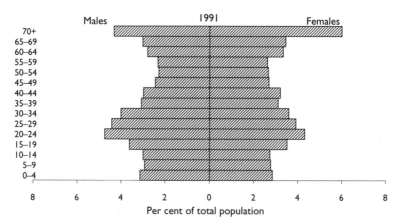

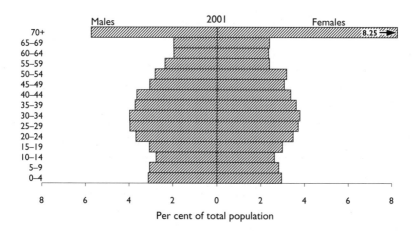

Figure 5.2 (cont.)

percentages of people in the 45–64 and over 64 age groups, and few children. Some had experienced large population losses through falling occupancy rates as children left the parental nest.

The new outer suburbs were the only areas of significant population growth, dominated by growing families in the child-bearing and child-rearing stages of the life cycle. Areas such as Campbelltown and Penrith in Sydney, Cranbourne and Berwick in Melbourne, Logan City in Brisbane, Wanneroo and Cockburn in Perth, and Morphett Vale and Golden Grove in Adelaide had high percentages of the population in the 0–4 and 5–14 age groups, and continued to experience population increase through new housing development.

Things are now very different. Patterns of variation in age structure and household composition have become much more complex since the mid 1980s, to the extent that the concentric rings shown in figure 5.1 are increasingly hard to recognise. The new patterns partly reflect changes in the location of new housing. But they are also strongly influenced by changes in household size and structure in established suburbs. These changes result from complex combinations of *migration*, where households leave an area and are replaced by others with different characteristics, and *ageing in place*, where households do not move but simply become older. Overall, what has happened?

The inner suburbs

The residential revitalisation of the inner suburbs had begun with the gentrification process in the 1970s and 1980s (chapter 1). It accelerated during the 1990s with the encouragement of state governments, whose *urban consolidation* programs promoted higher-density residential development in the existing built up area as an alternative to continued growth on the urban fringe (the debates about urban consolidation as a planning policy will be covered in chapters 7 and 8). In addition, one reaction to the financial crisis in 1987 and the fall in demand for CBD office space was to promote the conversion of some office buildings into city-centre residential apartments (figure 5.3). Melbourne City Council in particular encouraged such developments through its *Postcode 3000* scheme, and Adelaide City Council followed suit.

Several inner-city residential renewal schemes on old industrial land were also begun during the early 1990s under the Labor federal government's Better Cities program, as joint ventures with state governments, local councils, and private developers. Ultimo–Pyrmont, an area of old docklands and associated factories immediately west of the Sydney CBD, is by far the largest of these schemes (figure 5.4). Mile End in Adelaide's inner western suburbs, and East Perth (figure 5.5) are smaller examples. Similar projects not directly funded by Better Cities include Southbank and Docklands in Melbourne (figure 5.6),

Figure 5.3 Conversion of offices into residences, Melbourne, 1995. At the height of the CBD residential boom, this railway office building in Spencer Street was to be converted to apartments; but the proposal was delayed by the discovery of large amounts of asbestos in the ceilings and eventually the building was converted into a hotel.

Source: Clive Forster

Figure 5.4 Inner-city redevelopment, Ultimo–Pyrmont, 2003: the Jacksons Landing high-rise residential development. Note the old factory façade incorporated into the building on the right, and the Anzac Bridge in the background.

Source: Clive Forster

Figure 5.5 Inner-city redevelopment, East Perth, 1998: a medium-density residential development around Claisebrook Cove, two kilometres from the CBD.

Source: Clive Forster

Figure 5.6 Inner-city redevelopment, Melbourne, 2004: early stages of the Docklands project centred on Victoria Dock; Telstra Dome football stadium, dockside high-rise apartments, and, in the background, the Bolte Bridge carrying the CityLink tollway.

Source: Clive Forster

and a range of riverside developments in Brisbane. The Southbank–Docklands census area (SLA) in Melbourne contained only 146 private dwellings in 1991. By 2001 the area housed almost 5000 people in 2623 private dwellings, 2194 of which were flats over three storeys high. The southern part of the City of Sydney, including Ultimo–Pyrmont, grew in population from 4200 in 1991 to almost 25 000 in 2001, in 12 000 private dwellings, 11 000 of which were flats over three storeys.

Ultimo–Pyrmont, Southbank–Docklands (both of which will be much larger when completed), and the similar smaller developments elsewhere represent new types of Australian residential environment, dominated by high-rise apartments. City centres that once had very few residents have become, in population terms, the fastest-growing parts of our metropolitan areas. Meanwhile the surrounding inner suburbs have also continued to grow in population (albeit more slowly) through continued gentrification and small-scale redevelopment. Figure 5.7 shows that between 1996 and 2001 all Melbourne's inner suburbs gained population. The same is true of most inner suburbs in our other large cities. The Victorian government, in a publication titled *From Doughnut City to Cafe Society* (1998), welcomed the inner-city revival as a sign that Melbourne is adapting to the needs of a globalised world and providing the type of residential environment favoured by people working in the booming finance, producer services, tourism, and entertainment sectors.

Titles such as *From Doughnut City to Cafe Society* suggest that inner-city revitalisation represents a fundamental change in the nature of Australian cities, and the impact of residential revival on the landscape of the inner city is undeniable (figures 5.3–5.6). But it is important to remember that the *absolute number* of people involved is quite small. The population of the area described in the *Doughnut City* document rose by 43 000 between 1991 and 2001, from 216 000 to 259 000. This represents an increase from 7.2 to 7.7 per cent in the area's share of Melbourne's total population of over 3 million. So even though revitalisation is re-shaping the inner suburbs of Australian cities, its overall importance should not be overstated.

Until recently the inner suburbs had high percentages of residents aged over 64. But residential revitalisation has affected their age structure as well as their socioeconomic composition. The proportion of aged persons, though still high, has tended to fall and the areas have become increasingly dominated by young adults. In Ultimo–Pyrmont and Southbank–Docklands in 2001 approximately 25 per cent of the population were sharing accommodation as members of group households, 25 per cent were couples (some young, some older empty nesters), and another 17 per cent were living alone. Only 15 per cent were members of families with children. The result, as shown in figure 5.8, is a polarised age structure with a classic 'Christmas tree' shape: aged

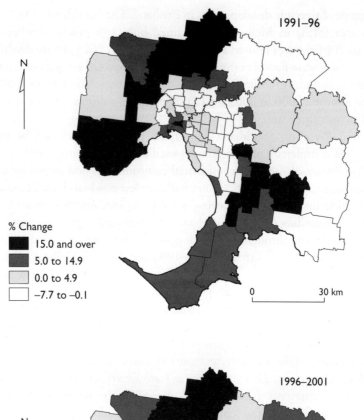

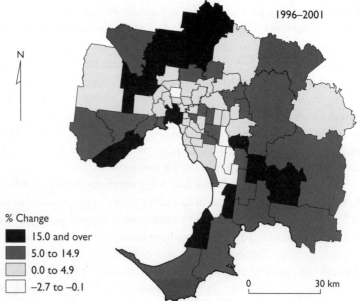

Figure 5.7 Patterns of population change, Melbourne, 1991–2001

Source: ABS 2001 Census, Time Series Community Profiles

people, young adults, and little else. The few families with young children are increasingly confined to areas of public rental housing. The inner suburbs in general, and the new high-rise projects in particular, have high rates of population turnover and therefore experience little *ageing in place*. Households regularly move out to be replaced by new but similar households, thus maintaining the age structure.

The middle suburbs

The middle suburbs, in contrast to the inner suburbs, have historically been characterised by relatively low rates of household turnover and therefore significant ageing in place. By the early 1990s they had become the main areas of population decline in our cities, as children grew up and left home and many households moved into the post-child stages of the life cycle. For example, figure 5.7 shows a distinctive belt of population decline in Melbourne's middle suburbs between 1991–96. But since then many middle suburbs have been affected by a complex combination of (a) the continued ageing of established households, (b) the replacement of old households by younger newcomers, and (c) various forms of housing redevelopment ranging from major schemes

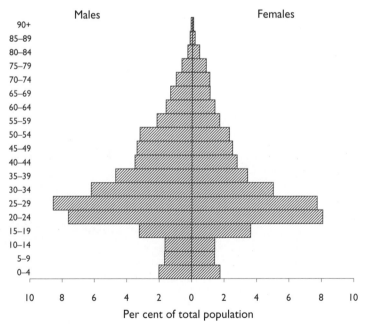

Figure 5.8 Age–sex structure of Ultimo–Pyrmont, 2001

Source: ABS 2001 Census

such as the Westwood project in Adelaide described in chapter 4 (figure 4.8), to the replacement of individual houses by Tuscan-style duplexes (figure 5.9). Figure 5.7 shows that many of the areas in Melbourne that experienced population loss in the early 1990s had begun to gain population by 2001, with continued decline confined to Coburg in the middle north, and to a belt of four SLAs in the south east around Waverley and Dandenong.

In some middle suburbs there is evidence of a new life cycle starting, as the original residents die or move into retirement accommodation and younger families move in. For example a belt of suburbs stood out particularly clearly in the 1996 social atlas of Melbourne, about 15 kms east of the city centre, extending from Brighton and Sandringham through Caulfield and Malvern to Camberwell and Heidelberg. This belt not only showed signs that population decline has slowed or reversed, but also that it had higher percentages of families with dependent children than newer suburbs farther east.

The outer suburbs

The character of suburbs on the urban fringe is shaped by the in-migration of new households. Research carried out for the National Housing Strategy in the early 1990s showed that households moving to the outer suburbs were smaller

Figure 5.9 Redevelopment in Adelaide's middle suburbs, 2002: old villas demolished and replaced by Tuscan-style townhouses.

Source: Clive Forster

and older than during the long boom, and fewer were first-home buyers. These trends have intensified. The 2001 census shows that while some outer and fringe suburbs are growing significantly in population (figure 5.7) and contain high percentages of families with young children, age structures are much more varied than in the classic 'nappy valley' fringe suburbs of the 1960s. Many new houses in fringe suburbs are now being bought by older households trading up in the housing market, rather than first home buyers. Also, lower rates of city growth mean that the areas we think of as the outer suburbs retain that status for longer, rather than being rapidly redefined as middle suburbs. So areas such as Tea Tree Gully in Adelaide are still thought of as outer suburbs, even though their oldest parts were first settled over thirty years ago and are now areas of population ageing and decline.

So there is no longer a simple progression from old, declining inner suburbs through stable middle suburbs to young, rapidly-growing fringe areas. The inner suburbs have become an intricate patchwork of population growth and decline, but with growth predominating. The middle suburbs have passed their peak period of ageing and population loss, are increasingly affected by redevelopment and urban consolidation, and in many areas new young families are beginning to move in. Some outer suburbs are still young and growing, but nuclear families with young children are much less dominant than during the long boom, reflecting the increasing diversity of household structures and of ability to reach the home ownership rungs of the housing ladder. If one looks within the large SLAs shown in figure 5.7 and examines trends in individual suburbs and localities, the 2001 census shows that areas of population growth, stagnation, and decline now exist alongside one another throughout our cities—including the outer suburbs.

Changing patterns of socioeconomic status

It is important not to exaggerate the degree of socioeconomic segregation in Australian cities. They are less segregated than most American cities, for example, and most suburbs contain a range of income groups. Nonetheless, we are used to thinking of our cities as containing, as suggested in figure 5.1, distinct sectors of contrasting socioeconomic status. The upper-status sectors have high percentages of people in professional and managerial occupations, earning high incomes and holding formal educational qualifications. In the lower-status sectors, large percentages of people have low incomes, blue-collar jobs (or no jobs), and no qualifications.

In each capital city the general pattern of wealthy and poorer sectors has a long history, beginning in the nineteenth century and persisting through the period of rapid suburban growth during the 1950s and 1960s (chapter 1). In a general sense the patterns continue today, still reflecting the ability of higher-income households to capture the more pleasant residential environments on higher land or near good beaches, and away from industry and areas with a poor 'image'. For example, clear contrasts still exist in Melbourne between the wealthy eastern and bayside suburbs and the low-status west, north, and south-east (figure 5.10). Similarly, in Sydney the northern and eastern suburbs are still affluent, the western and south-western suburbs generally low status. Low-status areas still lie to the south-west and south-east in Brisbane and Perth, with higher-status areas to the west. In Adelaide, too, long-established patterns persist. The western, northern, and to a lesser extent southern sectors of the city still contain the main concentrations of lower-income housing, with wealthier areas to the east and south east. But there have been some significant recent changes in patterns, with accompanying debates about causes and consequences.

Globalisation and social polarisation

For some years, researchers both in Australia and elsewhere in the developed world have presented evidence that the gap in living standards between rich

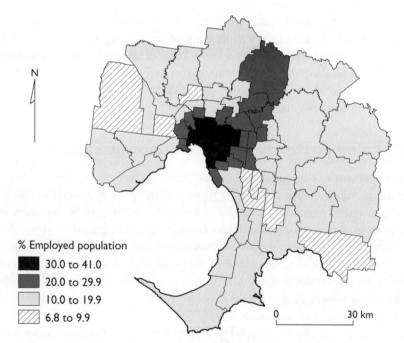

% Employed population

- ■ 30.0 to 41.0
- ■ 20.0 to 29.9
- ☐ 10.0 to 19.9
- ▨ 6.8 to 9.9

0   30 km

Figure 5.10 Workers in professional occupations, Melbourne, 2001
Source: ABS 2001 Census

and poor areas in cities has widened, and have argued that this increasing *social polarisation* results largely from the uneven impact of globalisation.

> Sydney has been experiencing rapid structural economic change in the 1980s. This has influenced conditions in the labour market and the housing market, resulting in significant redistribution of income. One clearly observable dimension of these changes is growing spatial inequality between the component local government areas. (Stilwell 1989, p. 3)

Gregory and Hunter (1996) carried out a study based on income data from the 1976, 1981, 1986, and 1991 censuses. They analysed almost 10 000 Collection Districts (CDs)—small areas containing 2–300 dwellings—in all Australian cities with populations over 100 000. The CDs were ranked according to socioeconomic status using a standard ABS index. The results suggested that over the fifteen-year period, in constant dollar terms, incomes fell most in the poorest CDs and increased most in the richest. In 1976 the mean household income of the lowest 5 per cent of CDs ranked by socioeconomic status was 60.4 per cent of that of the highest 5 per cent of CDs. In 1991 it was only 37.9 per cent (Gregory & Hunter 1996, p. 6).

It seems clear that economic, social, and demographic changes in how households participated in paid work, as discussed in chapter 3, had impacted unevenly to produce increasing inequality and polarisation in Australian cities. And statistical measures do not tell the whole story. Studies examining *geographical patterns* of changing inequality in Australian cities during the 1970s and 1980s revealed some consistent trends. The inner suburbs—whether originally high or low status—tended to move up the social scale as the gentrification process described in chapter 2 continued. But in the middle and outer suburbs, the rich areas got richer and the poor, poorer. In Adelaide, for example (Forster 1991), the established high-status suburbs to the east and south-east experienced a further increase in the percentage of wealthy people and a decline in the percentage of poor residents. In most of the low-status industrial suburbs to the west, north, and south, on the other hand, the already low proportion of wealthy people fell and the already high proportion of poor people rose. But in all the inner suburbs—whether originally rich or poor— the proportion of high-income persons rose significantly while the proportion of low-income residents fell. Stilwell (1993) reported similar trends in Sydney.

The trends have continued since 1991. As Badcock (1997, p. 245) puts it 'urban restructuring is forming "cones of wealth" in the inner areas, and selectively dispersing the "new urban poverty" to the suburbs'. These two rather different phenomena—the prosperity and booming property markets of the inner suburbs and the increasing polarisation of the middle and outer suburbs—are worth examining in more detail.

The inner suburbs: 'cones of wealth'?

During the early 1990s some North American writers (see Bourne 1993) questioned whether gentrification and inner-city revitalisation would continue, arguing that the development arose from specific economic and demographic conditions during the 1970s and 1980s, and that those conditions had changed. But there has been no sign of slackening in Australia. In all our major cities the 2001 Census shows that the inner suburbs and even the CBD environs themselves now contain the main concentrations of people with high incomes, professional jobs, and university degrees. Property markets in the inner suburbs have boomed, though by 2003 there were signs in Sydney and Melbourne that demand for inner-city apartments—largely fuelled by property investors—was falling. The inner suburbs and adjoining prosperous middle suburbs are, as Badcock and others suggest, the areas to have gained most from the growth in advanced producer-services jobs linked to the evolving global economy. And, increasingly, lower-income households are being priced out of these areas unless they get access to the declining stock of public rental housing.

The middle and outer suburbs: polarisation?

Gentrification and inner-suburban revitalisation have fascinated recent writers—perhaps because many are gentrifiers themselves! But, as discussed earlier in the case of Melbourne, the great majority of Australian city-dwellers do not live in the inner suburbs. For them, what is happening in the middle and outer suburbs is much more important. The more affluent sectors of our cities have generally prospered since 1991, having weathered the economic storm of the 1980s. Unemployment rates are well below average. Workforce participation rates are above average, and most people work in the expanding service sectors of the economy. Residential property values may not have kept pace with the inner suburbs, but have risen more rapidly than the metropolitan average or, at worst, have maintained their real value.

In the lower-income sectors, which grew up in association with manufacturing industry during the long boom, the story since 1991 has been more complex. As discussed in chapter 3, despite recent falls in unemployment, a fifth of the labour force in areas such as Elizabeth in Adelaide and Broadmeadows in Melbourne is still officially out of work, and there are high levels of hidden unemployment. Those in employment often depend on insecure jobs in stagnant or declining sectors of the economy. The housing trust or commission estates built during the long boom have suffered from the changing role of public housing, as discussed in chapter 4. Some have been redeveloped but the remainder house increasing proportions of welfare-dependent households, in dwellings suffering from obsolescence and poor maintenance.

People buying houses in nearby suburbs had been hard-hit by rising interest rates in the late 1980s, with many people in areas such as Salisbury in Adelaide losing their homes through mortgage foreclosures because they were unable to keep up with loan repayments. Even people who owned their houses outright saw their property values rise at below-average rates, or even fall in real terms. Low interest rates during the 1990s and rising property values in the early 2000s have removed some of the pressure, but the areas remain vulnerable to any economic downturns.

The experience of many low-income middle and outer suburbs therefore represents the converse of the inner suburbs, both in the impact of economic restructuring on employment, and in changes to the levels of housing investment and capital appreciation. But other parts of what are generally seen as low-status sectors such as western Sydney and Melbourne, or northern Adelaide, have recently emerged as enclaves of relative affluence, often in the form of so-called *master planned communities*.

Master planned communities: 'privatopias' or aspirations realised?

Master planned communities (MCPs) are large, comprehensively planned residential developments. Although not cut off from surrounding suburbs by security systems, like the *gated communities* found in some US cities, they are designed to be physically distinctive and separate. The estates typically have elaborate, titled entrances and abundant signage emphasising the key words such as 'sense of community', 'lifestyle', 'convenience', and 'security' that feature in their advertising. They are elaborately landscaped, often incorporating an artificial lake, and feature restrictive covenants that enforce minimum standards of building materials and design. The houses are generally project homes marketed as standard designs by large building companies. Referred to sneeringly as 'McMansions' by professionals living in the gentrified inner suburbs, they tend to be large (figure 5.11), often two-storey, and leave very little room for back yards.

Elements of the MPC concept, such as restrictive covenants, have been used for many years. But the first true large-scale MPC was West Lakes, a project with 20 000 residents developed in the 1970s in Adelaide's western suburbs by the company that later became the Delfin Corporation. Delfin went on later to develop projects in every major Australian city, often in joint ventures with state governments who ensured the provision of infrastructure. The West Lakes site was essentially a swamp in a working class sector of town, adjacent to large estates of public rental housing and with declining factory areas nearby. But by careful marketing of a comprehensively planned 'image', Delfin showed it was possible to create a high status residential environment where people such as tennis player Lleyton Hewitt are now willing to spend millions of dollars on a residence.

Master planned communities are now a familiar part of the urban land-scape, both on the fringe and as infill redevelopment projects in the middle suburbs. Some, such as Blackwood Park in Adelaide (figure 5.11) are in estab-lished middle-class areas. But many have emerged in the traditional low income sectors of our cities, for example Glenmore Park, Harrington Park, and Garden Gates in western Sydney, Caroline Springs in western Melbourne, and Mawson Lakes to the north of Adelaide. Research by Gwyther (2003) suggests that families moving into MPCs in western Sydney are often Australian born, Christian, nuclear families fleeing from older suburbs, which they now see as dominated by welfare-dependent households and/or ethnic groups who they regard as alien or threatening. They see the MPCs as offering a secure residen-tial environment where they are part of a community of owner-occupiers with similar incomes and values: 'people like them'. In this respect the newer MPCs differ significantly from early joint ventures such as West Lakes and Golden Grove in Adelaide, where a proportion of public housing was an integral part of the design. The absence of public housing is now a selling point.

One view about MPCs is that they are a good thing, breaking down old stereotypes about the low-status nature of whole sectors of a city. Politician Mark Latham welcomes them as an indication that 'aspirational' families who succeed financially can now satisfy their desire for a higher standard of living without leaving Sydney's western suburbs.

> When I grew up in Green Valley in the 1970s, our values were based on the politics of us versus them—the working class versus the North Shore. Now, when a young person grows up in my electorate, they can see prosperity in the neighbourhood next door. Social mobility has become more tangible and achievable. The politics of envy has been replaced by the politics of aspiration. (Latham 2003, p.111)

In contrast, Gleeson (2003), from the Urban Frontiers research unit at the University of Western Sydney, portrays them as more sinister 'privatopias', signs of a new, finer-scale pattern of polarisation and inequality, with stark contrasts in living standards increasingly emerging between adjacent suburbs. But whichever view one takes, the sector model shown in figure 5.1 is becom-ing an increasingly unsatisfactory oversimplification.

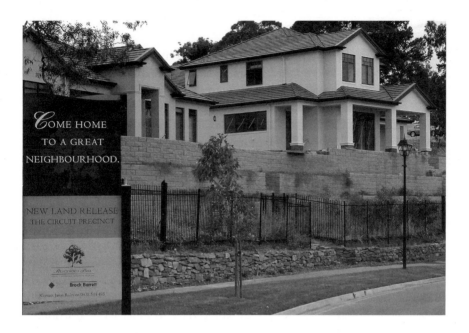

Figure 5.11 Master planned communities, 2003: 'McMansions' at Blackwood Park in Adelaide (above) and Garden Gates in western Sydney (below)

Source: Clive Forster

Changing ethnic patterns

Australia's major cities were already ethnically diverse by 1971 (table 1.4). In Melbourne, Sydney, and Adelaide especially there were marked concentrations of Italians, Greeks, and other nationalities in particular suburbs. Since then the ethnic structure of the cities has, like age structure and socioeconomic composition, become much more complex. As noted in chapter 2, the main countries of origin of migrants are now very different from the 1960s and, although most migrants still settle in the major cities, they are distributing themselves differently between those cities (tables 2.2 and 2.4). In Sydney and Melbourne, which have been capturing an increasing share of the migrant intake, almost a quarter of the population at the 2001 Census was born in non-English-speaking countries and over a quarter spoke a language other than English at home.

Table 5.1 shows the degree of spatial segregation of the main ethnic groups in Sydney and Melbourne, when compared to the Australian-born population using the Index of Dissimilarity (ID). The ID, which ranges from 0 to 100, shows the percentage of a group that would have to move to be distributed between sub-areas in exactly the same way as the Australian-born population. A value of 100 therefore means that a group is totally segregated, whereas a value of 0 shows that a group is shared between sub-areas in exactly the same way as the Australian-born. We generally interpret ID scores over 30 as suggesting significant segregation and scores over 50 as showing a very significant

Table 5.1 Indexes of dissimilarity between the Australian-born and selected major overseas-born groups, Sydney and Melbourne, 1991–2001

	Sydney		Melbourne	
	1991	*2001*	*1991*	*2001*
UK and Ireland	11.8	14.9	16.1	15.4
Germany	13.1	12.4	13.7	13.8
New Zealand	20.2	16.3	15.3	15.8
India	23.0	32.0	27.3	27.9
Philippines	35.7	37.2	34.6	37.6
Italy	35.8	35.7	37.8	37.4
Hong Kong	39.4	45.3	38.6	44.7
China	43.8	43.4	40.3	39.3
Greece	49.8	49.4	36.7	38.7
Lebanon	52.2	55.0	47.4	51.5
Vietnam	67.0	66.8	54.9	55.7

Data are for SLAs within the respective Statistical Divisions in 2001; 1991 data were recalculated to the 2001 boundaries

Source: ABS 2001 Census, Time Series Community Profiles.

degree of segregation. Therefore table 5.1 suggests that migrants from English-speaking and northern European countries are relatively unsegregated; that most southern European and Asian groups still show significant segregation; and that persons born in Lebanon and Vietnam (and the Greek-born in Sydney) are highly segregated. It also appears that people from China, Greece, Lebanon, and Vietnam are more highly segregated in Sydney than in Melbourne. But such comparisons must be made with caution because the ID is affected by the size and nature of the areal units for which it is calculated, and these vary from city to city.

The statistical degree of segregation of most groups did not change much between 1991 and 2001, but the spatial character of ethnic concentrations has changed significantly since the long boom. As figure 5.12 shows, there are distinct clusters of suburbs in both cities where between 30 and 50 per cent of the population were born in non-English-speaking countries. The inner suburbs, which had held the highest percentages of southern European immigrants during the long boom, are now not the main areas of ethnic concentration. Immigrants were attracted to the inner city by cheap housing and local jobs, particularly in manufacturing. Many of these original immigrants have now moved to the middle and outer suburbs, and the appeal of the inner suburbs to new migrants has fallen because of the massive losses of manufacturing jobs and the impact of gentrification on house prices. Some cheap private rental housing remains, together with high-rise public housing estates in areas like Richmond, Collingwood, and South Sydney. Because the high-rise flats (figure 1.8) were unpopular and had high turnover rates in the 1970s and 1980s, they tended to become occupied by recent arrivals, particularly the Vietnamese, who were in desperate need of housing. Overseas-born residents therefore still make up moderately high *percentages* of the total population of some inner suburbs, but their *absolute numbers* are small and declining.

The largest and most rapidly growing ethnic concentrations are now located in the middle and outer suburbs, particularly in western and south-western Sydney and south-eastern, northern, and north-western Melbourne (figure 5.12). In some areas, for example Melbourne's northern suburbs, the overseas-born population consists largely of long-established southern European migrants who have moved out from their original locations in the inner city, together with Lebanese and Turkish immigrants who arrived during the 1970s and followed the same path. Many Australian-born residents of those suburbs also have at least one overseas-born parent. As the 2001 social atlas shows, there are relatively few recent immigrants. Adelaide's eastern suburbs are similar, with a high percentage of Italian-born residents and people of Italian parentage, but few recent migrants.

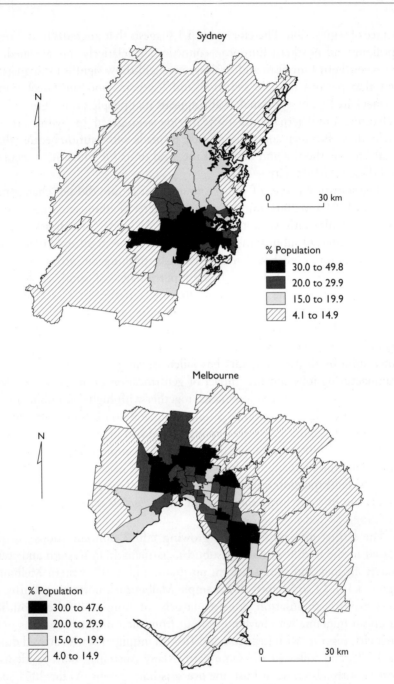

Figure 5.12 Persons born in non-English-speaking countries, Sydney and Melbourne, 2001

Source: ABS 2001 Census

The most striking feature of the ethnic geography of Australian cities in recent years, however, has been the development in some middle and outer suburbs of large concentrations of recent immigrants from the new countries of origin in South-East Asia and Latin America. These suburbs—for example Fairfield in Sydney, Springvale and Dandenong in Melbourne, and Enfield in Adelaide—share some significant characteristics. They are working-class areas dating from the long boom. They grew up alongside suburban manufacturing estates, and contain significant amounts of public rental housing. Vitally, they were close to major migrant hostels during the 1970s and 1980s. These hostels served as the entry points of refugee migrants, particularly from Vietnam, who tended subsequently to move into more permanent accommodation in the nearby public housing estates. Vietnamese shops and restaurants, religious institutions, and community facilities then developed, and the areas became a focus for later immigrants, and even for Vietnamese moving from elsewhere in the same city. By 2001, almost 25 000 Vietnamese-born people, representing 41 per cent of the total Vietnamese population of Sydney, lived in Fairfield local government area, mainly in or near the suburb of Cabramatta (figure 5.13).

Figure 5.13 Cabramatta, western Sydney, 2003: scenes in and around Cabramatta Mall

Source: Clive Forster

Figure 5.13 (cont.)

Suburban concentrations of new immigrants and the areas of secondary settlement of older established ethnic groups are not mutually exclusive. The largest and most complex concentrations of overseas-born people now consist of areas of major secondary immigrant settlement that have also received new influxes. The belt of local government areas in Sydney's middle western suburbs, centred on Fairfield and Auburn (figure 5.14), serves as the most spectacular example. The 2001 Census revealed that over half of Fairfield's and Auburn's total populations of 182 000 and 57 000 respectively were born overseas. In addition to the large and recently arrived Vietnamese, Chinese, Turkish and Filipino populations, there are significant numbers of people from Italy, Malta, Lebanon, Chile, and Croatia, most of whom had arrived in Australia before 1981. In both areas around 65 per cent of the population speak a language other than English at home.

The western suburbs of Melbourne, centred on Sunshine, have similarly complex ethnic compositions. So to a lesser extent do Adelaide's western suburbs and Salisbury, on Adelaide's northern fringes, is an area of low-cost

Figure 5.14 The Gallipoli Mosque, Auburn, 2003: a mosque mainly serving the local Turkish community

Source: Clive Forster

housing whose heterogeneous overseas-born population is growing particularly quickly. These, and similar areas in the suburbs of all the major cities, now reflect:

> the cumulative impact of generations of settlement of the multiplicity of ethnic, birthplace, religious and cultural groups which make up contemporary, multicultural Australia. The mix in each sub-area is a complex result of the nature and location of the area, its socio-economic structure and land use, local state and national government policies, the operation of labour, land and housing markets, and the influence of the myriad of specific forces which encourage various ethnic groups to settle in some places and not in others. (Hugo 1989, p. 352)

Another often forgotten aspect of the changing ethnic composition of Australian cities is the recent influx of higher-income people from Malaysia, Singapore, and Hong Kong as 'skilled' migrants, who have gained admission to Australia because of their educational qualifications and business skills. Significant numbers have come in under this category or its earlier equivalents in recent years, together with business people here as long-term temporary migrants. These people have tended, in complete contrast to South-East Asians who have mainly come in as refugee or family-reunion immigrants, to cluster in the wealthier suburbs. Students from Malaysia, Singapore, Indonesia, China, and India have also congregated in areas of rental housing close to university campuses.

Urban Aborigines

Relatively few Aborigines and Torres Strait Islanders live in the major cities. Only in Brisbane (1.7 per cent) and Perth (1.5 per cent) do they make up more than 1 per cent of the total population. However the numbers have grown significantly in recent years. The increase appears to be partly due to people being more willing to identify themselves as Aboriginal in their census returns, but also reflects a tendency for Aborigines to move to the big cities in search of employment, housing, and social services. Each major city now constitutes the largest single concentration of Aborigines in its respective state.

Within the capital cities, the Aboriginal population shows a moderate degree of residential concentration and segregation. The Index of Dissimilarity between Aborigines and the rest of the Australian-born population in 2001 was 29.1 in Sydney and 24.4 in Melbourne. Neither had changed significantly since 1991. The oldest-established concentrations are in inner suburbs such as Redfern in Sydney, but Aboriginals have been increasingly priced out of these areas by gentrification. The largest concentrations are now in middle and outer suburbs: Blacktown, Campbelltown, and Penrith in Sydney; Ipswich, Inala, and Wacol in Brisbane; Port Adelaide-Enfield, Playford, and Salisbury in Adelaide; and Stirling and Swan in Perth. The pattern largely reflects the dependence on public rental housing caused by low incomes, high unemployment rates, and discrimination—despite legislation to the contrary—in the private housing market.

A new mosaic?

> Contrasts between different areas of the cities have become starker…Australian cities have begun to reflect the stark realities of the economic changes which have transformed so many aspects of the western world. (Daly 1988, p. 160)

During the late 1980s, commentators on the impacts of economic restructuring on cities in Europe and North America saw widening economic inequality as linking with ethnic segregation to produce increasingly divided cities. The contrasts were depicted memorably in Tom Wolfe's novel *Bonfire of the Vanities*, set in inner New York: on one hand, the gentrified inner city and enclaves of luxury housing protected by fences and security services; on the other, low-income tenements, public housing projects, and the 'abandoned city' of the homeless and destitute. Short (1989) pointed to similar—but non-fictional—contrasts between the territories of 'yuppies' and 'yuffies' (young urban failures) in inner London. Since the early 1990s, more and more concern has been expressed about the links between globalisation, the *new urban poverty*, and the emergence of an urban *underclass* whose exclusion from the economic and social mainstream of society is reinforced by socioeconomic and racial segregation.

Australian cities, which have never been as segregated as their European and North American counterparts, have not suffered to nearly the same degree. But, as Daly suggests, they have not gone unscathed. Here, too, the media have seized on research showing increasing levels of inequality in incomes, and have run 'shock-horror' stories about divided cities. Figure 5.15 shows a selection of newspaper headlines from the 1990s.

The gentrified parts of Australian inner suburbs certainly contrast sharply—though not to the extent described by Short and Wolfe—with surviving areas of low-income housing and ethnic enclaves. But the most important changes in our cities have occurred, through a mutually reinforcing combination of economic and demographic trends, in the lower-income sectors of the middle and outer suburbs. The numbers of aged persons, families on supporting parents' benefits, and other people on low incomes have risen sharply in the

THE GREAT DIVIDE

■The rich get richer
and the poor have
children

Life gets tougher on the wrong side of the tracks

Wealth gap widening amid ghetto fears

The haves and the have-nots

Researcher examines our "divided cities"

Suburbs show growing gap between rich and poor

Figure 5.15 Newspaper headlines on urban inequality

Source: miscellaneous Australian newspapers 1990–96

areas already hardest hit by job losses—especially public housing estates. The largest and fastest-growing ethnic concentrations now lie in some of these same areas. Within each major city, large sub-regions with increasingly distinctive economic, social, and cultural characters now exist.

> The local government areas of Fairfield and Liverpool, contiguously situated on Sydney's south western boundary, are good illustrations of the character of change. They have a combined population of 300 000, making them larger than any city in New South Wales outside of Sydney, and larger than any cities in the other states outside of the capitals. Between them the two LGAs have 125 different ethnic groups resident; in some localities the majority of the people do not speak English. The populations are amongst the youngest and fastest growing in Sydney but unemployment is double the city's average and youth unemployment stands at about 50 per cent. (Daly, et al. 1993, p. 19)

Overall, the concentric rings, sectors and patches shown in figure 5.1 are becoming less and less recognisable in today's residential mosaic. Patterns have changed in scale and complexity. Individual local government areas—inner, middle or outer—are increasingly likely to contain areas of growth and decline, areas of wealth and deprivation, and areas of ethnic diversity. The changes in age structure and household composition are obviously significant for service provision, as will be discussed in chapter 6. To take one example, the proportion of aged people in the middle and outer suburbs has risen greatly. This has produced new demands for accommodation and services in areas that, because of their low-density, car-dependent nature, pose severe problems for old people who can no longer drive or are not confident driving at night or in bad weather. If *absolute numbers* of aged people are considered, rather than percentages, it becomes clear that the major, and growing, areas of demand for services for the aged now lie in the middle and outer suburbs rather than the inner city and the seaside.

Ethnic concentrations, particularly in Sydney and Melbourne, have increased in scale and changed in composition. They have also changed in significance. An *assimilationist* or 'melting pot' attitude prevailed towards immigration during the long boom. Migrants—and especially their children— were expected to blend over the years into the mainstream of Australian society and culture. In the 1980s and 1990s this view has been replaced by *multiculturalism*, a concept emphasising the right of all Australians, whatever their origins, to preserve and express their cultural heritage. Multiculturalism has now been officially embraced, though not without considerable opposition. And much of the criticism of multiculturalism has been directed at the development, especially within Sydney and Melbourne, of concentrations— often dubbed 'enclaves' or 'ghettos'—of immigrants from Asia and the Middle East who are visually distinctive and have languages, cultures, religions, and lifestyles very different from the Anglo-Celtic mainstream (figures 5.12–5.14). This opposition has also been fed by the massive media coverage of drugs-related violent crime in Cabramatta and rapes committed by Lebanese youths in western Sydney. It is significant that the Australians Against Further Immigration Party did well in several federal by-elections in suburban seats during 1994. They outpolled the Australian Democrats in the northern Adelaide seat of Bonython and attracted 11 per cent of the vote in the Sydney seat of Warringah. Pauline Hanson's One Nation party, which specifically opposed multiculturalism, Asian immigration, and Aboriginal land rights, was phenomenally successful in the 1998 Queensland state election. And more recently no issue has been more prominent in Australian federal politics than the debates over border protection and the mandatory detention of illegal immigrants.

Concentrations such as the Vietnamese in Cabramatta have been viewed negatively, not just by people who see them as threats and symbols of an immigration policy they dislike, but also by those who fear that 'enclaves' serve further to disadvantage and marginalise immigrants, and to slow their economic and social adjustment. Immigration officials in the 1980s deliberately attempted to reduce the degree of concentration by dispersing incoming migrants to a wider range of migrant hostels. However Dunn (1993, p. 242) argued strongly that the Vietnamese themselves value concentration for the support it provides, not just as 'a place of social and economic adjustment to a new society, but…also a celebrated spatial contribution to cultural diversity'. Ethnic concentrations such as Cabramatta, Dunn claimed, did not arise simply because of proximity to migrant hostels and the availability of cheap housing. They represent a deliberate, and sensible, choice by the communities concerned. As such, they may well prove to be long-lasting features of the multicultural social geography of our cities, rather than temporary 'problem' phenomena (Healy & Birrell 2003).

There is no simple answer to the question of how segregation by social class or socioeconomic status has changed since 1991. Gentrification means that most inner-city LGAs have continued to move up-market, but the 2001 Census social atlases still reveal complex patterns of segregation between the rich and the remaining poor at the more finely tuned collection-district level. The scale of socioeconomic segregation on the urban fringe has, as we have seen, also become more fine-grained, not only through the development of segregated master planned communities but also because of general planning and housing policies in force for some years in most states. Public housing authorities—if they get the chance to build any new housing—now scatter their rental stock more widely, rather than building vast segregated estates as in the 1950s and 1960s. Planners encourage a wider range of house styles and densities in new private developments. In the middle suburbs, the patterns of large-scale segregation inherited from the long boom are also being affected, not just by major redevelopment projects such as Westwood in Adelaide (see chapter 4), but also by a rash of smaller consolidation and infill developments.

So what?

> Public influence on residential patterns should be increased; it should always be used to encourage mixtures; it should absolutely prohibit large-scale low-income segregations; with skilled attention to the local facts of each case, it should generally try for the best mixture that can survive without self-defeating backlash. (Stretton 1989, p. 96)

Does socioeconomic segregation *matter*? Can and should we attempt to reduce it? Stretton's views, first expressed in 1970, were based on the belief that the large expanses of low-income housing that had been built in the 1950s and 1960s imposed significant and avoidable further disadvantages on their residents. Inadequate access to health care, underfunded local schools with 'rough' reputations, and poor access to facilities of all kinds accompanied poor local council services (see chapter 1). This essentially 'small-l liberal', reformist belief came to be accepted in principle by most metropolitan planning authorities and public housing bodies, and—as discussed in chapter 4—has had some effect on the nature of new residential development during the past three decades.

Subsequently, however, a concern with residential segregation has been criticised from both the left and right ends of the political spectrum. Marxists have rejected it as *spatial fetishism*, arguing that residential segregation and inequality are the inevitable results of an unjust capitalist society, and that attempts to reduce segregation are irrelevant tinkerings, incapable of significantly changing levels of inequality. Conservative writers have referred disparagingly to *social engineering*, portraying segregation as the 'natural' outcome of people's housing preferences.

Some aspects of changing residential patterns have also called into question the significance of segregation. The inner city, thanks to gentrification, has become more mixed. Similarly, master planned communities and urban redevelopment projects in the middle and outer suburbs have injected patches of more expensive housing into previously low-status areas. Residential differentiation has become more local in scale. Some of the concerns expressed by Stretton and others therefore seem to have been addressed. Local government areas are less likely to be wholly poor or rich, and regions such as Sydney's west or Adelaide's north are less easy to stereotype and stigmatise as wholly lower-class (though it takes time for media and public perceptions to change). But are low-income households any better-off? It is hard to see how the poor, apart from those who had housing to sell, have benefited from gentrification in the inner suburbs. Some have been displaced, unable to afford the higher housing costs. Those who remain have to pay higher rents and rates, while their established community networks are replaced by services and shops catering for the incoming gentrifiers. In the middle and outer suburbs, there is a danger that the people who have been able to escape the lower-status areas, in both the public and private housing stock, and flee to the new MPCs or redevelopment projects will be replaced by poorer, often welfare-dependent households, further increasing the inequalities between localities (Gleeson 2003). So more mixing at the local government area scale does not necessarily reduce inequality.

Segregation is not necessarily bad. Dunn's study of Cabramatta suggests that ethnic concentrations are seen as beneficial by many of their residents, who oppose and resent official attempts to reduce the degree of segregation. And it is important to remember that areas labelled 'low status' can still have a rich and varied culture that is valued by their inhabitants (Powell 1993). But, as we have seen, some of the 1950s and 1960s public housing estates that led to the concerns about socioeconomic segregation in the first place have suffered severely from the combined impacts of global economic restructuring and demographic change. Their unemployment rates, income levels, and degrees of welfare-dependence contrast even more starkly than before with their middle-class counterparts, some of which are now highly visible nearby.

Figure 5.16 suggests the cumulative process by which residents in such areas have become further disadvantaged. The process starts with rising unemployment and falling incomes among existing households, as economic restructuring undermines the local employment base. Incomes also fall as more and more people reach retirement age. At the same time, because waiting lists for public housing are now dominated by welfare-recipients (chapter 4), new residents moving into the areas are often not in employment. Bray and Mudd (1998) suggest that up to 40 per cent of the total income coming into areas such as Elizabeth in the mid 1990s was derived from welfare benefits. An increasing percentage of households therefore have no one in paid work, and lose contact with the 'world of work', through which information about job opportunities is often gained. Remoteness from areas of job growth, and low levels of car ownership, make it even harder for school leavers and older unemployed people to search for work. High levels of unemployment become entrenched.

Local government is caught in a two-way squeeze. As incomes fall, the need for local services rises—but the ability to raise money to pay for them falls because residents cannot afford to pay higher local rates. At the same time, the areas are particularly vulnerable to cuts in federal and state services such as education, health, and public transport.

Finally, the areas become stigmatised by the media and, ironically, further labelled as 'disadvantaged' in programs attempting to provide assistance. The media have seldom been able to resist stereotyping residents in stories about 'welfare ghettos', crime, vandalism, child abuse, teenage gang warfare, and—inevitably—the alleged emergence of an *underclass* (figure 5.15). Anecdotes abound of school leavers being refused job interviews simply because of their home address, and of investors refusing to set up businesses in the areas because of their poor 'image'. This labelling makes it even harder for residents to compete for jobs, and makes it likely that only people with no choice will move into the areas, further increasing the level of welfare dependence.

Under such circumstances, questions of social mix and residential segregation again appeared on the political agenda in the early 1990s, in federal and state social justice policies. The South Australian Housing Trust, for example, gained funding from the Labor federal government's Better Cities program to diversify the socioeconomic structure of Elizabeth by redeveloping areas of old

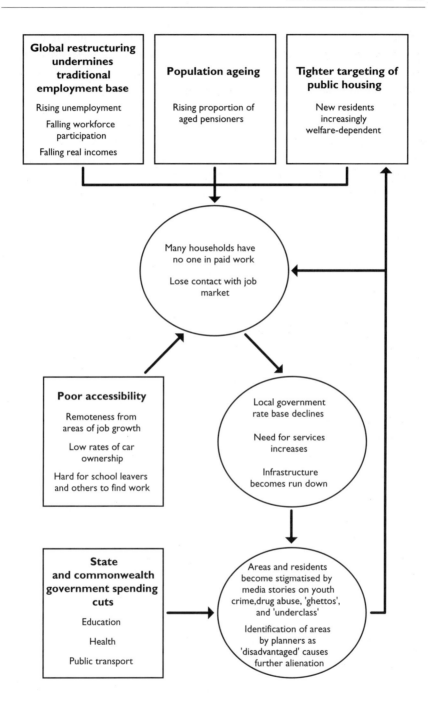

Figure 5.16 The cumulative process of disadvantage affecting public housing estates

Source: Clive Forster

public housing, as described in chapter 4. More recently, Australian researchers (Randolph & Judd 1999) have applied the UK concept of *social exclusion* to issues of segregation and disadvantage like those summarised in figure 5.16. Social exclusion, and social inclusion policies, will be discussed in chapter 8.

Intervening with the explicit aim of changing the nature of residential segregation in established suburbs is, to say the least, ambitious, and some of the problems that arise when redeveloping public housing estates were discussed in chapter 4. In any case, the coming to power of the Howard Coalition government in 1996 abruptly ended federal interest in urban inequality as a policy issue. But existing patterns of residential segregation and social exclusion cannot simply be regarded as 'natural', or as the inevitable result of the forces of globalisation. True, they constitute the outcome of people's struggles for shelter over the years, as shaped by the nature of the parent society. Manchester's residential mosaic in the 1840s, as described so vividly by Friedrich Engels, did reproduce 'on the ground' the class structure and the distribution of wealth and power in industrial capitalist society. Similarly, patterns in Melbourne or Sydney in the 1890s or the 1960s reflected contemporary class structures and technology (and ethnic and gender relations). Today's cities certainly reflect the impacts of recent economic, demographic, and cultural change. But the degree and nature of inequality and segregation is also vitally affected by government policies, and decisions are taken every day that will maintain patterns or change them. Within limits, we do have choices. We shall examine these choices in more detail when discussing policy options for the future in chapter 8.

6

Governing the Cities

Australia's major cities are the products of a capitalist society, but the state— broadly defined as governments, public bureaucracies, and public institutions at all levels—has always played a significant role in their development. Governments founded and laid out our capital cities, whose status as administrative centres was then instrumental in maintaining their primacy in the Australian settlement pattern. During the nineteenth century, colonial and local governments assumed the two classic roles of the state in modern cities. First, they provided *public goods* or items of *collective consumption*: essentials such as sewerage systems that the private sector could not easily supply and charge for on an individual basis. Second, they imposed controls over building and land use to avoid undesirable *externality effects*: the costs imposed on neighbours by someone starting a noxious industry in a residential area, or building a house that was a fire hazard, or discharging effluent into the streets or waterways.

Later, during the long boom, the era of the *state-managed capitalist metropolis,* the state expanded its role massively, to become the dominant force shaping the nature and quality of urban life (chapter 1). Commonwealth government policies on trade, industrial development, immigration, and housing had direct impacts on the rate, location, and nature of urban growth. State and local governments continued through town planning and building regulations to control the physical structure of the cities. State governments in particular also became the main providers of services such as public transport, education, and health. These are not intrinsically public goods. They can be, and often are, provided by the private sector. But governments decided that they were what economists call *merit goods*—things that for the general benefit of society should be available to everybody, rather than just those who could afford them through the private market. With the growth of the welfare state, the provision of such merit goods by public authorities increasingly determined standards of living—and variations in standards of living—in our cities.

Since the end of the long boom, the demands upon government services have grown and become more complex. As we have seen, the numbers of aged, unemployed, and otherwise welfare-dependent people have increased enormously, with obvious impacts on the need for housing, health, and welfare services. At the same time, there has been growing conflict between environmental concerns and the desire to encourage new economic investment and employment. Ironically these challenges have arisen during a period of declining political enthusiasm for 'big government', characterised by falling levels of taxation and public expenditure, and by the privatisation of many public services. This chapter examines how government in Australia's major cities is responding to these changes in the demand for and supply of public services. The first section discusses Australia's particular, not to say peculiar, system of urban government. The following section analyses the impacts of recent changes, and the conclusion raises some key issues facing urban government in the twenty-first century.

The organisation of urban government

The major cities are affected by three levels or tiers of government: Commonwealth (federal), state, and local. Commonwealth government, the highest level, sets the context within which the cities develop through its policies on immigration, trade, housing, and welfare. Much of the money for the provision of public services is also raised by the Commonwealth as tax, then passed on to state and local government in the form of grants. The Commonwealth government also controls the amount of money states can borrow to fund major capital expenditure on things such as public transport. But the Commonwealth generally leaves direct policies on how cities should grow and how services should be provided to the state and local levels (table 6.1). The main exceptions have been during the Labor administrations of the 1940s, the mid 1970s and, to a lesser extent, the early 1990s.

State governments form the second or middle level, but are the main players in the game. They are responsible for metropolitan planning strategy. They run the public housing bodies. They are the direct providers of public education, health, police, transport, and recreational and cultural services (table 6.1). State governments and bureaucracies devote most of their time— as country people are quick to point out—to running the cities, where most of their electorate lives.

Local government is the third and least powerful level of administration. The various colonial governments set up local councils during the nineteenth century to make communities fend for themselves. Councils were expected to provide services such as road maintenance, drainage, and sewage disposal. Their funds came mainly from *property rates*, paid by local landowners in proportion to the value of their property. They also administered local building regulations and health by-laws. Local councils retain these functions today, leading to the common jibe that their only concerns are the 'three rs': roads, rates, and rubbish. But they now also provide a range of community, recreational, and cultural services (table 6.1) and receive funding assistance from the higher levels of government (McNeill 1997).

The most significant geographical aspect of local government is its fragmented nature. As the cities grew, original councils such as the City of Melbourne became surrounded by other independent inner-suburban councils: Fitzroy, Richmond, South Melbourne, and so on. Later, particularly during the long boom, once-rural shires or district councils were engulfed by suburban expansion to become part of a complex patchwork quilt of local government authorities—a *jurisdictional partitioning*—within each capital city. In the early 1990s, fifty-seven local councils lay within the Melbourne Statistical Division. Sydney contained forty-four, Perth twenty-six, and Adelaide thirty. Brisbane differed from the other cities because in 1925 the twenty local council areas that comprised the urban area had been merged to form one large City of Brisbane. Even there, however, subsequent suburban expansion resulted in seven additional councils lying partly or totally within the Statistical Division. During the 1990s the Victorian and South Australian governments undertook local government amalgamation programs that, as discussed later, reduced the number of local councils to thirty-one in Melbourne and nineteen in Adelaide. Minor changes in the number of councils also took place in the other capitals.

Table 6.1 General government expenses on major services, 2001–2

Purpose	% Local	% State / Territory	% Commonwealth	% multi jurisdictional*	Total $A million
Defence	0.0	0.0	100.0		12017
Health	0.5	46.3	53.1		51955
Education	0.1	49.5	27.4	23.0	42648
Transport and communications	27.6	56.6	15.8		16786
Social security and welfare	1.2	8.2	90.6		76231
Housing and community amenities	31.7	49.9	18.4		12011
Recreation and culture	31.9	38.2	29.9		6794
Total**	5.1	32.2	59.7	3.1	324205

* jurisdiction shared between levels; mainly comprises public universities
** Includes other expenditure categories not shown in table

Source: ABS 2003b

But urban local government is still fragmented, with each local government authority (LGA) seeing itself as an independent mini-state, complete with elected councillors and in most cases a mayor and official regalia.

Australian urban government therefore has a Commonwealth level that raises much of the money but is only sporadically involved in direct urban policy, a middle (state) level that delivers the bulk of the key services (table 6.1), and a highly fragmented but relatively unimportant local level. Other countries do things differently. The United Kingdom has only two levels of government: national and local. Local government is much more significant than in Australia, accounting for approximately 25 per cent of all government expenditure and traditionally taking responsibility for major functions such as health, education, police and fire services, local public transport, and public housing. But local government in British cities, apart from Greater London, is relatively unfragmented. Cities such as Birmingham and Manchester are covered by one or two major councils, plus a handful of others at the fringes.

The USA has a federal system like Australia's, with three levels of government. But the local level is more important than ours, accounting for about 26 per cent of all expenditure, and the state level is less important, accounting for about 21 per cent. In most American cities, local government possesses the extensive powers and responsibilities of the British system, but with an even greater degree of fragmentation or jurisdictional partitioning than in Australia. Typically, a large central-city council is surrounded by dozens of small suburban councils, each responsible for raising its own revenue and providing a full range of services.

There has been a long-standing debate, particularly in the USA, between supporters of the fragmented system of local government within cities and advocates of centralised or unified city-wide government. Critics of fragmentation argue that it is inefficient, because services can be provided more cheaply by a large, city-wide authority able to take advantage of economies of scale than by small individual councils. They also accuse the fragmented system of leading to uncoordinated development because each individual council pursues its own interests, irrespective of its neighbours. Finally, fragmentation is portrayed as inequitable, because councils serving wealthy areas with high property values can afford to provide better local services than councils serving low-income areas. In other words, fragmentation causes the rich to get richer and the poor to get poorer. Centralised urban government, the critics argue, would be more efficient, better coordinated, and fairer. It would provide cheaper services on an equal basis, or on the basis of need, rather than according to ability to pay. Supporters of fragmentation counter by arguing that centralised service-provision and planning are remote and bureaucratic, lacking the accountability and sensitivity to local needs provided by small local councils.

A similar debate has existed in Australia, but less is at stake here because local government provides relatively few services. Some writers have even suggested that the unique Australian system may, perhaps accidentally, provide us with the best of both worlds. The really important services such as education and health care are provided centrally, by state governments using money raised through Commonwealth and state taxes and charges. The states, in other words, serve as de facto centralised urban governments. But less important services—road maintenance, garbage collection, parks and gardens, recreational facilities, and so on—are in the hands of small, flexible, locally responsive councils. Local councils also exercise a degree of control over building and planning regulations, within the broad framework of metropolitan strategies set by the state governments.

This is not to say that our system has been problem free. The literature on urban government and service provision cites three specifically geographical factors—jurisdictional partitioning, externality effects, and tapering—that can magnify inequalities within cities. All operate in Australia. The high degree of *jurisdictional partitioning* in all the cities except Brisbane means that inequalities in service provision still exist between rich and poor councils, despite funds being passed down from state and Commonwealth governments in an attempt to redress them.

Lobby groups from wealthy suburbs, and the wealthy and powerful local councils they support, are generally more successful in keeping their areas clear of developments that produce *negative externalities* than residents of poorer, less influential suburbs. Local independence (or bloody-mindedness) can also obstruct coordinated metropolitan planning.

Nor does the centralised administration of a service guarantee its equal provision. Many services such as hospitals, universities, museums, and public cultural facilities can only be provided from a very limited number of points. Access to them therefore *tapers* with distance: the farther away you live, the less access you have, even though your taxes are paying as much for the service as people living close to it. Rural people suffer worst from tapering, but the historical concentration of many major public institutions in the city centres means that residents of the outer suburbs are also affected. Residents of the western suburbs of Sydney and Melbourne have also persistently argued that when universities and hospitals did decentralise during the 1960s, they went mainly to the other, wealthier, sectors of the cities, creating disparities in access that persist today despite more recent developments such as the University of Western Sydney.

There have therefore been long-standing concerns about the degree to which the Australian system of urban government provides unequal levels of services, and about the tendency for that inequality to be inequitable, in that it makes the poor poorer (though to a lesser extent that some other systems of government). In addition, economic restructuring and demographic change have combined to transform both the demands upon governments and the levels of funding available to provide services. As a result, the past ten years have seen major changes in the ways our cities are governed.

The restructuring of urban government

As pointed out in chapter 2, all levels of government in Australia have been under pressure from the forces of globalisation. In particular, governments have sought to maintain the international competitiveness of their local economies by reducing levels of expenditure so as to avoid debt and keep taxes low. British geographer Steven Pinch (1989) argues that public services, faced with the resulting funding cuts, have had to restructure in the same ways as private businesses in attempts to lower costs and increase productivity. He suggests that restructuring in the public sector can occur in five main ways: rationalisation, privatisation and subcontracting, intensification, adoption of new technology, and increasing self-reliance.

Rationalisation in the manufacturing sector involves closing factories and concentrating production in fewer locations. In the public sector, rationalisation means reducing the number of points from which a service is provided by closing some schools, hospitals, and branch offices of other departments. It has also involved the merging of government departments and pressure for the amalgamation of local councils.

Privatisation and subcontracting is one public sector equivalent of post-Fordist flexible production strategies. Government departments cut their permanent pay rolls by allowing private companies to take over completely the provision of some services (privatisation), or by hiring subcontractors or casual staff to carry out some of the work previously done by public servants.

Intensification involves attempting to increase individual productivity through reorganising how departments operate. Flexible production strategies such as multi-skilling and 'flatter', less hierarchical bureaucratic structures are again involved. But typical results are also higher workloads and worsening staff–client ratios as retiring staff are not replaced and as full-time staff are replaced by part-time and casual workers.

The *adoption of new technology* involves workers being replaced by investment in capital equipment. The replacement of routine clerical workers by computers and telecommunications systems is the most obvious example of this trend. Another is the adoption of automated ticket systems on public transport in an attempt to cut the number of staff.

Increasing self-reliance is rather different. It involves cutting costs by shifting responsibility for providing a service, for example care for the aged, away from the public sector and back to individual households or voluntary institutions.

Pinch argues that different combinations of these processes will occur in different places, producing outcomes that will vary geographically according to economic and demographic structure and trends, prevailing political attitudes, and the power held by public sector trade unions. His model of public sector restructuring was not proposed with Australian cities specifically in mind, but it provides a useful framework for understanding recent changes in the three levels of urban government, and the impacts of those changes on different parts of our cities.

The states

Since the mid 1980s, cuts in Commonwealth government funding and tighter limits on their ability to borrow money have caused the states great stress. Because the states, as discussed in chapter 2, are competing against one another to attract investment capital, they have also sought to keep their own taxes and charges to a minimum. State government departments have therefore been under pressure to restructure their activities in some or all the ways Pinch suggests.

Public authorities providing physical infrastructure in the major cities (sewerage, water supply, electricity, etc.) have responded to the shortage of funds by shifting more of the cost of servicing new housing areas onto the private developers, who then pass the costs on the home buyer. More services are now provided on a 'user pays' basis. Some new roads in Sydney and Melbourne are being paid for by collecting a toll from the motorists who use them. As will be discussed in chapter 8, cutting expenditure on new infrastructure was also the main initial motive behind state governments adopting *urban consolidation* policies. Consolidation policies seek to reduce the rate of suburban expansion by encouraging more people to live in higher density housing in the inner and middle suburbs, where infrastructure is already in place.

In government departments providing 'human services', such as education, staff ceilings were imposed during the 1980s to restrict the number of public servants. Staffing rates in most services fell by attrition as retiring staff were not replaced and new technology and work practices were adopted. The de-institutionalisation of care for aged persons and the mentally ill also had the effect of shifting responsibility for service provision to individuals, voluntary organisations, and local government. The proportion of the employed population working for the state government fell in all the mainland states, though in 1991 (table 6.2) it still ranged from 16 per cent in New South Wales to almost 21 per cent in South Australia, and state governments still employed most of the public servants involved in delivering urban services.

During the recession of the early 1990s the pressure to economise and restructure became much greater, especially in Victoria and South Australia where Liberal governments came to power following the collapse of state financial institutions. At Commonwealth level the Keating Labor government strongly supported privatisation. It sold off Qantas and the Commonwealth Bank and generally advocated the exposure of traditional public sector functions to competition from the private sector through *competitive tendering*. Competitive tendering enables private and public organisations to bid against one another for the contract to provide a service. It allegedly improves efficiency and cost effectiveness, but with the dangers of poorer quality of service and the replacement of public accountability by concern for private profit. The Howard Coalition government, when it came to power in 1996, endorsed competition and privatisation even more strongly, and resolved to reduce still further the size of the public sector workforce.

As Hayward (1997, p. 55) so vividly describes, the Kennett government in Victoria led the way in seeking every opportunity to privatise, rationalise, and intensify.

In five years, the Kennett government has split up and sold into foreign control most of its electricity industry (the gas industry is currently being prepared for sale); it has sold off ports (at Geelong and Portland), the TAB, the Grain Elevators Board, Bass ticketing, and part of the state's bus and train networks. It has deregulated shopping hours, the driving school industry, the planning and building approval process, and, after suspending local democracy for some three years, has forced competitive tendering onto local government. It has also substantially privatised the Victorian prison system, has begun to privatise the state's public hospital system, and has contracted out part of the ambulance system and the whole of the state's emergency dispatch system. It has also begun to privatise the state's road building function, in the form of CityLink, a $1.7b privately built, owned and operated toll-based freeway system.

Other state governments—South Australia for example—followed the Victorian lead to some extent. Table 6.2 shows that between 1991 and 2001 the percentage of wage and salary earners who were state government employees fell significantly in all the mainland states, though the fall was particularly steep in Victoria. Commonwealth government employment also fell sharply. As Hayward (1997, p. 55) puts it: '...we have reached a new phase in Australian urban history, with the private sector now responsible for the provision and/or management of an unprecedented proportion of our urban infrastructure, both social and economic'.

Local government

Local government experienced something of a renaissance during the 1970s and 1980s, following a long period of being criticised as inept, inconsequential, and often corrupt. Localism and 'small is beautiful' came into vogue, as residents' associations and other pressure groups took a more active part in local politics. The Australian Local Government Association raised public awareness of the role of local councils, tirelessly proclaiming that local government was the level of government 'closest to the people'. A campaign emerged for the formal recognition of local government in the Australian Constitution. However it failed to get the necessary support when put to a referendum in 1988. State governments could still, if they wished, legislate to abolish local government altogether.

Since 1973 the Commonwealth government has made grants to local councils, via state Grants Commissions that distribute the money according to complex formulae based partly on population size and partly on assessed need. These funds have come to make up about 10 per cent of council funding. Local government has expanded its role as a provider of human services, particularly in the community development, recreation, and aged care fields. And, as will be discussed in chapter 7, local councils have became increasingly involved in environmental issues such as kerbside recycling of domestic waste, catchment management, and Agenda 21 programs. In economically depressed areas, councils have joined together to pursue *local economic development* initiatives in attempts to attract investment and jobs. Multicoloured signs have

Table 6.2 Employment by sector, wage and salary earners in mainland states, 1991–2001 (%)

	New South Wales		Victoria		Queensland		Western Australia		South Australia	
	1991	2001	1991	2001	1991	2001	1991	2001	1991	2001
Public sector										
Commonwealth	6.0	2.7	5.1	2.7	5.0	2.4	4.5	2.3	5.7	2.9
State	16.0	14.5	17.4	11.7	19.2	16.4	23.1	15.8	20.6	16.0
Local	2.7	1.9	2.5	1.7	2.9	2.8	2.0	1.8	1.5	1.5
Private sector	75.3	80.9	74.9	84.0	72.8	78.4	70.4	80.1	72.2	79.7
Total	100	100	100	100	100	100	100	100	100	100
Number employed ('000)	2277.4	2441.7	1811.4	2014.6	985.1	1363.7	555.0	768.5	556.2	557.8

Source: ABS 2002

proliferated at council boundaries (figure 6.1), carrying coats of arms and slogans. During the early 1980s Sunshine, in Melbourne's western suburbs, proclaimed itself *The Multicultural City of Victoria. A Nuclear-Free and Peace City.* Less ambitious councils settled for simple nuclear-freedom or environmental awareness. The number of workers employed by local government grew during the 1980s, though in 1991 (table 6.2) the numbers were still very small compared with state government.

Figure 6.1 A local council boundary sign, Adelaide, 2003
Source: Clive Forster

State governments have had an ambivalent attitude to the expanding role of local councils in the major cities. (Queensland should not be included in the generalisations that follow, because the relationship between the state government and the large Brisbane city council, though often turbulent, is rather different—See Stockwell (1995).) The states, in general, have been more than happy to pass some functions and responsibilities down to the local level. But they have tended to regard most councils as too small to be economically efficient. They have also seen local economic development programs as exercises in 'robbing Peter to pay Paul', with councils competing against one another to attract development but producing no net gain to the state as a whole. More importantly, state governments have for many years perceived local councils as unduly parochial and obstructive in their attitudes towards development. They accuse councils of having a NIMBY (not in my back yard) attitude towards anything that local residents might see as a LULU (locally unwelcome land use) capable of generating negative externalities. Commercial developments, medium density housing, public housing, and facilities for stigmatised groups such as Aborigines can all be LULUs. Some exasperated developers and state officials have described council attitudes as BANANAs (build absolutely nothing anywhere near anybody)! State governments, desperate to attract economic development, have been particularly concerned that so-called mega-projects, especially major CBD property developments funded largely by overseas capital, might be obstructed by the city-centre councils.

Local councils have been under the same economic pressure to restructure their operations as state governments, and have responded much as Pinch (1989) suggests. Services such as garbage collection have been subcontracted. Councils have rationalised by providing some services jointly with neighbouring councils. Staff loads have increased. Small councils in particular have had to fight for their very existence, as the states' concerns about local government intensified under the pressures of their own economic restructuring. Conflicts over development policy in the CBD prompted state governments to use their powers to dismiss the elected councils of both Melbourne and Sydney during the 1980s, and replace them for a time with appointed administrators. Perth suffered the same fate in the early 1990s. Throughout Australia, major CBD development proposals have been 'fast tracked' by passing special Acts of Parliament exempting them from the normal planning controls operated by local government. State governments have also changed the boundaries of the city centre councils in Sydney, Melbourne, and Perth. Many of the residential areas surrounding the CBDs have been gentrified for some years, and their residents elect councillors who tend to oppose major development projects on heritage and environmental grounds. Re-drawing boundaries to pass some residential areas over to adjoining inner suburban councils reinforces the power of CBD property-owners on the city centre council. But the most visible result of the pressure to restructure local government was the rash of council amalgamations during the 1990s.

Council amalgamations

New South Wales, Victoria, South Australia, and Western Australia all held at least one inquiry during the 1970s and 1980s into the structure of local government. The inquiries focused largely on the arguments in favour of large government units, based on economies of scale. None went so far as favouring the Brisbane style of metropolitan-wide government, but all recommended that the number of local councils in the major cities should be reduced, and their average size increased. For example in Western Australia the 1974 Royal Commission on Metropolitan Municipal Boundaries recommended that the number of councils in Perth be reduced from twenty-six to eighteen.

The amalgamation proposals met with outraged protests from officials and residents of councils that would have been abolished in the mergers. The state governments, afraid of an electoral backlash, ruled that mergers would only go ahead if a majority of the residents involved were in favour, and quietly allowed the recommendations to lapse. But in 1993–94 the newly elected Kennett government in Victoria finally decided, as part of its overall rationalisation program, to grasp the nettle. Local government throughout the state was transformed by a series of enforced amalgamations, the replacement of elected councils by state-appointed administrators for a three-year period, and the imposition of compulsory competitive tendering for a wide range of council functions. Within the Melbourne Statistical Division the number of local councils fell from fifty-seven to thirty-one.

In South Australia the state Liberal government signalled its desire to follow the Victorian path. But, unlike the Kennett government, it did not control the upper house in state parliament. It was therefore unable to enforce council amalgamations because they were opposed by Labor and the Australian Democrats. Instead, a combination of persuasion and threats of economic sanctions was used to bring about a series of amalgamations that reduced the number of local councils in the Adelaide Statistical Division from thirty to nineteen.

The Commonwealth

During the early 1990s the Commonwealth government became more directly involved in urban policy than at any time since 1975 (when the dismissal of the Whitlam government led to the abolition of the Department of Urban and

Regional Development). A specifically 'urban' ministry was not re-established. The departments responsible at various times for housing, community services, immigration, and industry, together with the Department of the Prime Minister and Cabinet, were all involved, although a series of departmental reshuffles culminated in 1994 in the formation of a Department of Housing and Regional Development with major responsibility for urban affairs. A series of inquiries and research projects were set up into urban issues related to the government's three major policy concerns of microeconomic reform, social justice, and environmental sustainability. These initiatives also sought ways to reduce the cost of building cities. The most tangible outcome was the Building Better Cities program announced in the 1991 Budget. The program, later simply renamed 'Better Cities', made over $A800 million available over five years for grants to the states, to fund projects encouraging urban consolidation, improvements to public transport, ecologically sustainable urban development, and a more diverse housing stock. Matching financial contributions from state and local government brought total funding to $2.3 billion.

Better Cities funds were used in a range of ways. Some went to the redevelopment of old public housing estates in Adelaide and Melbourne (chapter 4). Several major redevelopment and urban consolidation projects were carried out in the inner suburbs (figures 5.4 & 5.5), for example in East Perth, Ultimo–Pyrmont in Sydney, and Lynch's Bridge in Melbourne. These and a number of other projects—for example Patawalonga and Elizabeth–Munno Para in Adelaide—also involved improvements in urban water catchment management. Some projects involved new or extended public transport lines.

Critics of Better Cities have argued that the projects were small scale and did little to address basic urban problems. They pointed out that the amount of funding involved was much less than the cuts in general grants to the states that were needed to fund basic urban services.

> There is a recurring problem of incoherence, which is exemplified by the Building Better Cities program. Social justice objectives are stressed, together with reducing the costs of peripheral metropolitan expansion and providing more diverse housing to cater for the population structure. But an interventionist approach to urban policy is basically incompatible with 'economic rationalism' and the ideology of a 'level playing field' that have been the hallmark of the Hawke and Keating government's economic policies. (Stilwell 1993, p. 196)

Despite such criticisms, however, individually worthwhile projects were carried out in each of the major cities and in some smaller centres. But whatever the merits or deficiencies of Better Cities, the program was short-lived. The incoming Howard Coalition government announced in 1996 that no further funding would be forthcoming, once existing commitments had been met. At the same time the Department of Housing and Regional Development was abolished, its responsibilities shared amongst other departments, and its staff transferred or dismissed. The Commonwealth once more withdrew from active involvement in the planning and management of our cities. The main Commonwealth impacts are now:

1   the flow-on effects of overall 'economic rationalist' financial and fiscal policies, which have forced state governments in particular to restructure the provision of public services and infrastructure
2   immigration, housing, trade, and industry policies that, as always, markedly affect the nature of economic development and population growth, and therefore the need for services and infrastructure.

Urban government in the twenty-first century

It has become fashionable to refer to the end of 'big government' and the 'shrinking state'. However, about 20 per cent of all jobs are still in the public sector (table 6.2), and further significant reductions will be hard for governments to achieve. The economist's classic justifications for urban government in capitalist cities—the provision of public and merit goods (see p. 141) and the control of externalities—are still, despite privatisation, competitive tendering and 'user pays', very much with us. But the roles of all three levels in Australia's peculiar system of urban government have, like the cities they serve, been markedly affected by globalisation and economic restructuring.

> Cities like Liverpool are at the cutting edge of [the] downturn: not only feeling unemployment first and hardest, but being less equipped to cope with decreases in government funds. With lower family incomes, so much of our quality of life in Liverpool depends on opportunities which only the public sector can provide: quality education, health care, transport access, family support and recreation. (Latham 1992 p. 31)

This *cri de coeur* from Mark Latham, current federal Labor leader, was made when he was Mayor of Liverpool in Sydney's industrial western suburbs at the height of the early 1990s economic recession. Latham's views about the role of government have changed considerably since 1992, but his statement highlights a vital point. The parts of our cities that have been the 'losers' from the changes in employment, housing, and population discussed in earlier chapters are those most vulnerable to the changes in service provision and government we are discussing now. Some, such as Elizabeth in Adelaide's north, may have 'scored' Commonwealth money for a Better Cities demonstration project. But their local councils face increasing demands for services coupled with declining ability to raise rate revenue from their residents. Falling levels of provision of state government services such as education and health, plus meaner Commonwealth unemployment relief programs, will also hit them hardest, reinforcing the cumulative process of increasing disadvantage set out earlier in figure 5.16. More affluent suburbs, which are less dependent on public education and health services, are not as vulnerable to cuts at the state and Commonwealth level and can afford the rates to pay for local services.

Another aspect of the uneven impact of the restructuring of service provision is that women bear a triple burden. Women still take the main responsibility within households for child-rearing and care of the aged, so are most affected by cuts in public services for those groups, and have been particularly hit by cuts in Commonwealth funding for child care. The majority of voluntary workers are women, so any shifting of responsibility for service provision from the public to the voluntary sector also falls mainly on them. And a significantly higher proportion of women workers is employed in the public sector than men, so they also bear more of the burden of job losses, higher workloads, and more demanding working conditions. As governments retreat from the role of cushioning the unequal impact of economic restructuring and globalisation on urban communities, it seems inevitable, as discussed in chapter 5, that Australian cities in the twenty-first century will become more polarised and unequal.

A second key point about the restructuring of urban government is the heightened conflict between the desires for local autonomy on the one hand, and rationalisation and metropolitan-wide efficiency on the other.

> Local government exists to allow local voters control over some aspects of their lives. (Jones 1989, p. 143)

> Because local government is residentially based, it tends to give too much weight to the views of existing residents at a cost to overall planning objectives and, in particular, the facilitation of economic development. (Victoria, Ministry for Planning 1993, p. 13)

The second quotation states the centralist position in stark terms. This view seeks fewer, larger local government areas, with more of their service functions privatised and more of their control functions vested in state governments. The Victorian government pushed through such a rationalisation in the mid 1990s. South Australia followed suit and other states may be tempted to do the same. However, as Jones suggests, we prize a sense of control over the local urban environments within which we live much of our lives. It can be argued that in post-modern cities characterised by diversity, flexibility, and tolerance for (even a celebration of) difference, local democracy is particularly appropriate. Perhaps the largest urban local government areas, with over 100 000 residents, are already too large and should be split up, rather than merged with their neighbours. This has happened recently in Sydney, with Pittwater splitting away from the City of Warringah (total population over 170 000) to form a new council with only 50 000 inhabitants.

The claims of localism are related to demands for public participation in decision-making, as opposed to the centralised 'government knows best' style of administration characteristic of the modernist city—the *state managed capitalist metropolis*—of the long boom. During the 1970s and 1980s, individuals and lobby groups succeeded in having processes of public participation—or at least consultation—built into most state and local planning decisions. But state governments in the 1990s became increasingly impatient with local attempts to frustrate metropolitan-wide policies such as urban consolidation, and changes to planning law in several states weakened the power of local communities. The local response, particularly in Victoria, was not long in coming.

The suburban backlash: Save Our Suburbs

Residents, particularly in Melbourne's higher-status eastern suburbs, felt that the character of their local environment was being destroyed by poorly designed higher-density infill development encouraged by the Victorian government's urban consolidation policy. The book *Suburban Backlash* (Lewis 1999) summarises the residents' concerns, while also conveying their feelings in its title. The *Save Our Suburbs* organisation (SOS) was founded in 1998 to oppose what members saw as inappropriate developments in established suburbs, and to lobby for changes in planning legislation and policy. Other SOS groups were founded later in Sydney, Perth, and Adelaide, but SOS Melbourne has been the most influential. The group was a vocal and effective opponent of the Kennett government's urban development policies, and may have played some part in the government's surprising defeat in the 1999 state election. Since then, the group has continued to lobby against policies it sees as threatening the traditional character of the Australian suburb.

The various SOS groups may represent an understandable response to state government policies that threaten established local environments, and their success, particularly in Melbourne, is a timely reminder of the danger of alienating local communities. But the danger with localism, particularly in hard economic times, is not simply that it can frustrate the economic 'master plans' of state governments. It also increases the ability of affluent communities to insulate themselves from change, while leaving low-income communities in charge of their own problems but without enough resources to tackle them.

Similarly, public participation and consultation processes can be 'hi-jacked' by articulate and well-organised middle-class groups whose interests are not necessarily representative.

It is perhaps ominous that in Adelaide, for example, it is the more affluent councils that have most successfully withstood pressure to amalgamate. If the pre-merger councils are ranked according to the percentage of individual weekly incomes that were above $700 at the 1996 Census, it emerges that six out of the top eleven—including three of the top four—have avoided amalgamation. Some councils in higher-income areas such as the Adelaide Hills and the inner eastern suburbs have chosen to merge, but others have so far withstood the pressure. On the other hand, of the bottom eleven councils in the income table, only Salisbury has not been involved in a merger. And as it was by far the largest pre-merger council, with a population of 110 000, it was under little pressure to do so. Is truly *local* local government becoming a luxury only the rich can afford?

People living in Australian cities, like people living anywhere, cherish their own rights and freedoms. Yet they still wish to be protected from the harmful actions of others. They recognise the need for locally unwelcome facilities to be located *somewhere*, yet—as the success of the SOS groups shows—they still wish to protect the character and amenity of their own residential environments (figure 6.2). Recent conflicts over the roll-out of overhead telecommunications

Figure 6.2 Local residents protest against a new housing development, southern Adelaide, 1992 (the protest was unsuccessful)

Source: Clive Forster

cables in residential areas and the location of transmission towers for mobile phone systems show that new issues will continue to arise as the impacts of globalisation affect local communities.

As Australian cities become more complex and diverse, it is increasingly difficult to get a good balance between the rights and responsibilities we should possess as individuals, as members of a local community, and as residents of the city as a whole. As we enter the twenty-first century we need to seek that balance, as well as demanding efficiency and cost-effectiveness. We need a locally accountable form of urban government capable of dealing effectively with conflicts and dilemmas—in poor as well as rich areas—rather than one that is justified simply in terms of greater size providing economical road mending and garbage collection services, plus vague promises of more 'clout' in economic development and environmental protection matters.

7

Sustainable Cities?

Big cities have always produced environmental problems. As the ancient Romans found, the concentration of large numbers of people into a small area has some inevitable consequences. Vast amounts of sewage and other waste must be disposed of. Fresh water supplies must be safeguarded. Some of the Romans' greatest engineering achievements came from meeting these challenges. As discussed in chapter 1, similar problems reached new heights in the nineteenth century. Industrial urbanisation in Britain and elsewhere produced severely degraded urban environments with high levels of air and water pollution, and modern town planning emerged as an attempt to tackle the mess.

Even in low-density cities such as we have in Australia today, millions of people living close together produce enormous amounts of waste, the disposal of which threatens local land, rivers, and oceans. Those same people pollute the local atmosphere by burning fossil fuel to generate the energy they need for heating and cooling their houses, and for transport, industry, and commerce. As cities grow and spread, they take up good agricultural land and threaten fragile natural ecosystems. In built-up areas, concrete, tarmac, and other impervious materials cover the land surface and radically change the nature of stormwater runoff. Tall buildings in city centres produce 'wind tunnel' effects and areas permanently in shade. Cities generate their own 'heat islands' of raised local temperatures.

For most of the twentieth century these environmental issues have been seen as engineering and town planning problems, to be tackled by a combination of improved technology and stricter building and planning legislation. But during the last twenty-five years or so a significant change has occurred. Researchers began to argue that the nature of urban development in countries like Australia was producing serious and irreversible environmental harm, not only to the local environment but on a global scale. Cities were increasingly viewed as key contributors to problems such as global warming, acid rain, damage to the ozone layer, depletion of resources, and loss of biodiversity. Urban planning authorities throughout the world were urged to strive for *environmentally* (or *ecologically*) *sustainable urban development.*

Environmentally sustainable urban development

Most people first became aware of the concept of environmentally sustainable development following the publication in 1987 of *Our Common Future* by the UN World Commission on Environment and Development, chaired by the Norwegian prime minister Gro Harlem Brundtland. The book, also known as the Brundtland Report, defined environmentally sustainable development as development that 'meets the needs of the present without compromising the ability of future generations to meet their own needs'. The report argued that current levels of resource depletion and waste production are not sustainable, and that the greatest challenge facing the world is to tackle poverty and inequality—particularly in developing countries—while maintaining environmental quality for the future. One chapter concentrated specifically on environmental problems in cities, dealing with both developing and economically advanced countries. But the whole report stressed the *global* significance of urban environmental issues. It suggested (accurately) that by the year 2000 over 50 per cent of the world's population would be living in cities, and pointed out that cities are destined to be the major generators of future world environmental problems.

The United Nations 'Earth Summit' held in Rio de Janeiro in 1992 gave further impetus to the call for sustainable urban development. In particular the summit encouraged governments at all levels, but especially local government, to adopt the Agenda 21 program (produced by the conference) as a practical blueprint for communities to improve environmental sustainability through local actions such as kerbside recycling, stormwater management, tree planting, coast protection, and the development of cycleways. 'Think globally, act locally' became a common slogan for environmental activists.

The messages from the Brundtland Report and the Rio Earth Summit found a ready audience in Australia, where researchers had been arguing for some time that our low-density, suburbanised cities use too much energy, especially in fuel for cars, and generate too much waste and pollution. As early as 1980, planning proposals for metropolitan Melbourne had incorporated environmental concerns as a major part of their 'five E' key principles: efficiency, equity, employment, energy, and environment. As Newton (1997, p. 2) puts it, 'three energy-related issues [had] emerged to signal a halt to "business-as-usual" thinking about the future pattern of development of cities…' These three issues were:

1   the threat to world oil supplies in the 1970s
2   the threat of global warming from the greenhouse effect in the 1980s
3   increasingly serious levels of local air pollution.

In 1989, Newman and Kenworthy produced the influential and controversial *Cities and Automobile Dependence—An International Sourcebook*. They argued that the Australian capitals compared badly with cities in most other parts of the world on measures of energy consumption and waste production, and that we urgently needed to increase residential densities and encourage the use of public transport.

When state governments produced new metropolitan planning policies in the 1990s, they almost invariably adopted environmental sustainability as a major objective. For example the New South Wales Department of Planning's *Cities for the 21st Century* (1995, p. 4) stated that 'Environmental Quality—using integrated environmental management to strive for ecologically sustainable development' was one of four basic goals for the Sydney region. The federal government's Australian Urban and Regional Development Review (AURDR) (1995) *Green Cities* report took a similar approach and the first Australia: State of the Environment report, produced for the federal government in 1996 by the State of the Environment Advisory Council, included a 'Human Settlements' chapter stressing the need to reduce urban resource inputs and waste outputs. Earlier a National Strategy for Ecologically Sustainable Development had been adopted in 1992. Its core objectives were to:

* enhance individual and community well-being and welfare by following a path of economic development that safeguards the welfare of future generations
* provide for equity within and between generations
* protect biological diversity and maintain essential ecological processes and life support systems.

In addition, at the local level, many local councils in the major cities had adopted Local Agenda 21 programs (see p. 149) by the late 1990s.

Further United Nations environmental conferences, in Kyoto in 1997 and in Johannesburg in 2002, were less successful than the Rio Earth Summit. Some developed countries, including Australia, proved reluctant to commit themselves to international agreements to tackle issues such as global warming. Nonetheless it has become conventional planning wisdom for all three levels of government in Australia to be committed to *environmentally sustainable urban development.* But how meaningful is this concept, and how much progress are we making? The rest of the chapter will attempt to answer these questions.

Cities and metabolic flows

Most discussions of urban environmental issues begin with a diagram similar to figure 7.1. Cities are depicted as systems that require huge inputs of resources: water, raw materials, energy in the form of fuel or transmitted power, food, and so on. These resources are essential to produce and support the reasons people live in cities (the 'good' outputs of economic productivity and high standards of living). But the concentration and transformation of resources that happens in big cities also produces waste outputs, with the environmental consequences already discussed. Put simplistically, if we want more sustainable cities (without sacrificing living standards) we need to reduce the size of the *resource inputs* and *waste outputs* boxes in figure 7.1, while somehow maintaining or even increasing the size of the *'good' outputs* box. And the key to achieving this is found in the *city structures* box, through changes to transport technology, urban form and density, social customs and cultural norms, economic policies, and structures of government.

Measures of actual metabolic flows (inputs and outputs) are harder to produce than the simplified model shown in figure 7.1, but table 7.1 (based

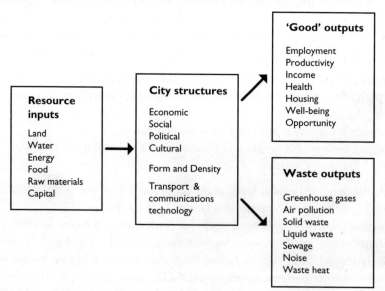

Figure 7.1 Cities and metabolic flows

Source: Adapted from Australia, Department of the Environment, Sport and Territories, 1996, p. 3–5 and Aplin et al. 1995, p. 134

on the first Australia: State of the Environment report, published in 1996)
attempts a comparison between levels of resource input and waste output in
Sydney in 1970 and in 1990. Intakes per person of energy, water, and food all
increased, as did outputs of sewage, solid waste, and atmospheric waste. Given
that the total number of people also increased, table 7.1 suggests that Sydney
(and by implication the other major Australian cities) became less rather than
more environmentally sustainable over the twenty-year period. Despite reductions in some types of air pollution, it appears that local urban environments
were deteriorating and our cities were making an increasing contribution to
global problems such as the greenhouse effect and the depletion of fossil fuels.

The data in table 7.1 are now out of date, but the second State of the
Environment report, published in 2001, unfortunately does not provide
comparable information. Nevertheless, in assessing whether our cities are

Table 7.1 Trends in resource flows, Sydney, 1970–90

	1970	1990
Population (million)	2.79	3.66
Resource inputs per person		
Energy (mj)	88 589	115 377
% domestic	10	9
% commercial	11	6
% industrial	44	47
% transport	35	38
Food (tonnes)*	0.52	1.00
Water (tonnes)	144	180
% domestic	36	44
% commercial	5	9
% industrial	20	13
% agriculture/gardens	24	16
% miscellaneous	15	18
Waste outputs per person		
Sewage (tonnes)	108**	128***
Solid waste (tonnes)	0.59	0.77
Air waste (tonnes)	7.6	9.3
carbon dioxide (kg)	7210	9050
carbon monoxide (kg)	205	178
sulphur oxides (kg)	21	5
nitrous oxides (kg)	20	18
hydrocarbons (kg)	63	42
particulates (kg)	31	5

* reflects increased use of primary foodstuffs such as grains in production of meat and processed foods
** includes stormwater
*** waste water within sewerage systems only

Source: Australia, Department of the Environment, Sport and Territories 1996, p. 3–34.

environmentally sustainable, we clearly still need to consider the interrelated issues arising from the patterns of resource input and waste output suggested by figure 7.1 and table 7.1:

- energy use
- greenhouse gas emission
- air pollution
- water use
- sewage disposal
- water catchment pollution
- solid waste disposal

Energy use

Figure 7.1 shows that per capita energy use increased significantly in Sydney up to 1990. The main users were industry and transportation, both of which increased their percentage share, whereas domestic energy use made up a declining share of the total. Energy use has continued to grow since 1990, and dependence on fossil fuels has not declined, despite a growing interest in developing renewable power sources such as solar and wind power (Australian State of the Environment Committee 2001, pp. 100–2). Table 7.2 reveals that

Table 7.2 Transport fuel use and population densities in Australian and overseas cities

City	Total transport fuel use per person (GJ)*	Total car use per person (km) 1990	Population density (persons per ha) 1990
Sydney	34.66	5885	16.8
Melbourne	34.24	6436	14.9
Brisbane	37.30	6467	9.8
Perth	40.25	7203	10.6
Adelaide	35.21	6690	11.8
Houston	84.20	13 106	9.5
Los Angeles	65.50	11 587	23.9
New York	52.09	8317	19.2
Hamburg	23.07	5061	39.8
London	18.72	3892	42.3
Amsterdam	10.47	3977	48.4
Tokyo	15.35	2103	104.4
Singapore	11.04	1864	86.8
Hong Kong	5.41	493	300.5

* Data are for various years from the early 1980s onwards

Source: Australia, Department of the Environment, Sport and Territories 1996, p. 3–37 and Newton 1997, p. 166.

Australian cities are particularly heavy users of transport energy compared with European or Asian cities, though they lag behind North American cities. The demand for transport energy, particularly fuel for road vehicles, is met largely by consuming fossil fuels and is therefore placing increasing pressure on non-renewable global resources.

Greenhouse gas emission

Naturally occurring gases in the atmosphere, mainly carbon dioxide, nitrous oxide, and methane (plus water vapour), act like the glass in a greenhouse. Energy from the sun, in the form of short-wave radiation, passes readily through these gases to be absorbed by the Earth. Some of the energy is then emitted from the Earth's surface in the form of heat. This long-wave (infra-red) radiation is absorbed by the greenhouse gases, to be re-emitted and trapped in the atmosphere as a warming 'blanket'. The greenhouse effect is vital to maintaining liveable temperatures at the Earth's surface. Without it, temperatures would on average be over 30°C lower and the Earth would be covered in ice.

The problem with the greenhouse effect is that most scientists now believe it is intensifying (*the enhanced greenhouse effect*) because human activities such as burning fossil fuels and clearing forests are causing more greenhouse gases to be emitted into the atmosphere. As a result, global temperatures appear to be rising, threatening significant changes in climatic regimes and rises in sea levels through the expansion of the oceans as their temperatures increase.

The enhanced greenhouse effect is a global environmental sustainability issue *par excellence*. Climatic change and rising sea levels do not recognise national frontiers. Greenhouse gases generated in the cities of Europe and North America (and Australia) will threaten the very existence of people living near the sea in Asia and the Pacific if the predicted rise in sea levels of up to 30 cm by the year 2030 takes place. Australia is a high per capita producer of greenhouse gases, emitting 33.3 tonnes of carbon dioxide, methane, and nitrous oxide per person in 1990, compared with 23.0 tonnes in the United States of America and 15.4 tonnes in Germany (Newton 1997, p. 4). Approximately half the emissions result from urban energy use, either as fuel for motor vehicles or as electricity generated by burning coal, oil, or gas and used in industry, commerce, transport, and the home. Table 7.1 shows that carbon dioxide emissions increased significantly in Sydney between 1970 and 1990, and later data show that Australia's total greenhouse gas emissions rose by 17 per cent between 1990 and 1998 (Australian State of the Environment Committee 2001, p. 25).

Air pollution

Air pollution results from the release of noxious gases and fine solid particles (soot, smoke, dust, and so on) into the atmosphere. Motor vehicles produce the bulk of air pollution in Australian cities, contributing over 75 per cent of carbon monoxide emissions (Australian State of the Environment Committee 2001, p. 28), plus over 40 per cent of unburnt hydrocarbons, and between 50 and 80 per cent of nitrous oxides (AURDR 1995, p. 56). Photochemical smog, which forms when nitrous oxides and hydrocarbons react in the presence of sunlight, is a significant problem, particularly in western Sydney. Legislation enforcing higher standards of emission control for motor vehicles, plus the banning of backyard burning and restrictions on industrial pollution, produced improvements between 1970 and 1990 (table 7.1). These improvements have continued with the phasing-out of leaded petrol by 2002, and air quality in Australian cities compares well with large cities elsewhere in the world. But air pollution still forms the most widely recognised local environmental problem—and a potentially serious health hazard—in our cities.

Water use

Australian cities are extremely thirsty consumers of water and, as table 7.1 shows, that thirst grew between 1970 and 1990. Levels of use have generally fallen in recent years, but remain unsustainably high. The most significant demand is for domestic use, particularly the irrigation of large, European-style lawns and gardens. Each city depends on an expensive infrastructure of dams, reservoirs, and pipelines, extending the city's *ecological footprint* over many kilometres as it sucks water in from surrounding catchments and rivers. Adelaide, for example, is highly dependent on the already depleted and degraded Murray–Darling system, and restrictions on water supply form a significant limiting factor on future urban growth.

Sewage disposal

For cities to be liveable, sewage—water contaminated by human waste including faeces and urine—must be disposed of in a way that does not pose a health hazard. Most areas in Australia's major cities are now connected to deep sewerage. A system of pipes collects sewage from each dwelling and channels it to a treatment plant, from where it is usually discharged into the nearby ocean. Despite occasional leakages and overflows, such systems adequately safeguard the health of city dwellers. But there are significant environmental problems. Because sewage treatment is incomplete, it has been estimated that 10 000 tonnes of phosphorus and 100 000 tonnes of nitrogen are discharged into the oceans each year (Australia, Department of the Environment, Sport and Territories 1996, pp. 3–42). The impact of this discharge on marine ecosystems is obviously a matter of concern.

Water catchment pollution

During the nineteenth century, rivers and streams in Australian cities became heavily polluted by industrial waste and sewage. Deep sewerage systems and tougher controls on industry now prevent the worst of this pollution, but less obvious problems remain. The replacement of open land by impervious surfaces such as roads, parking areas, and roofs greatly increases the rate of stormwater runoff and reduces the amount of infiltration. To deal with the resulting flood danger from heavy rains, many urban streams have been turned into concrete-lined drains, further increasing the speed of runoff. Moreover, the stormwater runoff picks up large quantities of material such as litter, rubber, metal fragments, oil and lead from roads and chemicals, fertiliser, and other nutrients from gardens. As a result, urban waterways carry significant amounts of pollution into estuaries and the ocean, and urban catchment areas suffer changes to water tables because of loss of recharge by infiltration. It is only in the last ten years or so that these problems have begun to be addressed by setting up urban water catchment management boards and through Local Agenda 21 programs (see p. 149).

Solid waste disposal

Australian cities produce large amounts of solid waste, consisting of household garbage, waste from industrial and commercial premises, and building and demolition waste. Table 7.1 suggests that the output of solid waste rose between 1970 and 1990, and more recent data for Adelaide show a 14 per cent rise between 1998 and 2002 in the amount of solid waste needing to be disposed of (South Australia Environment Protection Authority 2003). As with most measures of urban resource flows, the Australian levels are significantly higher than European cities and are second only to the United States of America (Australia, Department of the Environment, Sport and Territories 1996). OECD data for the mid 1990s suggests that Australian local councils collected on average 620 kg of waste per person per year, including material such as car tyres as well as domestic garbage. Overall, 40 per cent of urban solid waste is 'municipal waste', collected and disposed of by local councils. Construction and demolition activities generate 37 per cent, and the remaining 23 per cent is derived from commercial and industrial activities (Newton et al. 2001, pp. 125–7).

Most urban solid waste is dumped in landfill sites in and around the cities. These sites, unless carefully (and expensively) managed, produce environmental problems such as harmful materials being leached into the water table and methane discharge, as well as smell, noise, and visual pollution. In some cities the lack of suitable sites for infill within a reasonable distance will become an increasing problem in the future.

Summary

Overall, a pattern emerges of high levels of resource inputs and waste outputs in Australian cities compared with most other countries. Some recent improvements have been achieved through catchment management programs, the widespread adoption of kerbside recycling, tighter pollution controls, and higher charges for domestic water. On the other hand, as discussed in chapter 3 (table 3.3, p. 67), dependence on the automobile remains extremely high, with ominous consequences for energy use, air pollution, and greenhouse gas emission. Despite making some progress since 1990, there is still plenty of cause for concern. We cannot see into the future, so it is not possible to know *for certain* whether or not our current style of urban life is environmentally sustainable. However, given the serious potential threats posed by global warming, air and water pollution, and the depletion of finite energy, raw material, and water resources, it seems only prudent and sensible to aim for reduced levels of resource inputs and waste outputs. As Giradet (2003, p. 2) puts it: 'Modern cities have a linear metabolism, demanding huge quantities of resources and discharging wastes into nature. Future cities need to develop a circular metabolism to become sustainable, using resources efficiently, recycling waste and running on renewable energy.'

In search of sustainability

Approaches to creating more sustainable city environments vary widely. So-called *deep green* activists call for radical change to the whole economic system and see the adoption of low-energy, low-consumption, lifestyles as the only path to true environmental sustainability. But such a change threatens the 'good' outputs in figure 7.1—the productivity, wealth, and opportunity that attract people to live in big cities in the first place. For most people, the aim is to reduce resource inputs and waste outputs while maintaining these 'good' outputs.

Several pressure groups have also raised the general issue of immigration levels and sustainable urban development. They argue that the environmental impact of our cities can only be controlled by stopping them getting any bigger, and that halting immigration is the way to do this. As discussed in chapter 2, immigration certainly continues to make a major contribution to population growth in Australian cities, particularly Sydney and Melbourne. But tables 7.1 and 7.2 show that it is not the *number of people* that is the main problem. If our cities are environmentally unsustainable it is mainly because *per capita* levels of resource consumption and waste production are too high. If we do not cut down these metabolic flows, reducing population growth through immigration will not help very much. At most it might provide a little 'breathing space' before problems become intolerable (Burnley et al. 1997, p. 110). However, there is some merit in the New South Wales government's repeated claim that federal funding for environmental (and social and other) programs should reflect the degree to which recent immigrants have flocked to Sydney.

Most recent discussion has focussed on two approaches to improving sustainability, both of which are implied in the 'city structures' box in figure 7.1. The first concentrates on *economic, social, political, and cultural structures*, and on *technology*. Supporters of this approach see changing human behaviour and improving technology as the keys, and advocate legislation, pricing policies, research, and education programs as the best ways to improve sustainability. The second approach focuses on urban *form and density*. Its supporters regard low-density, suburbanised urban structure and the associated dependence on the automobile as the root cause of unsustainability. They argue, therefore, that differently structured cities are needed to reduce energy consumption, water use, and pollution levels. We shall examine this second approach first.

The urban form debate

City planners have tried for many years to shape the spatial relationship between jobs and housing, so as to improve accessibility to employment and reduce the time and energy spent travelling to work. The main approaches have been *decentralisation, multi-centralisation,* and *consolidation*.

Decentralisation

Decentralisation policies are based on the premise that our major cities are too big. They therefore seek to encourage the growth of smaller cities, or even create totally new cities of limited size as first proposed by the nineteenth-century British writer Ebenezer Howard. If people (and sufficient jobs) locate in these smaller settlements instead of adding to the expansion of large cities, both they and the residents of the large cities should benefit from shorter journeys to work, less energy consumption, and lower levels of congestion and air pollution.

Decentralisation policies have a long history in Australia, dating back to Decentralisation Leagues set up as political organisations in the nineteenth century to oppose the dominance of the colonial capital cities. The Victorian and New South Wales governments pursued decentralisation policies during the long boom, offering incentives for businesses to set up in country towns, but with no real impact on the growth of Melbourne and Sydney. The Whitlam federal government established an ambitious New Cities program in the mid 1970s, but Albury–Wodonga is its only real legacy. Recently the federal government has also attempted to persuade immigrants to settle in smaller centres rather than the large cities, but again with little success.

It has proved very difficult, in the absence of draconian controls on further metropolitan growth, to counter the attractions of the major cities. It would also require an unprecedented amount of growth in established smaller centres and new cities to have a significant impact on the growth of the major cities. The latest planning document for Melbourne estimates that by 2030 the city will grow by 1 million people or over 600 000 households—the equivalent of over four new Canberras. In any case smaller cities and rural areas, because of their lower levels of congestion and lack of public transport, tend to have higher rates per person of automobile dependence and energy use than the big cities. According to Moriarty (2002) 'Only near-subsistence living, with a high degree of self-sufficiency, would make rural areas more environmentally sustainable than cities'. So decentralisation is unlikely to provide the answer to the sustainability problem.

Multi-centralisation

Multi-centralisation, in contrast to decentralisation, accepts the continued growth of major cities and seeks to encourage the development within them of strong suburban employment centres, well served by public transport and therefore providing access to jobs and services while reducing dependence on the automobile. For example, Melbourne's metropolitan strategy of the early 1980s designated fourteen suburban *district centres*, all served by public transport, and sought to channel new retail and office development into them. But, with the exception of Box Hill, the centres have been largely shunned by private office developers, who prefer to build on individual sites at or near major intersections in the arterial road system. Public sector offices remained, with government encouragement, heavily concentrated in and near the CBD, and major retailers such as Myer had opted since the 1960s for car-oriented suburban shopping centres on their own sites. The designated centres therefore attracted a disappointing share of employment and services. Moreover the development they did attract has been mainly car-oriented, producing parking problems rather than the hoped-for boost to public transport.

Official policy in the other cities up to the end of the 1980s also favoured concentrated suburbanisation of jobs and the encouragement of access to public transport. Sydney can point to some success in the emergence of Parramatta (figure 3.7, p. 62), St Leonards, and Chatswood, the first in particular aided by an energetic policy for the relocation of government offices. But, as discussed in chapter 3, the actual location of suburban employment has been much more dispersed than the planners intended. Australian suburban landscapes may not match Los Angeles's post-modern assembly of retail supermalls, technology parks, entertainment theme parks, and edge cities, but they are also far removed from the neat, polycentric hierarchy of district centres envisaged in the planning documents of the 1970s and 1980s. Multi-centralisation, like decentralisation, has so far proved difficult to achieve and disappointing in its effects.

Consolidation

Urban consolidation policies concentrate on increasing housing densities in the large cities to produce more compact development, shorter travel distances, and less dependence on automobiles. All the mainland state governments held reviews and inquiries into metropolitan development during the late 1980s and early 1990s, and released new or modified strategy plans embracing, with encouragement from the federal government, some aspects of consolidation. The media also became increasingly interested in debates about whether our cities were too sprawling and needed to move towards higher densities. The following quotation is from a book based on a Triple J radio documentary produced in association with the Better Cities program.

> Australian cities have reached a mid life crisis. Two hundred years after European invasion and the beginnings of urban development in this country, we are looking down at the sprawling belly of our cities and exclaiming, 'Oh my God, how did that happen?' We are full of regret for our gluttonous consumption of space and now we are questioning the ideology on which our lifestyle has been based. (Collins 1993, p. 30)

Many conservationists believe that more compact urban development is essential for environmental sustainability. They argue that in more compact, higher-density cities, journeys would be shorter and public transport would be more viable, thus reducing car use and easing pressures on non-renewable fossil fuels, while cutting atmospheric pollution and the emission of greenhouse gases. More compact development would reduce the rate at which urban expansion consumes good agricultural land and threatens sensitive natural environments. It would also reduce the demand for water, much of which in urban areas is used to irrigate large gardens.

Newman and Kenworthy (1989; 1992) have been particularly strong advocates of the argument that energy consumption and urban densities are closely linked, and that only by increasing densities can our cities become more sustainable. They contend that Australian cities have an average population density of only fourteen persons per hectare (table 7.2, p. 164), compared with fifty-four in European cities, and that this is a basic reason why only 8 per cent of our urban travel is by public transport, compared with 25 per cent in Europe. Newman and Kenworthy have proposed a series of radical changes in urban planning and transport policies, designed to produce more energy-efficient and equitable cities. They advocate increasing residential densities so as to reduce suburban expansion and improve the viability of public transport. They propose discouraging the use of cars by switching expenditure from roads to public transport systems, while imposing strict controls on parking and even car access in city centres and sub-centres. They favour encouraging employment to locate in the city centre, in major regional centres, and in *urban villages*: mixtures of medium-density housing and employment-generating activities located along light rail systems. Their ideas, not surprisingly, receive strong support from conservationists and supporters of public transport.

Troy (1992; 1996) rejects the notion that there is a necessary connection between urban density and ecological sustainability. He argues that higher residential densities can make it more difficult to develop sustainable policies such as reducing stormwater runoff and disposing of domestic waste by composting. Troy and other critics also view Newman and Kenworthy's claims about the relationship between urban densities, dependence on the automobile, and energy use as too simplistic. They point to the increased use of cars in the inner suburbs following gentrification (see chapter 5) and the falling duration of journeys to work in low-density suburbs in recent years (see chapter 3). Overall, Newman and Kenworthy are accused of portraying an idealistic, even romanticised view of life in denser European-style cities while unfairly condemning as 'urban sprawl' the dispersed but well-designed suburban environments most Australians prefer.

Brotchie et al. (1995) and O'Connor (1992) also reject the consolidation argument. They contend that the continued suburbanisation of employment during the 1980s was associated with stabilising journey-to-work distances, showing that the low-density, suburbanised metropolis represents an efficient, sustainable structure. Both writers relate the continuing suburbanisation of jobs and work trips to the transformation of Australian cities from industrial to post-industrial 'informational' economies, strongly influenced by technological changes in communications and information-processing. O'Connor (1992, p.93) argues that in Melbourne and Sydney in particular, 'it may be more appropriate to view the present suburban structure as a means by which

Australia's bigger cities will be more productive and internationally competitive...' rather than as a 'problem' to be addressed by consolidation policies.

The various 'urban form' proposals are not mutually exclusive. Newton (1997) advocates a combination of centralisation and multi-centralisation. This is less extreme than Newman and Kenworthy's proposal for urban consolidation and urban villages, and meets some of O'Connor and Brotchie's concerns about retaining the economic benefits of a suburbanised structure. Newton's views arise from a study estimating the levels of air pollution and energy consumption that would probably result from a growth of 500 000 in Melbourne's population by the year 2011 under five different scenarios:

1 *Business as usual* current trends continue
2 *Compact city* increased population in the inner suburbs
3 *Edge city* increased population, housing densities, and employment at selected centres within the city
4 *Corridor city* growth along linear corridors radiating from the CBD with upgraded public transit
5 *Fringe city* growth accommodated predominantly on the fringe

For each scenario, a computer model allocated housing and employment to their likely locations, then calculated the transport flows that would be expected to occur. Levels of air pollution were then estimated, assuming some technological improvements in fuel efficiency and emission control.

Newton estimates that under the 'business as usual' scenario, risks of photochemical smog will worsen by 71 per cent, exposure to particle concentrations will increase by 61 per cent, carbon dioxide emissions will rise by over 25 per cent, and fuel consumption will rise by 25 per cent. The 'compact city' scenario (urban consolidation) delivers significant improvements in each measure except exposure to particle concentrations. 'Edge city' (multi-centralisation), 'corridor city', and 'fringe city' all do better than 'business as usual' on each measure, though they do worse than 'compact city' except for exposure to particle concentrations.

Summary

Despite the well-publicised calls for more compact urban development, there is no clear consensus about the most sustainable and efficient future structure for Australian cities. As discussed in chapter 4, the amount of medium- and high-density housing in Australian cities, particularly Sydney and Melbourne, has increased since 1991. But low-density houses still dominate, and we cannot assume that planners in future would be *able* to produce significant changes in structure given the unimpressive track record of decentralisation, multi-centralisation, and consolidation policies in the past. Moreover, there is no guarantee that changing urban structure will change human behaviour sufficiently to produce a significant improvement in environmental sustainability. Throughout history, changes in transport technology have produced changes in urban form and structure. We saw this in chapter 1, with the change from the compact *walking city* to the starfish-shaped *public transport city* during the nineteenth century and then the change from the public transport city to the sprawling *automobile city* during the 1950s and 1960s. Advocates of the 'urban form' approach to environmental sustainability essentially believe that this relationship can be reversed: that by changing urban form and structure we can produce different patterns of transport use and energy consumption. But will this necessarily happen? Some people believe it is better to aim directly at changing human behaviour and encouraging the development of better technology through market forces, legislative controls, and education.

Changing human behaviour and improving technology

Market forces

Economists have long argued that people over-consume resources and cause pollution because of *market failure*: pricing systems that do not reflect the true cost of one's actions. Until recently householders paid only a fraction of the true cost of water. Motorists pay nothing directly to compensate for the air and water pollution they cause. There is no financial incentive to reduce the amount of garbage a household produces. All these behaviours would, it is argued, change if a realistic sliding scale of charges existed. For example, households in Australia traditionally paid a 'water rate' in proportion to the value of their house, rather than a charge related to the amount of water they actually used. In the Newcastle region in the early 1980s the introduction of a partial 'user pays' system resulted in a 20 per cent reduction in total water consumption compared with expected trends (Pigram 1986, p. 116).

Pricing systems that incorporate the cost to society of pollution and wasteful energy use would also encourage the development of new technology. There would be more incentive for builders to produce energy-efficient housing, and for companies to develop and market 'clean', energy-efficient cars. However, we should not rely too much on a 'technological fix' to environmental problems. It is tempting to argue that affordable solar-powered vehicles will inevitably be developed some day. But their manufacture will still consume a significant amount of energy, and if their availability encourages us to maintain a high-consumption lifestyle in low-density cities, they may simply delay the attainment of truly sustainable urban development.

There are problems with using market forces to encourage environmentally responsible behaviour. 'Polluter pays' charges are hard to calculate and enforce, and economic sanctions in general are politically unpopular and risk hurting people on low incomes more than the affluent. Charges also may have to rise significantly in order to change deeply entrenched behaviour patterns. Increases to water charges in Adelaide in the 1990s only produced a marginal reduction in average domestic use, from 460 litres per day in 1993–4 to 442 litres in 1996–97 (SA Water 1997, p. 75).

Legislative controls

Governments can legislate to impose minimum standards of pollution control, energy efficiency, and resource conservation. This already happens in the case of car engines, and has helped to reduce levels of air pollution (table 7.1). Also, several state governments have recently introduced restrictions on domestic households' use of water. In Adelaide, for example, households in 2004 can only use garden sprinklers before 10.00 a.m. or after 6.00 p.m., and cars can only be washed if parked on permeable surfaces. As a further example, several states have, with federal encouragement, made it compulsory for new houses to have a five-star energy efficiency rating. There is plenty of scope for further legislation. Cars could be banned from city centres. Minimum standards for engine efficiency and emission control could be toughened. Rainwater tanks, solar hot water systems, and efficient insulation could be made compulsory in new housing. Governments in the 1990s favoured deregulation and reliance on market forces rather than the imposition of new controls. But recent trends suggest that state governments in particular are increasingly willing to adopt legislation as the most effective and equitable way to modify behaviour.

Education

Everyone agrees that educating people to take more responsibility for the environmental sustainability of their actions is a good thing. Governments at all levels have put a lot of effort into environmental education programs, especially since the 1992 Rio Earth Summit. Sceptics doubt the effectiveness of education in changing people's behaviour, compared with the heavier weapons of legislation or market forces, and suspect that governments may opt for education because they lack the courage for more direct action. However, no one who works with young people can doubt the change in attitudes over the past twenty years, reflected in a massive rise in enrolments in environmental science or environmental management degrees, and in personal commitment to conservation, recycling, and waste-reduction programs.

So governments—federal, state, and local—can act in a range of ways to change how individuals, households, and businesses affect the environment by their behaviour. The following examples examine some of the successes and failures.

Urban water catchment management

The management of urban water catchments is a specific area where a combination of legislation and education has produced visible results. Until recently, urban rivers and creeks were perceived as little more than natural drains and convenient routeways for freeways or public transport lines. Very often they served as boundaries between local council areas and, guaranteeing a lack of coordinated management, the catchment areas themselves were usually further divided by other local council boundaries that followed the straight lines of nineteenth-century land surveys. But we have finally begun to think of catchment areas as significant sub-regions within major cities, with particular management needs. For example, a Metropolitan Sydney Catchment Authority was established in January 2004, and Catchment Water Management Boards were set up in Adelaide under the powers of the 1997 *Water Resources Act*. Householders in Adelaide pay a catchment environment levy through their local councils to support the Boards, whose activities include constructing trash racks and pollution traps, revegetation projects, running community education programs, and seeking to reduce industrial pollution. The past decade has also seen a large number of *wetlands* created in urban catchments— open water bodies that act as natural filters by holding water during wet seasons and allowing pollutants to settle out rather then being rapidly washed downstream (figures 7.2 and 7.3). Wetlands also act as habitats for native flora and fauna species, and as recreational and educational resources.

Many householders only became aware that they lived in something called a catchment when maps appeared in local newspapers. 'Why am I paying more money because of a map they've drawn?' asked one indignant resident in a letter to the Adelaide *Sunday Mail* (2 April 1995). But catchment management has now become an accepted part of the urban scene.

Local Agenda 21

Local Agenda 21 arose from the 1992 Rio Earth Summit. At the summit the Australian government undertook that by 1996 every local council in the

Figure 7.2 Urban wetlands in construction, 1998, on the Sturt River in Marion LGA, southern Adelaide, as part of a catchment management strategy

Source: Clive Forster

Figure 7.3 Regent Gardens, Adelaide, 1998. Note the small wetland that collects stormwater runoff from the housing development

Source: Clive Forster

country would consult with the local community and prepare a Local Agenda 21, defined by Kupke (1996, p. 183) as 'a long term strategic program for achieving sustainability by the 21st century which integrated environmental, social and economic objectives'. The aim has not been met fully, but an increasing number of local councils in Australian cities have now adopted Local Agenda 21 as a community-based approach to improving sustainability at the local level. Typical activities include revegetation projects, developing and looking after wetlands (figure 7.2), cleaning up streams and coastal areas, environmental education programs, projects to reduce pollution from industrial areas, and plans to encourage bicycle use and reduce energy consumption.

Recycling of household waste

Many local councils have introduced kerbside recycling programs, where materials such as paper, glass, plastics, tins, and garden waste (which makes up 40 per cent of domestic solid waste) are collected separately from other household garbage (figure 7.4) and recycled rather than dumped as landfill. For example Marion council in southern Adelaide has achieved a 60 per cent reduction in the amount of solid waste now going to landfill. Over 90 per cent of households participate in the program by sorting their waste into separate

Figure 7.4 Kerbside recycling, 1998
Source: Clive Forster

bins for collection, even though there is no direct financial benefit. But Australia as a whole fell well short of the national target of reducing the amount of waste going to landfills by 50 per cent between 1992 and 2000 (Australian State of the Environment Committee 2001, p. 106), and more direct legislation or financial incentives are needed.

Environmentally sustainable housing

Housing has a major influence on how much energy, water, and land our cities consume, as well as affecting waste emission (solid, liquid, and atmospheric) and stormwater runoff. If we look at figure 7.1, housing therefore contributes significantly to both the 'input' and 'waste output' sides of the urban metabolic flow model. The sustainability of our cities depends on the houses we live in. Much of the housing and sustainability debate has, as we have seen, focussed on housing density and the merits or otherwise of urban consolidation. But, irrespective of density, there is plenty of evidence that the design of Australian housing is nowhere near as sustainable as it should be. Addressing this problem is a major test of the ability of the three tiers of government to change how our behaviour affects the environment.

What is wrong with our houses? Generally, they are not well designed. Correct orientation and the use of verandahs or eaves should make maximum use of sunlight for lighting and winter warmth in living rooms, while giving maximum protection from summer sun and taking advantage of through ventilation for cooling. Good insulation (including double glazing) can significantly cut power use for heating and cooling. But most modern houses do not have these features. Developers do not take account of orientation factors when laying out streets. Design fashions seem more important than function, and home buyers place short-term cost considerations ahead of long-term benefits. Air conditioners therefore become almost essential, and heating and lighting take more power than necessary.

The choice of building materials is also important. There are three issues here: thermal mass, embodied energy, and harm to the environment. Parts of buildings with significant *thermal mass*, such as solid, thick walls and foundations, act as heat and coolness 'stores' and cut down on the fluctuations in internal temperature that require energy for heating or cooling. *Embodied energy* is the energy needed to build the house, including the energy used to manufacture building materials. Some materials such as concrete, steel, bricks, and tiles require a lot of energy to produce. Building a house from them can represent a significant expenditure of energy and emission of greenhouse gases, representing a significant proportion of the total energy used and emissions produced in a building's lifetime (Troy et al. 2003). Some building materials should also be avoided because of *harm to the environment*. For example using non-renewable, old growth hardwood timbers threatens biodiversity. Some glues, paints, plastics, and synthetic building materials incorporate harmful substances, or their manufacturing produces harmful wastes. High mass/low embodied energy materials such as mud brick, rammed earth, and straw bales should therefore be encouraged, together with plantation timber or recycled wood. But the building industry, and until recently many local councils when considering applications to build houses, tend to be suspicious of innovative, environmentally sensitive, building materials and design.

In addition to the demands of heating, cooling, and lighting, our houses are packed with an increasing array of appliances—mainly electrical—and domestic energy use continues to climb. To meet these energy needs, houses depend almost totally on mains power generated by burning fossil fuels and thus depleting non-renewable resources and producing greenhouse gases. 'Smart housing' systems where computers control lighting, heating, cooling, and other appliances, can reduce power needs but are uncommon. Another approach is for houses to generate some or all of their own power from renewable, non-polluting sources. Solar hot water systems have been on the market for over thirty years, and photovoltaic cells for general domestic power generation are now available, but are still not widely used because of short-term cost, and aesthetic considerations. Some housing developments even specifically prohibit units on roofs facing the street.

Our conventional suburban gardens demand a lot of water, especially in Melbourne, Adelaide, and Perth where summers are very dry. Yet few houses now have rainwater tanks and few houses are designed to retain and absorb stormwater on site, although some whole subdivisions have system of wetlands. Almost all houses in our cities are attached to mains sewerage, and have weekly collection of solid waste that must go to landfill. Kerbside recycling is almost universal, and some households have compost bins or worm farms. But grey water is seldom recycled and sewage is almost never treated on-site.

So to be more environmentally sustainable our housing should be designed and built to minimise energy consumption for lighting, heating, and cooling. Building practices should make maximum use of recycled and low-energy building materials with good thermal mass, whose manufacture is not harmful to the environment. Houses should use renewable energy sources where possible. We should minimise the use of mains water by good design of gardens and appliances, by recycling, and by storing stormwater. We should absorb and recycle as much waste water, sewage, and solid waste as possible. The question is; how to get closer to these standards? What are the possible policy approaches, and how successful have they been so far?

Improving the sustainability of housing involves a wide range of players. All three levels of government are involved (chapter 6) plus developers, builders, and the financial institutions responsible for housing loans, as well as the householders who make the final decisions about the type of dwelling to buy or rent. There are many possible reasons why sustainability measures have not been incorporated into houses: lack of awareness of the issues; concerns about cost; inflexible local building regulations; poor energy-pricing policies; and the inherent conservatism of the building industry and householders.

Until recently, governments have mainly concentrated on encouraging better housing design by education programs and demonstration projects. During the 1990s the federal government's Green Street and AMCORD projects for new residential development standards demonstrated the possibility of more compact, energy-efficient, and water-efficient (yet basically conventional) housing. Regent Gardens (figure 7.3), 8 km from the centre of Adelaide, is a mixture of 1200 small-lot, medium-density, and conventional houses on the site of an old public hospital and institution. A small wetland filters stormwater before it drains to an artificial aquifer, from where it can be pumped to irrigate surrounding reserves. The Sydney 2000 Olympic village became, after the Games, the focus of the new suburb of Newington, with a similar range of sustainability features plus solar power generation (figure 7.5).

Figure 7.5 The Newington sustainable housing development, Sydney, 2003: note the main stadium for the 2000 Olympic Games in the background.

Source: Clive Forster

More ambitious demonstration projects such as the New Haven Village at Port Adelaide show that it is possible to make major savings in energy consumption through better insulation, better use of sunlight for winter light and warmth, and more efficient heating and cooling systems. At the same time, outputs of stormwater, sewage, and solid waste are almost eliminated by recycling and reusing on site. Some of these features have now been incorporated into the Delfin Lend-Lease company's master planned community at Mawson Lakes.

Perhaps the most ambitious demonstration project of all is the privately developed Christie Walk EcoCity development in central Adelaide, founded by Urban Ecology Australia (figure 7.6). In Christie Walk, day-to-day inputs of resources and energy and outputs of waste are minimised, both through recycling and by careful design to reduce the need for heating and cooling. The houses also incorporate a minimum of embodied energy. They make extensive use of low-energy materials such as straw bales and lightweight building blocks, as well as recycled material such as salvaged hardwood, and renewable resources such as plantation timber.

Figure 7.6 Christie Walk, Adelaide, 2003: environmentally sustainable housing incorporating solar power systems, stormwater capture and storage, and extensive use of recycled materials

Source: Clive Forster

There is no doubt that the better housing design represented by these projects can make our cities more sustainable. But ordinary developers, builders and householders have been slow to adopt the ideas they demonstrate, generally for short-term cost reasons. Governments have attempted to overcome this reluctance by financial incentives such as subsidies for householders installing solar power systems, and water-saving devices such as low-pressure shower heads and dual-flush toilets. In addition, rising 'user pays' prices for water and power under new privatisation or outsourcing arrangements (chapter 6) provide incentives for householders to cut consumption. And state governments in particular, as discussed earlier, are increasingly willing to legislate to enforce better minimum standards of housing design. In 2003 the Victorian Department of Sustainability and Environment set specific targets for reducing water and energy conservation, for example to reduce Melbourne's drinking water use per capita by 15 per cent by 2010; and to be recycling 20 per cent of Melbourne's wastewater by 2010. Such targets will only be possible with specific financial incentives, and with legislative sanctions to change the decision-making behaviour of individual households, both when choosing housing and when deciding how to live in it. But legislation and incentives designed to improve environmental sustainability will also need to take account of economic and social issues in an era of declining housing affordability and increasing housing inequality, as discussed in chapter 4. It is also important not to concentrate solely on new housing. Most of the houses we will be living in twenty years from now have already been built and residents need assistance and incentives to undertake the often expensive task of retrofitting their dwellings to make them more sustainable (figure 7.7)

Transport and sustainable cities

Transport is clearly a key issue in determining how environmentally sustainable Australian cities will be in future. Our current high level of dependence on the automobile (table 7.2) is a major cause of demand for resource inputs of non-renewable fossil fuels, and waste outputs of greenhouse gases and atmospheric pollution (figure 7.1). In recent years, policies to tackle automobile dependence have largely concentrated on attempting to change urban form, particularly through the adoption of urban consolidation. But, as discussed earlier, the problems involved with urban consolidation suggest that more direct attempts to change people's transport choices and behaviour are also needed. What are the options?

Unfortunately for transport planners and environmentalists, most of us like cars. For a lot of our transport needs they provide unrivalled convenience and flexibility. Cars are also heavily marketed as status symbols, as sexy, and as

Figure 7.7 Retro-fitting for sustainability, Adelaide, 2003: a conventional 1970s house with roof and rooms re-oriented to face north and fitted with solar panels for power generation

Source: Clive Forster

just plain fun to own and drive. Critics can point to the falseness of the advertising, the high real costs of using cars, the environmental issues, the deaths and injuries through road accidents, the congestion, the parking problems, and so on. But most of us still happily buy and use cars. We support the idea of public transport, but for most of our transport needs it seems inconvenient, even unsafe (particularly for women travelling at night), or simply unavailable when and where we need it. Cycling or walking may be wholesome and virtuous, but impractical for most needs. Even car-pooling is unappealing, given the complex nature of our transport needs. Our attitudes towards the alternatives to driving resemble the general attitude towards Brussels sprouts. We acknowledge in the abstract that they may be good for us, but on any given day we prefer not to consume them.

Persuasion and education have made little impact on our love of the automobile for personal transport. According to a survey in the 1990s (quoted in Newton 1997, p. 154) only 5 per cent of Australians would be willing to drive less in order to reduce air pollution, compared with almost 70 per cent who are happy to participate in recycling programs. In the outer suburbs, young people grow up associating car ownership with freedom and mobility and often have negative attitudes towards public transport. In a study by Bickl (1997, p. 47), school students in southern Adelaide were asked about their attitudes towards public transport. One replied as follows: 'public transport is the last thing you try if you haven't got anything else to go by'. According to another respondent: 'sometimes you don't want to be around anybody and you have to go on public transport and sit next to full-on ferals...' Faced with these attitudes, governments can adopt three main approaches. They can attempt to make public transport, cycling, and walking more attractive. They can attempt to make car driving less attractive. And they can continue to educate and persuade.

Mees (2000) argues that public transport can be a viable alternative to the car, even in low-density cities, providing the service is fast, frequent, and reliable, with the different modes (bus, tram, train, and ferry) integrated into one system of routes, timetabling, and ticketing. Integration may be achieved through better planning, but making public transport more attractive generally costs money. It is very expensive to extend networks, increase the frequency of services, upgrade the rolling stock or vehicles, improve safety, and so on. Because the services are heavily subsidised (for example in Adelaide it is estimated that fares cover only 20 per cent of the cost of providing the service), state governments must meet the cost of improvements. But, as discussed in chapter 6, governments have been under heavy pressure to reduce public spending, not increase it. In Victoria the state government privatised Melbourne's tram and rail services in 1998, having already sold off the public bus services. In both Adelaide and Perth, the bus services have been contracted-out to private companies, though the state governments retain control over network planning (Mees 2003).

Given the above circumstances, the state governments are probably doing as much as they can. Systems are now being maintained rather than cut back, and there has been some new investment. The Perth railway system was significantly improved in the 1980s (chapter 3). Melbourne's tram fleet has been partly upgraded and a line extended to Box Hill in the eastern suburbs (figure 7.8). In Sydney a new light rail line (figure 7.9) has been built from the city centre to Lilyfield via Ultimo–Pyrmont. Similarly, all states now recognise in their planning documents the need to encourage cycling and walking by providing more dedicated cycleways, secure cycle storage at public transport interchanges, pedestrian overpasses, and other minor infrastructure improvements.

There are recent signs of slightly reduced car dependence, or at worst no significant increase (tables 3.3 and 3.4). But the changes are marginal. The South Australian government aims to increase public transport's share of

Figure 7.8 The new tram line to Box Hill, Melbourne, 2004

Source: Clive Forster

Figure 7.9 The Sydney light rail system, 2003: the line runs from Central Station to Lilyfield via Star City casino and Ultimo–Pyrmont. Note also the Darling Harbour monorail.

Source: Clive Forster

weekday passenger trips in Adelaide from the current 5 per cent to 10 per cent by 2018, and to double the use of bicycles (Government of South Australia 2003). Melbourne's target is that by 2020 the share of all motorised trips taken by public transport will be 20 per cent, compared with 9 per cent in 2002 (Victoria Department of Infrastructure 2002). If these and similar targets are to be met, moderate improvements in services and infrastructure will not be enough.

To look at the other side of the equation, can (and should) governments make driving cars less attractive? One line of argument is that motorists do not pay for the real social and environmental costs of using cars and that if they were compelled to do so, other forms of transport would be used more. Petrol is already taxed heavily, partly on environmental grounds, but the rate could be increased. Vehicle registration fees and parking charges could be raised. Motorists could be charged for entering city centres. In 2003 London introduced a Congestion Charging scheme under which people living outside the inner city are charged the equivalent of $A12 per day if they drive a car into the inner area. After six months of operation, the number of vehicles entering inner London had fallen by 15 per cent and congestion was reduced by 30 per cent. The revenue raised will pay for improvements to public transport.

There are several problems with such schemes. In cities with very high levels of car ownership they are bound to be politically unpopular. Any individual state government would be concerned that imposing much higher charges on motorists would damage its capital city's attractiveness to potential business investors or migrants if other states kept their charges low. City centre businesses are afraid of losing customers to suburban centres if driving or parking is made too expensive or difficult. Equity is also involved. Fees or fuel taxes that apply equally to everyone will hit low-income people hard, while rich people can afford them easily. If people are to be priced out of their cars, we also need to be sure that alternative forms of transport are actually available. There is a case for making car driving and parking more expensive and difficult, especially in the inner areas of the larger and more congested cities of Sydney and Melbourne, but the equity issues need to be addressed. In all the cities there is a strong case for encouraging the use of smaller, more fuel-efficient, and less polluting vehicles, including hybrid cars running partly on electric power.

All the mainland states continue to run advertising and education campaigns attempting to woo drivers out of their cars and on to public transport, bicycles, or their own feet. Measures range from advertisements on the backs of Adelaide buses highlighting the high real costs of running a car, to the *TravelSmart* programs operating in every state and the ACT, with the support of the federal Australian Greenhouse Office. The *TravelSmart* programs vary in nature, but all aim to bring about voluntary changes in travel behaviour in targeted suburbs, schools, or workplaces. They mainly work by analysing people's current travel patterns and discussing with them how car use can be reduced, while stressing the environmental and health benefits of such a reduction. Road transport planning now concentrates on *demand management*, rather than the old approach of *predict and provide*: predicting demand for car traffic and then providing the roads and other infrastructure to meet that demand.

Improving the sustainability of urban transport clearly needs a multifaceted approach. Planning authorities should continue low-key consolidation policies such as medium-density infill developments on vacant urban land; redevelopment of old public housing estates, with mixed uses and higher densities; and the encouragement of mixed densities and land uses on the urban fringe. Some of these developments could profitably incorporate 'urban village' ideas. Planning authorities should also encourage the growth of district centres where these have had some success, and reinforce their role as nodes in the public transport system. They should develop more cycleways and seek other means of encouraging cycling and walking. They can expect some increase in the small proportion of people who currently use telecommunications and computer technology to work at home, and it may be possible to encourage this.

But it is vital to recognise that most households in Australian cities will, for the foreseeable future, continue to live in conventional low-density suburbia. Their members will need to travel at various times of the day—for work and other things—to a range of destinations difficult to reach at present except by private car. To change this, as Stretton (1994) suggests, will require policies directly addressing the comparative costs and benefits of cars and public transport. State governments should increase investment in metropolitan public transport and seek arrangements with local government and private enterprise to diversify the nature of services. On the other hand, they should not build commuter freeways or tollways because they unavoidably increase car dependence and the low-density fringe expansion that feeds it (figure 7.10). Excessive car use should also be discouraged by fuel pricing policies, parking restrictions, and traffic calming devices. But, because even then most people will still treasure the convenience and flexibility of the private car, governments will need to enforce higher standards of fuel efficiency and pollution control and encourage research into alternative power sources.

Summary

Education, legislation, and, to a lesser extent, pricing policies have produced some improvements in the environmental sustainability of Australian cities, particularly better water catchment management and some reductions in

Figure 7.10 The Southern Expressway, Adelaide, 1998
Source: Clive Forster

domestic water use and the production of solid waste. But their impact on the major problems of energy use, atmospheric pollution and greenhouse gas emissions has so far not been great, and governments, particularly in the vital areas of housing and transport, have tended to favour the 'softer' approach of education rather than the less popular but more effective weapons of legislation and market forces.

Sustainability, equity, and prosperity?

Although it seems at first glance impossible to disagree with, environmentally sustainable development is a *political* concept, and a controversial one at that. It implies that we can combine long-term environmental sustainability with economic development. But, as we have seen, measures to reduce resource inputs and waste outputs often conflict with economic development. They can also threaten equity or social justice. Figure 7.11 summarises these conflicts.

As Campbell (1996, p. 298–9) puts it, writing from a North American viewpoint:

> The economic development planner sees the city as a location where production, consumption, distribution and innovation take place. The city is in

competition with other cities for markets and for new industries. Space is the economic space of highways, market areas, and commuter zones.

The environmental planner sees the city as a consumer of resources and a producer of wastes. The city is in competition with nature for scarce resources and land, and always poses a threat to nature. Space is the ecological space of greenways, river basins, and ecological niches.

The equity planner sees the city as a location of conflict over the distribution of resources, of services and opportunities. The competition is within the city itself, among different social groups. Space is the social space of communities, neighbourhood organisations, labor unions, the space of access and segregation.

The three perspectives should be easily recognisable from earlier parts of this book. Economic development and competition was discussed in chapters 2 and 3, equity in chapter 4, and environment in this chapter.

Conflicts between the economic growth and equity perspectives are not hard to find: for example, in the uneven impacts on rich and poor areas of economic restructuring and reduced spending on public services. Conflicts between the economic growth and environmental perspectives are easy to envisage, too. Business interests often argue that tough anti-pollution laws will scare off investment and cost jobs. Conflicts between environmental and

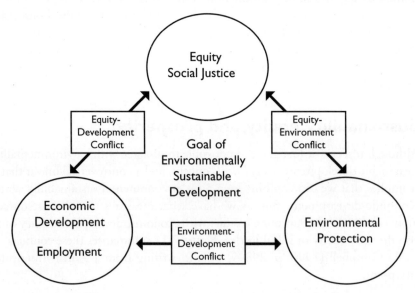

Figure 7.11 Conflicts between environmental protection, equity, and economic growth
Source: adapted from Campbell 1996, p. 296

equity perspectives are perhaps less obvious. However, they can happen where 'user pays' policies discourage the over-use of resources such as water or fuel. The wealthy can afford higher charges without much difficulty, leaving poor households to bear the burden of reducing consumption.

More complex *inter-generational equity* issues can also arise. Cities would expand less rapidly and probably be more environmentally sustainable if all new housing on the city margins was subject to tough 'user pays' charges for connection to power, water, roads, and other services. But this would force house prices up, particularly affecting young people buying their first house. At the same time older people in the inner suburbs, who did not have to pay such charges when their houses were built years ago, would receive a windfall gain as the rising price of new housing makes their houses worth more on the market.

The search for environmental sustainability therefore seems inevitably to involve some conflicts with other goals such as equity and economic development. The concept of environmentally sustainable *development* implies that these conflicts can be resolved successfully without major sacrifice, and therefore has obvious appeal. But advocates of more radical 'green' policies doubt this, and argue that true sustainability will require significant changes to society's commitment to economic growth and high levels of consumption.

Conclusion

Governments in Australia have endorsed the goal of environmentally sustainable urban development for well over a decade. In that time, what has been achieved?

- Legislation has forced car makers to produce vehicles that are more energy efficient and emit less pollution.
- The move towards 'user pays' water rates has produced slight reductions in use by domestic consumers.
- Kerbside recycling of domestic waste is now the norm.
- Catchment management programs are beginning to reduce levels of water pollution, via wetlands, trash racks, and clean-up schemes.
- Local Agenda 21 programs have raised public awareness about environmental issues and helped start coastal management, revegetation, and other measures at the community level.
- Young people are much more conscious of environmental problems.
- Urban consolidation policies pursued by state governments and sponsored by the federal Better Cities program have produced modest increases in residential density.

- A significant percentage (up to half in Sydney) of new dwelling approvals are now for medium-density housing (chapter 4) and inner suburban areas have experienced some revitalisation (chapter 5).
- There have been a few improvements in public transport systems, particularly in Perth (chapter 3).

The above list is in some ways very impressive. But the 2001 Census shows that car dependence continues at very high levels (table 3.3). The level of urban water use remains high and wasteful. Air pollution is a serious health issue. Australian cities continue to generate increasing amounts of greenhouse gases, an issue largely ducked by the federal government at the 1997 Kyoto Climate Change Conference. Levels of energy use remain high by international standards. Urban expansion still threatens biodiversity through vegetation clearance and the pollution of marine and coastal ecosystems. A survey in 1999 (ABS 1999) showed that even though 43 per cent of Australians believed that environmental quality had fallen over the previous ten years, only 9 per cent regarded it as the most important social issue facing us (compared with 30 per cent for health, 26 per cent for crime, 17 per cent for education, and 13 per cent for unemployment). Also, the level of concern about individual issues such as air pollution was almost invariably lower than in a similar survey carried out in 1992.

We have, it seems, adopted the relatively painless environmental policies while ducking the hard issues that challenge our comfortable way of life. At one level, we are happy to recycle our rubbish and join local volunteer groups to clean up catchments, and we put up with higher water charges. At another more abstract level, most of us seem to accept the 'conventional wisdom' that urban consolidation is a desirable long-term planning policy—providing it does not change how *we* live. Neither of these things affects our individual daily lives very much. Most of us cling to a suburban lifestyle based on high levels of energy consumption and waste production. And we are not enthusiastic about the prospect of using public transport instead of our beloved cars.

As the recent report *Creating a Sustainable Adelaide* (Giradet 2003) stresses, there is no one key to more sustainable cities. To tackle the hard issues of significantly reducing resource inputs and waste outputs, planning policies that encourage changes in urban structure along the lines Newton (1997) suggests have their place. So have education programs, demonstration projects, and the like. But these policies will not suffice on their own. They must be pursued in conjunction with harnessing market forces, and enacting legislation to encourage better technology and change people's behaviour in our existing suburbs. There is much to do.

8

Urban Futures?

In our examination of the changing geography of Australia's major cities we have looked in turn at five major topics:

1 employment, workforce participation, and urban structure
2 housing supply and demand
3 patterns of residential differentiation and inequality
4 urban government and service provision
5 urban environmental issues.

Those earlier chapters suggest that Australian cities have changed significantly since 1991. In retrospect, the 1990s was a watershed decade. As pointed out in the Introduction, we have experienced one of the longest periods of economic growth in Australia's history. But the benefits of that growth have been unequally shared and some taken-for-granted aspects of our quality of urban life seem under threat: decent employment prospects; affordable home-ownership; high quality public education and health services; reliable and affordable power and water supplies. At the same time we have become acutely aware of the environmental problems created by our cities. What are the key changes?

Economically, the period since 1991 has seen the strengthening impact of globalisation on Australian cities. Our cities' economies have restructured to become increasingly dominated by professional and administrative employment in producer and consumer services, at the expense of blue-collar jobs. There are also signs, especially in Sydney and Melbourne, of emerging 'dual economies' in a spatial sense: the prosperous core and inner regions, like Sydney's 'Global Arc', whose businesses and residents have benefited most from increasing integration into the global economy, are increasingly divorced from the remaining middle and outer suburbs. The nature of work itself also continues to change. More people work long hours while at the other extreme more people don't work at all, despite falling unemployment rates. More jobs are insecure, part-time, or casual in nature. Overall, work is shared more unequally and household incomes reflect this.

Chapter 3 argued that the 1990s was definitely a watershed decade for housing. The supply of public rental housing declined significantly as the federal government slashed funding and state governments pursued policies of sales and redevelopment of old estates. Private rental housing became more difficult to access. And, despite low interest rates, by 2003 the affordability of home ownership was at its worst for thirteen years. The average size of new houses continues to grow, but medium- and high-density apartments now make up an increasing percentage of new dwellings, especially in Sydney and Melbourne. As the same time, households have become smaller and more varied in composition as the population structure ages. Are we seeing the end of the Great Australian Dream of families owning their own house in the suburbs?

Patterns of residential segregation are also changing. The inner suburbs continue to prosper through gentrification and new high-rise residential projects such as and Sydney's Ultimo–Pyrmont and Melbourne's Southbank–Docklands (figures 5.4 & 5.6). Many older middle suburbs are undergoing redevelopment and urban consolidation (figures 4.8 & 5.9). The character of outer and fringe suburbs is becoming more varied as master planned communities (figure 5.11) create patches of affluence in once-working-class sectors of town. Ethnic diversity continues to increase, particularly in Sydney and Melbourne, with controversies about multiculturalism and enclaves. Areas of population growth and decline can now be found throughout the inner, middle, and outer suburbs. The old generalisations about sectors of different social status, concentric rings of different age structure and growth rates, and patches of different ethnic composition are being replaced by a finer-grained and more complex residential mosaic. But there are still significant concentrations of disadvantage, and in the 1990s we invented the term *social exclusion* to describe the phenomenon and its consequences.

Our cities are governed and managed differently. The 1990s was the decade of the 'shrinking state', with what Gleeson and Low (2000) refer to as the rise of neoliberalism and increasing reliance on market forces rather than government direction. At the federal level the decade began with a Labor government committed to 'Building Better Cities', but the victory of the Howard-led Coalition in 1996 saw an almost complete retreat from federal involvement in urban policy. State governments, led by the Kennett government in Victoria, slashed their workforces, rationalised the provision of public services, and privatised or outsourced key utilities such as water, power, and public transport. Maintaining the economic competitiveness of their capital city in the national and global economic systems became the key aim. Local government came under heavy pressure to rationalise, led again by the Kennett government's forced council amalgamations and financial reforms in Melbourne.

On a different note, the 1990s saw environmental issues establish themselves firmly on the urban policy agenda. Metropolitan planning policies pledged themselves to pursue environmental sustainability. Urban water catchment management boards were set up. Kerbside recycling programs became almost universal. Housing demonstration projects like Regent Gardens and Christie Walk in Adelaide (figures 7.3 & 7.6) sprung up, pointing the way towards dwellings that used less energy and water, and recycled more of their waste. Urban consolidation actually began to happen. We even saw levels of car use peak by the mid 1990s and then begin slowly to decline, together with a rise in public transport patronage. But our cities continue, in the view of most analysts, to be environmentally unsustainable in their present form.

In addition, it can be argued that significant changes are occurring in the values or ideals that will shape our attitudes and expectations. One planner (Reynolds 2003 pers. comm.) summarises the changes as follows:

1990s	Future
home, family, stability	diverse, multiple, unstable values
egalitarian	differentiated
young	older: biggest age groups 55+
households as decision makers	individual decision makers
low-density suburbs	mixed-density suburbs
8 hour city	24 hour city
wasteful resource use	prudent resource use

Given the changes we have experienced, how are Australian cities likely to develop in the future? In considering that question and the policy issues it raises, there is a danger, as argued in the Introduction, that the conventional division of material into chapters, necessary as it may be for a thorough consideration of each topic, might cause us to lose sight of the connections between them. This final chapter therefore attempts to 'put it all together' by emphasising the interrelatedness of the topics, before examining some key debates about what Australian cities might be like in the future, and what public policy can, and should, do to shape that urban future.

Putting it all together

The topics covered in chapters 3–7 reflect a number of common themes. They all show clearly the impact of the global economic restructuring discussed in chapter 2. They all illustrate the relationship between that restructuring, with its predominantly economic and technological components, and important demographic changes. All reflect the actions of governments, and are key elements in policy debates about the efficiency, equity, and ecological sustainability of future urban development. But as well as sharing some common causes and raising some common policy issues, the topics also strongly affect one another. It is not simply that questions such as 'are our cities becoming more unequal?' and 'are our cities ecologically sustainable?' involve jobs, transportation, housing, segregation, government, and services. We can only address the questions properly by understanding how all these things interact in particular cities and parts of cities.

To illustrate the importance of the interactions involved, consider the relationships between employment, housing, and public services. Employment—or lack of it—determines income, which in turn determines the amount of choice one has in the housing market. The location of employment, particularly in the larger cities, can also restrict one's housing options. So 'work' tends to determine 'home'. But, conversely, people seeking to enter the labour force or to change jobs find that where they live determines the range of jobs within feasible travelling distance. 'Home' can therefore determine 'work', particularly in the case of people without cars, or part-time and casual workers who cannot afford to travel far.

The nature of public services also affects people's ability to participate in work. Public transport and the quality of local education and training programs are obvious examples. Fincher (1989) also points out that the availability of local child-care and aged-care services can have an important bearing on the ability of women to enter employment. But again the relationship is two-way. Areas where a high proportion of residents are in well-paid jobs can support better local public services, or can afford to pay privately for services. In low-income areas, policy changes such as a reduction or increase in support for child-care services will have greater impacts.

So 'home', 'work', 'services', transportation, and so on are all connected by a web of two-way relationships. It is not hard to see how this web can intensify the impact of economic restructuring on particular regions within cities. The preceding chapters have described how working-class suburban areas in western Sydney, western and south-eastern Melbourne, and northern Adelaide have suffered from changes in employment, housing, and service provision— changes that reinforce one another to maintain and intensify the 'disadvantaged' image the areas carry—to their further detriment (figures 5.15 & 5.16). It is an oversimplification to classify whole regions within cities as 'losers' and others as 'winners'. But there are stark and increasing contrasts between these working-class areas and more affluent suburbs. The contrasts show in income levels, unemployment rates, and other forms of welfare dependence. They show in the quality of housing and how desirable the areas are perceived to be as residential areas. They show in the quality of local services and in the nature of accessible job opportunities.

Clear linkages also exist, as discussed in chapter 7, between the nature of housing, the location of employment, questions of equity, and the environmental sustainability of our cities. Figure 7.11 (p. 190) summarises in a simplified manner the conflicts that need to be resolved.

With the admirable exception of bodies such as the Urban Frontiers Program at the University of Western Sydney, there tends to be an 'academic division of labour' between researchers working on economic development and employment, those working on housing and social structure, those whose main interests are in transportation, and those researching environmental issues. Geographers in particular should never lose sight of the interrelationships, and the significance for public policy of the outcomes they produce in different regions.

Shaping the future? Metropolitan planning strategies

Recent trends, as summarised in chapter 2, suggest that some of our major cities are going to grow more rapidly than others. ABS population projections published in 2003 (table 8.1) estimate that by 2021 Sydney will have a population of around 5 million, Melbourne over 4 million, Brisbane over 2 million, and Perth approaching 2 million. Adelaide, the slowest-growing major city, is expected to have a population of 1.1–1.2 million. Looking further ahead, Sydney is expected to have reached around 6 million by 2051, and Melbourne 4.5 million.

Even in the slower growing cities, the population projections, when combined with the continued decline demographers expect in average household size (chapter 4), suggest major demands for new housing. Perth is expected to need an extra 400 000 dwellings by 2021; even Adelaide will need almost 100 000. Sydney and Melbourne are already so big that even modest growth

Table 8.1 Major city population projections, 2021–51

	Projected population ('000) 2021		Projected population ('000) 2051	
	high estimate	*low estimate*	*high estimate*	*low estimate*
Sydney	5143	4987	6216	5705
Melbourne	4178	4102	4639	4493
Brisbane	2364	2083	3311	2511
Adelaide	1221	1142	1229	1031
Perth	1930	1725	2565	1982

Source: ABS 2003d, p. 117

rates will generate demand for large numbers of dwellings. The latest Melbourne planning strategy assumes that an extra 600 000 households will need to be housed by 2030, and Sydney expects to need 500 000 new dwellings over the next 20 years or so.

How do the various state governments intend to cope with these demands, not only for housing but for new roads, sewerage systems, water and power services, schools, hospitals, public transport, and other services? And how are the 'triple bottom line' aims of economic growth and efficiency, environmental sustainability, and equity (figure 7.11) going to be pursued and reconciled? Each state has a metropolitan planning strategy for its capital city, setting out aims for the development of urban structure over the next 20–30 years. The following strategies were available from the relevant departments' websites early in 2004:

- New South Wales: *Shaping Our Cities* (covering the period to 2021)
- Victoria: *Melbourne 2030: Planning for Sustainable Growth*
- Queensland: *SEQ 2021: A Sustainable Future*
- Western Australia: *Plan for the Sustainable Development of Greater Perth* (in preparation, but a series of published technical papers cover the period to 2031)
- South Australia: *Planning Strategy for Metropolitan Adelaide* (covering the period to 2016).

Naturally, the strategies reflect the differences between the major cities identified in earlier chapters. As we have seen, the cities do differ significantly, not only in projected rates of population and household growth, but also in economic structures and prospects, the nature of their current housing stocks, and the nature of their physical environments. But the various planning strategies also reflect a common set of key challenges, and to some extent a common set of philosophies and approaches to meeting the challenges. All stress, in their titles or their introductory vision statements, the aim of sustainable development and the importance of adopting the 'triple bottom-line' criteria of equity, environmental sustainability, and economic efficiency. For example the Premier's introduction to *Melbourne 2030* speaks of a 'vision that balances economic, social and environmental goals, so that our children will enjoy an even better quality of life'. All see more compact cities as a key to achieving these visions, and the Melbourne and Adelaide plans adopt urban growth boundaries to limit the extent of future fringe growth and direct more new housing into the already-developed urban area.

All the strategy documents emphasise the need for economic growth and employment. 'Economic activity' heads the list of priorities in the Adelaide plan, while the Sydney plan aims for 'a robust economy that can provide employment and a high quality of life for all people' and one of the Melbourne plan's key directions is 'a more prosperous city'. All recognise in various ways the need for a supply of affordable and appropriate housing. All express concern about automobile dependence. As discussed in chapter 7, several set targets for increased levels of public transport and cycle use, and all seek to encourage the growth of employment and services in clusters or centres served by public transport. For example, one of the Sydney plan's key principles is to 'identify and create opportunities for employment and business growth in locations that support access by public transport and minimise conflict with other uses'. Finally, all the strategies recognise heritage issues and seek to protect features of cultural and historical significance.

Implementation?

All the plans are laudable in their aims, but the means by which they seek to achieve those aims raise some important questions. O'Connor's (2003) review of the Melbourne 2030 strategy identifies a range of issues. His main concern, as discussed in more detail later in this chapter, is the strategy's reliance on more compact growth—in other words, urban consolidation—as a means of reducing automobile dependence and generally achieving more environmental sustainability. O'Connor also questions the feasibility of attempting to concentrate commerce, services, and higher-density housing into clusters or centres, given the disappointing history of previous attempts to do so (see the discussion of multi-centralisation in chapter 7). Finally, he argues that setting an urban growth boundary is likely to create a land shortage, force land prices up, and make housing even more unaffordable for low-income households.

The Melbourne 2030 strategy, like the other metropolitan plans, also faces some key problems of implementation. As O'Connor (2003) points out, urban development always involves large costs for new infrastructure or for upgrading old services, and the plan does not address how a state government is to meet these costs, other than implying that more compact development will keep costs down. The privatisation and outsourcing of services such as water supply, energy supply, and public transport has robbed the state of potentially powerful means of shaping the nature of future urban growth. O'Connor also raises the set of issues discussed at the end of chapter 6 in this book. Implementing the Melbourne strategy, or any of the other plans for the growth of a whole metropolitan area, will involve dealing with conflicts between overall aims, and the interests and attitudes of individual local communities. Each state has a different set of planning and development laws, but all face the dilemma of how to reconcile local government's day-to-day control of new development with the pursuit of longer-term and metropolitan-wide strategic aims. They also face the prospect of dealing with resident protest groups such as *Save Our Suburbs* (Lewis 1999), determined to defend their local neighbourhoods against what they see as undesirable and unfair changes in character. In practical political terms, achieving more efficient, equitable, and sustainable cities will depend largely on how we reconcile these dilemmas and problems.

Key debates: Economic development, sustainability, and equity

Three debates have dominated recent discussions about the future of our cities, and point to the most important challenges now facing urban policy-makers (Hall 1999). The first concerns the search for economic viability in an increasingly globalised world. The second is the long-running debate about urban form and urban consolidation. The third—social exclusion/inclusion—reflects the continuing concern about social disadvantage, and the recognition that the benefits of a decade of economic growth appear to have been shared very unequally within our cities. We shall examine each in turn.

Economic development, globalisation, and urban policy

As pointed out in the Introduction, globalisation became the buzzword during the 1990s. Academic writers, politicians, and the popular media alike saw the exposure of our cities to intensified international influence and competition as explaining many of the things discussed in earlier chapters. The decline of manufacturing and the rise of producer-services jobs (see chapters 2 and 3), increasing polarisation and social inequality, gentrification, and inner-city revitalisation have all been at least partly attributed to globalisation.

The forces of globalisation are also often portrayed as leaving urban policy-makers little choice: the *globalisation steamroller* or the TINA (there is no alternative) syndrome, as Stilwell (1997) caricatures it. According to the TINA view, the essential aim of urban policy must be to improve a city's global competitiveness so as to attract investment and employment. This means more than simply image-building and the other aspects of *urban entrepreneurialism* discussed in chapter 2. Because cities are competing against one another to have the lowest taxes and the best credit ratings, privatisation and reduced spending on public services are also portrayed as an inevitable result of globalisation. For urban planners, social and environmental considerations are also in danger of being regarded as unaffordable luxuries, because they might deter potential investors. The Kennett government in Victoria in the 1990s (chapter 6) epitomised the TINA syndrome, but all the states and the

Commonwealth have used the rhetoric of globalisation to justify so-called economic rationalist policies. According to the *Melbourne Metropolitan Strategy* document published in 1994:

> Melbourne's continuing competitiveness depends on enhancing its existing advantages and overcoming its disadvantages. The Government's role in this process is to establish a strategic framework that facilitates quality development and provides greater certainty for business. The role of business in implementing the strategy will be crucial (Victoria, Department of Planning and Development 1994, p. 1).

Critics of the TINA syndrome do not deny the existence of globalisation as a phenomenon. But they reject the view that reductions in government services, increasing reliance on the private market, and a retreat from concerns about equity and quality of life are the inevitable response. They point out that the liveability of Australian cities is one of their key comparative advantages (as acknowledged in the Victorian report quoted above). So is their political stability. Yet the over-enthusiastic pursuit of economic competitiveness can threaten both liveability and stability. Symptoms of this include the public disillusionment with both major political parties that stems from concerns about, among other matters, the sale of public assets such as Telstra and cuts in public health and education services. Other symptoms are increasing levels of local protest over aircraft noise near metropolitan airports, the building of telecommunication towers, cable roll-outs, freeway construction, and similar urban issues.

Stillwell (1997) argues that urban policy is now in a 'three-way squeeze' between a trio of competing forces. The first force is the desire for low costs and economic competitiveness so as to attract international capital investment. The second force is the increasing level of public concern about threats to liveability, equity, and environmental quality posed by cuts in government services and reductions in planning controls. The third force comes from what Stilwell sees as an often-forgotten aspect of globalisation—the increasing (although as yet small) pressure to develop international standards in areas such as environmental protection, human rights, and labour conditions. Australia is, for example, party to international agreements concerning targets for reduced emission of greenhouse gases and gases harmful to the ozone layer. Such standards currently have few 'teeth' when it comes to enforcement, but are likely to become increasingly influential.

The various state government documents that set out current planning strategies for Australia's major cities all express a commitment to what could be called the Holy Trinity of planning: economic efficiency, environmental sustainability, and equity. But, despite the rhetoric, efficiency very much dominated the other two during the 1990s. We need a more even balance between the three. If we are to have good urban environments in the twenty-first century, governments need to deal with the pressures and opportunities of globalisation while maintaining a concern with decent levels of public services and environmental protection, rather than using globalisation as a pretext for surrendering to market forces and the interests of international big business.

Environmental sustainability and urban consolidation

From the 1980s onwards, successive state governments, led by New South Wales, adopted urban consolidation as a key element in urban planning policy. The Commonwealth government's Better Cities program followed suit in the 1990s. At its simplest, urban consolidation involves attempting to reduce the rate of suburban expansion by:

- housing more people in the existing built up area
- reducing the average size of new housing allotments on the urban fringe.

Aspects of urban consolidation policy have been discussed in relation to the journey to work (chapter 3), housing (chapter 4), and environmental sustainability (chapter 7). But the policy was adopted originally in the hope of reducing expenditure on new physical and human services. Supporters argued that following many years of population decline in the inner and middle suburbs, services such as schools were underused. If more people could be housed in those existing areas, governments could avoid having to provide new services on the urban fringe. A number of studies in the major cities estimated that building houses within the existing urban area instead of opening up new suburbs on the fringe could produce major cost savings per dwelling. For state governments facing cuts in Commonwealth funding and severe restrictions on their ability to borrow money to pay for new infrastructure (chapter 6), the idea had obvious appeal.

As we have seen, additional claims for urban consolidation soon followed. It has been claimed to improve the *appropriateness* and *affordability* of housing. Supporters argue that increasing the number of small, medium-density dwellings will diversify the housing stock to match the increasingly diverse structure of households in Australian cities, and that putting more dwellings on a given area of land will reduce the cost of housing. Consolidation has, of course, been claimed as essential to improving environmental sustainability. More compact cities will, it is asserted, reduce our dependence on cars, and therefore our use of fossil fuels and emission of air pollutants and greenhouse gases, as well as reduce the amount of water put on gardens.

Consolidation is also claimed to produce more *equitable* cities, by reducing the locational disadvantage suffered by households living on the urban fringes far from services and facilities, and suffered by all people without access to cars. The spatial scale of residential segregation and inequality will also—as a matter of geometry—be smaller in more compact cities.

The so called *New Urbanism* movement, originating in the USA, has strong connections with urban consolidation, as does the newer American term *smart growth*. Supporters of new urbanism condemn conventional low-density suburbia as socially sterile and environmentally unsustainable, and call for a return to pre-automobile styles of neighbourhood rather like the urban villages advocated by Newman and Kenworthy (chapter 7). New urbanism neighbourhoods are envisaged as containing a housing stock with a range of prices and densities, plus local shops and services within walking distance and some local employment opportunities. Streets would be laid out to encourage walking and cycling rather than cars. Neighbourhoods would be connected to one another and to the city centre by public transport.

Urban consolidation sounds almost like a magic elixir: the cure for all known urban diseases. But can it live up to its promises or is it, as some critics claim, more akin to snake oil? Outright opponents such as Troy (1996) cast doubts on the savings in the cost of providing new services, pointing out that many services in the older suburbs are obsolete and would themselves need major expenditure to allow them to handle rising demand. They counter the claims about housing appropriateness by pointing out that small households still express a strong preference for conventional housing (chapter 5). They also dismiss the claim that urban consolidation improves affordability, by citing the high prices charged by developers for medium-density housing in the inner and middle suburbs.

Critics also deny that more compact cities will necessarily be more equitable, arguing that if consolidation involves restricting development at the urban fringe, it will inevitably cause property values in established suburbs to rise. This will, if anything, force *more* low-income households into the outer suburbs, where they will have smaller dwellings with less private space, and with poorer public services because of cuts in public expenditure. And as discussed more fully in chapter 7, Troy and others also reject the proposition that urban consolidation is necessary for ecological sustainability, and regard urban village or new urbanism ideas as naive and idealistic. Infill developments consisting of large houses crammed onto small blocks, with no back yards for recreation or children's play, also raise questions of social sustainability and health in a society where child obesity is causing increasing concern.

Other participants in the urban consolidation debate simply doubt whether the policies can have a significant impact on the rate of suburban expansion. Consolidation policies so far have involved:

- *infill*—the development of vacant sites in the existing urban area (figures 5.5 and 7.3, pp. 114 & 177)
- *conversion* of buildings from non-residential to residential use (figure 5.3, p. 113)
- *dual occupancy*—permitting landowners to subdivide an existing dwelling or block to produce two dwellings (figure 5.9, p. 118)
- *smaller blocks on the fringe*—incorporating a proportion of smaller villa (figure 4.3, p. 84) and courtyard blocks in new residential developments such as Golden Grove in Adelaide.

These policies have their merits, but they make little difference to the overall distribution of population. Between 1981 and 1991 a major infill program accomplished a 20 per cent increase in the number of dwellings in the inner Adelaide suburb of Hindmarsh, but because of falling occupancy rates the population only rose by 6 per cent—a total of 500 people in ten years. During the same period the population of Salisbury in the low-density outer northern suburbs was increasing by 2000 people *per year*. There are also only so many opportunities within the existing cities for infill development or conversion of non-residential property, and some of those have major problems of industrial contamination.

McLoughlin (1991) has also pointed out that smaller residential blocks will not, on their own, significantly reduce the rate of urban expansion because of the large proportion of land taken up by roads, schools, recreation parks, shopping centres, and other uses. As a result, even major reductions in block sizes will only reduce the spread of suburbia by a few hundred metres. In the absence of what Bunker (1986) called 'heroic measures' such as massive estates of high-rise flats and severe reductions in the amount of open space, urban consolidation seems unlikely to transform our cities.

Consolidation, therefore, is not likely to be the answer to all our urban problems. That is not to say that individual consolidation projects are worthless. The increasing supply of medium-density dwellings in our inner suburbs and on the urban fringe in developments like Golden Grove has usefully widened the range of housing choice for smaller households. Redevelopment projects like East Perth, Southbank–Docklands, and Ultimo–Pyrmont have brought life and prosperity back to some old industrial areas after decades of decline and neglect. Many infill developments do add to the available housing stock in accessible locations, while saving some infrastructure costs compared with fringe development. But impacts on housing affordability, equity, and environmental sustainability will depend on the precise nature of each development, and that is how they should be judged—on their individual merits. Urban consolidation as such does not guarantee better urban environments.

Despite urban growth boundaries and the commitment to more compact cities, a significant amount of new urban development over the next twenty to thirty years will still be in the form of new suburbs on the urban fringe. The Melbourne strategy estimates that over 30 per cent of the new dwellings built by 2030 will be on fringe 'greenfield' sites. And the housing most of us will be living in twenty years from now is already built. The most important questions therefore concern the nature of conventional suburbs. Will governments succeed in encouraging a more sustainable suburban structure of housing, jobs, and transport systems, perhaps incorporating some urban village ideas (chapter 7), or will they—while paying lip service in their plans to equity and sustainability—accept the market trends towards dispersed, unstructured, *post suburban* automobile dependence (chapter 3), and hope for the best?

Equity, locational disadvantage, and social exclusion

> Disadvantages can arise where people have limited access to services and recreational facilities or have poor employment, training and educational opportunities because of where they live. Locational disadvantage can reduce the quality of life for many Australians and can exacerbate other disadvantages, especially those associated with low income.

This quotation comes from the foreword to a series of reports issued in the early 1990s by the Hawke–Keating Labor government's Social Justice Research Program into Locational Disadvantage (Maher et al. 1992). Earlier, the National Housing Strategy had also identified locational disadvantage as a concern, arguing that the quality and appropriateness of housing could not be discussed without examining questions of location and accessibility.

The government's interest in locational disadvantage had a mixed reception at the time. Some geographers and planners welcomed it as a long overdue recognition of issues that have been neglected since the mid 1970s. Others, while agreeing that locational disadvantage could exacerbate inequalities based on income, feared that concentration on locational disadvantage would be at the expense of addressing the basic social inequalities that lay behind the spatial patterns. Their concern was that governments would direct resources to areas identified as disadvantaged, rather than taking the more difficult and expensive actions necessary to attack the social and economic causes of disadvantage wherever it occurred (Fincher 1991).

This initial debate was essentially about the relative importance of locational disadvantage and social inequality. Much stronger criticism emerged from the Industry Commission's (1993) *Report on Taxation and Financial Policy Impacts on Urban Settlement.* The commission claimed to identify 'general perceptions' that the outer suburbs of Australian cities contain large numbers of low-income households—particularly first-home buyers—suffering from locational disadvantage because they are unable to afford housing in more accessible suburbs. The commission dismissed these perceptions as 'myths', arguing that the Housing and Location Choice (HALCS) surveys carried out for the National Housing Strategy had found that, in general, residents of the outer suburbs are happy with their lot, cheerfully accepting long journeys to work and poor accessibility to services in order to achieve the Great Australian Dream of home ownership in a suburban setting. The report also claimed that both the HALCS surveys and census data showed that first-home buyers and low-income households are distributed throughout the major cities, rather than being 'forced' to live on the fringes. The outer suburbs, the report concluded, contain a diverse mixture of household types and incomes, and to suggest that they were disadvantaged would do great injustice, for example, to the many low-income people still living in much worse housing in the inner suburbs.

The Industry Commission Report and the HALCS results were eagerly seized upon by opponents of urban consolidation, aided by media headlines such as 'Survey Debunks Ownership Myth', 'Poorer Families not Fringe Dwellers', 'People Happy in Nappy Valley', and 'Roof Falls in on Urban Policy' (Badcock 1994). In any case, questions of locational disadvantage attracted less political interest in the last years of the Keating government and, together with the overall issue of social polarisation discussed in chapter 5, disappeared from the federal policy agenda altogether with the election of the Howard Coalition government in 1996.

But the equity issues raised by the locational disadvantage debate remain relevant today, particularly given continuing concern about the uneven impact on our cities of global restructuring. So, how valid are the Industry Commission's findings? They were based largely on taking survey responses and census data from all the outer suburbs—rich and poor—in each city, and averaging out the results. Yet no one has ever seriously said—or believed—that *all* low-income households live in the outer suburbs, or that the outer suburbs consist largely of low-income 'deprived' households and marginal first-time home buyers forced there against their will. What matters is that *some* outer and fringe suburbs undeniably do contain significant numbers of low-income households—more than in the inner city—and that their numbers are rising (chapter 5). The inner suburbs still have the highest *percentages* of low-income households. They also contain a lot of the very worst housing conditions and the very worst poverty. But the outer and fringe suburbs contain *in absolute numbers* more low-income households than the inner and core suburbs. Also, because outer suburban households are larger, low-income *people*—and especially their children—outnumber those in the inner suburbs to an even greater extent. Moreover both the absolute numbers and percentages of low-income households are falling in the inner suburbs and increasing in the outer and fringe areas.

Of course people living in the outer suburbs are not *all* permanently deprived through locational disadvantage. Some very wealthy people choose to live in fringe locations such as the Adelaide Hills or the Dandenongs. But other outer suburbs in each city do contain significant numbers of households on low incomes. Whether renting or buying their housing, their choice of alternative locations is very limited (chapter 4) and many do suffer locational disadvantage. As discussed in chapter 5 (see figure 5.16), there is evidence that spatial inequality is increasing in Australian cities because of the uneven impact of global economic restructuring, combined with demographic changes and reductions in government expenditure on urban services (chapter 6). In that case, residents of low-income outer suburbs will become even more vulnerable. Their claim for better access to services and jobs does not deserve to become a casualty in the war of words between supporters and opponents of urban consolidation.

Social exclusion

Locational disadvantage is but one component of a complex problem. The disadvantage faced by people living in the poorest areas of our cities is multifaceted in nature. Low incomes through lack of employment is the central issue. But that is then compounded by inaccessibility, poor housing, poor health, crime, drug abuse, lack of education, and so on. Stigmatisation and marginalisation are also, as suggested in figure 5.16, key mechanisms for perpetuating the problems of disadvantaged areas. Living in such areas means that people tend to be locked out of opportunities. Which is why they tend to benefit last—if at all—from overall improvements in the economy.

Some American writers have applied the term *underclass* to people who have become permanently disconnected from participation in the formal economy, and survive on a mixture of welfare, charity, casual employment, drug dealing, and other forms of crime. But the term has been widely criticised because it was taken to imply that these people—mainly Black single parent households—were somehow unfit to participate in mainstream society because of a breakdown in moral standards. In Europe, the term commonly adopted was the *socially excluded*. It originated in France, and may have changed meaning slightly in translation, but it appealed strongly to both academic researchers and politicians. (One suggested reason for the concept's appeal within the European Union was its relativism and its vagueness, compared with concrete measures of, for example, minimum incomes, which the member countries could never agree upon.) Social exclusion picked up the notion of marginalisation, while not 'blaming the victims' in the way 'underclass' did. People were being excluded from opportunity by social, political, or economic *processes*, not by their own shortcomings. So multiple disadvantage in British cities is now increasingly referred to as social exclusion. And the appropriate policy response—clearly—is to identify and attack the causal processes so that social *inclusion* is developed instead.

When the Blair Labour government came to power in the UK in 1997, one of its first acts was to set up a Social Exclusion Unit reporting directly to the Prime Minister. The Unit defined social exclusion as 'what can happen when people or areas suffer from a combination of linked problems such as unemployment, poor skills, low incomes, poor housing, high crime environments, bad health, and family breakdown' (UK Social Exclusion Unit 2000).

The Social Exclusion Unit sought to reduce social exclusion by producing 'joined up solutions to joined up problems'. The Unit was staffed by people from central government, local government, business, and the voluntary sector, across the areas of housing, education, law enforcement, health, and so on. Some of the Unit's work did not relate to disadvantaged areas or regions, but to general problems such as truancy and exclusion from schools, homelessness, teenage pregnancy, and 16–18 year-olds not in education, training, or employment. But a key element was to produce a National Strategy for Neighbourhood Renewal to tackle the worst spatial concentrations of disadvantage in the country—many of them older public housing estates.

The UK Neighbourhood Renewal Strategy is based on coordinated action on four fronts:

- *reviving local economies*—job creation, supporting local business, skills training, access to information technology, tackling the transition from welfare to work
- *reviving communities*—tackling crime and vandalism, reforming public housing allocation policies, preventing abandonment of dwellings, promoting local sport and the arts, developing local leadership and community involvement
- *ensuring decent services*—setting targets for core public-service standards (schools, police, health) supported by special funding, support for families and young people, bringing shops back into areas, improving access to financial services

- *leadership and joint working*—providing leadership from central government, building local strategic partnerships, encouraging neighbourhood management, getting businesses involved.

A target was set in January 2001 that within ten to twenty years no one in the UK should be seriously disadvantaged by where they live. Benchmarks have been set for measuring progress towards reducing the gap between disadvantaged areas and national average levels of unemployment, educational attainment, crime rates, morbidity, and mortality.

A key concept within the neighbourhood renewal approach to tackling social exclusion is *Social Capital*, defined as the contact, trust, and solidarity that enables residents to help, rather than fear, each other (Winter 2000). The erosion of social capital is seen as a major part of social exclusion. The theory is that in communities that are working well, there is a high level of interaction and participation in common activities, which in turn breeds trust and a sense of mutual support and obligation. You feel that you can depend on others for help and support, and in turn they can depend on you. People provide a resource for each other—hence the term 'social capital'. Some researchers argue that people living in areas with a good level of social capital are happier, healthier, more likely to find work when they need it, and suffer lower levels of local crime.

An element of social exclusion theory is that in excluded areas social capital has been eroded, and people no longer trust or support each other. This erosion is blamed on things like public housing allocation policies that concentrate the most severely disadvantaged households together; high turn-over rates that mean neighbours do not get a chance to know one another; unchecked levels of local crime and vandalism; and loss of faith in local services and local political institutions. Rebuilding social capital is therefore seen as a key element in reviving communities to build social inclusion.

Although the social exclusion approach has developed most strongly in the UK, the terminology is in increasing use in Australia, especially when discussing the redevelopment of public housing areas (Randolph & Judd 1999). In South Australia the Labor opposition adopted the UK social exclusion approach, and announced a Social Inclusion initiative as part of its policy platform for the 2002 state election. Following Labor's narrow electoral victory a Social Inclusion Unit was established, though its main activities so far have concentrated on general issues such as homelessness, low school retention rates, and drug abuse, rather than neighbourhood redevelopment.

The UK Social Exclusion program set up targets for outcomes over ten to twenty years, so it is obviously too early to judge the success of the approaches. Critics see the idea as either fruitless social engineering or the re-badging of existing policies. But the approach does recognise the 'joined up', complex nature of the problems and processes, and appreciates that broad economic policies alone will not trickle down far enough to help the most disadvantaged residents of our cities. Social inclusion programs do involve all levels and branches of government, together with business and voluntary community organisations. However a key issue will be the amount of hard cash committed to improving local services, re-training workers, fighting crime, and improving housing conditions. Without adequate resources, social inclusion is likely to become just another failed slogan.

Conclusion: Transition, continuity, and public policy

This book has attempted to examine some major issues in the complex and ever-changing geography of Australia's major cities. I hope it has convinced readers that the geography of our cities *matters*. The spatial structure of employment and the journey to work, the density and location of housing, patterns of residential differentiation, and the spatial organisation of urban government shape how we live. If they change, our lives change.

The future development and character of Australian cities will mainly be determined by the forces of economic restructuring, demographic change, and technological development discussed in earlier chapters. But, as also emphasised in those chapters, we do have some choices. The debates over policy issues such as social exclusion, urban consolidation and urban structure, the consequences of globalisation, and approaches to environmental sustainability reflect a range of visions concerning desirable futures.

As Peel (1995) points out, urban planning has always tended to identify the 'bad city' it wishes to avoid more clearly than the 'good city' that should be created in its place. He argues that Los Angeles has become the image of the 'bad city' we now wish to avoid: sprawling, car-dependent, polluted, and socially polarised. As this chapter has discussed, we are not clear what we should aspire to instead. But, whatever policy we pursue, we can be sure that it will involve conflicts. Figure 7.11, which summarises the conflicts between equity, efficiency, and environmental protection that arise when pursuing the goal of environmental sustainability, closely resembles Stilwell's 'three-way squeeze' model of the relationship between urban policy and globalisation. Both in turn resemble the commitments to equity, sustainability, and efficiency found in chapter one—often on page one—of most metropolitan planning strategies. Future policies must deal with this conflict, preferably not by simply giving in to the pressure for narrowly defined economic efficiency.

Whichever policies we decide to pursue, however, their impacts will be limited by the heritage of the past as well as the current forces of transition and restructuring. There is an apocryphal story of a lost traveller asking for directions, and receiving the answer 'Well, I wouldn't start from here!' The problem with visions of radically different cities in the future is that we do have to start from here. As Mees (1994b) points out, Australian cities have distinctive characters, neither North American nor European, which owe a lot to their particular pasts and individual environmental settings, and are not necessarily amenable to imported planning notions. Despite the significant recent changes identified in this chapter, our cities are still huge, sprawling, decentralised, and car-dependent, and have been so for some decades. They have complex patterns of ethnic and economic segregation that have also evolved over a long period of time, despite spectacular recent phenomena such as inner-city revitalisation and master planned communities. The current debates about urban policy are often conducted in simplistic terms—Maher (1993) coined the term 'planning by slogan'. If we are to develop realistic and effective urban policies, we need to understand more clearly the unique and constantly evolving structures of our cities, and how people actually live their lives in them.

Further Reading

Chapter I Foundations

For a more detailed discussion of nineteenth-century Australian urbanisation, see McCarty, J.W. 1970, 'Australian Cities in the Nineteenth Century', *Australian Economic History Review*, vol. 10, no. 2, pp. 107–37; Jackson, R.V. 1977, *Australian Economic Development in the Nineteenth Century*, Australian National University Press, Canberra; and the new perspectives developed in Frost, L. 1991, *The New Urban Frontier*, New South Wales University Press, Sydney. Berry, M. 1984, 'The Political Economy of Australian Urbanisation', *Progress in Planning*, vol. 22, pp. 63–147, provides a valuable interpretation of the whole history of Australian urbanisation from a political economy perspective, and Berry is one of the few authors to examine the interwar period. Freestone, R. 1982, 'The Garden City Idea in Australia', *Australian Geographical Studies*, vol. 20, no. 1, pp. 24–48, discusses the early history of town planning in Australia, as do the early chapters in Hamnett, S. & Freestone, R. (eds) 2000, *The Australian Metropolis: a Planning History*, Allen & Unwin, Sydney. McCalman, J. 1984, *Struggletown*, Melbourne University Press, Melbourne, is a vivid account of life in a working-class inner suburb during the Great Depression.

A vast body of literature exists on Australian cities during the long boom. This chapter has drawn extensively upon Burnley, I.H. 1980, *The Australian Urban System: Growth, Change and Differentiation*, Longman Cheshire, Melbourne; Maher, C.A. 1982, *Australian Cities in Transition*, Shillington House, Melbourne; Logan, M.I., Whitelaw, J.S. & McKay, J. 1981, *Urbanisation: the Australian Experience*, Shillington House, Melbourne; and Neutze, M. 1977, *Urban Development in Australia: a Descriptive Analysis*, George Allen & Unwin, Sydney. Badcock, B.A. 1984, *Unfairly Structured Cities*, Blackwell, Oxford, provides a more detailed account of the debates concerning the Marxist approach to postwar urban development. Hugo, G.J. 1986, *Australia's Changing Population*, Oxford University Press, Melbourne, deals in detail with demographic trends. Alexander, I. 1981, 'Post-war metropolitan planning: goals and realities', in P.N Troy (ed.) *Equity in the City*, George Allen & Unwin, Sydney, discusses postwar city planning. Jones, M.A. 1972, *Housing and Poverty in Australia*, Melbourne University Press, Melbourne, is the standard work on the development of public housing during the long boom, and Peel, M. 1995, *Good Times, Hard Times:*

the Past and the Future in Elizabeth, Melbourne University Press, Carlton, is an excellent account of the development of an outer suburban industrial region during that time.

Allport, C. 1983, 'Women and Suburban Housing: Post-War Planning in Sydney, 1943–61', in P. Williams (ed.) *Social Process and the City: Urban Studies Yearbook 1*, George Allen & Unwin, Sydney, and Harman, E.J. 1983, 'Capitalism, Patriarchy and the City', in C. Baldock & B. Cass (eds) *Women, Social Welfare and the State in Australia*, George Allen & Unwin, Sydney, are landmark papers dealing with feminist perspectives on Australian suburbanisation. Stretton, H. 1989, *Ideas for Australian Cities*, 3rd edn, Transit Australia, Sydney, remains the most provocative book on the general nature of Australian cities in the 1970s.

The urban restructuring that followed the end of the long boom is analysed in Fagan, R.H. & Webber, M. 1994, *Global Restructuring: the Australian Experience*, Oxford University Press, Melbourne. More detailed and specifically urban analyses can be found in Daly, M.T. 1988, 'Australian Cities: the Challenge of the 1980s', *Australian Geographer*, vol. 19, no. 1, pp. 149–61; Maher, C.A. 1993, 'Recent Trends in Australian Urban Development: Locational Change and the Policy Quandary', *Urban Studies*, vol. 30, nos. 4/5, pp. 797–825. Relph, E. 1987, *The Modern Urban Landscape*, Croom Helm, London, does not specifically examine Australian cities, but provides a good general discussion of modern and post-modern city landscapes; Soja, E.W. 1989, *Postmodern Geographies*, Verso, New York, provides a more advanced and complex discussion.

Smith, N. & Williams, P. (eds) 1986, *Gentrification of the City*, Allen & Unwin, London, is the most comprehensive work on gentrification as a world-wide phenomenon in the 1970s and 1980s. Badcock, B.A. 1995, 'Building Upon the Foundations Of Gentrification: Inner City Housing Development in Australia in The 1990s', *Urban Geography*, vol. 16, no. 1, pp. 70–90, reviews the Australian experience and Logan, W.S. 1985, *The Gentrification of Inner Melbourne*, Queensland University Press, St Lucia provides a longer view.

Chapter 2 Cities in a Globalising World

O'Connor, K., Stimson, R. & Daly, M. 2001, *Australia's Changing Economic Geography: a Society Dividing?* Oxford University Press, Melbourne, discusses in detail the impact of globalisation on Australian cities and regions. Brotchie, J., Batty, M., Blakely, E., Hall, P. & Newton, P. (eds) 1995, *Cities in Competition: Productive and Sustainable Cities for the 21st Century*, Longman Australia, Melbourne, is a very useful collection of detailed papers about the implications of globalisation for cities in Australia and elsewhere. For a critical discussion of the globalisation concept see Stilwell, F.J.B. 1997, *Globalisation and Cities: an Australian Political-Economic Perspective*, Urban Research Program Working paper 59, Australian National University, Canberra. Engels, B. 2000, 'City Make-Overs: the Place Marketing of Melbourne During the Kennett Years, 1992–99', *Urban Policy and Research*, vol. 18, no. 4, pp. 469–94, analyses in retrospect the urban entrepreneurialism of the Kennett years. Hall, P. 1992, 'Cities in the Informational Economy', *Urban Futures*, Special Issue No. 5, pp. 1–12, provides an international perspective. Kelly, P. 1994, *The End of Certainty: Power, Politics and Business in Australia*, Allen & Unwin, Sydney, gives a view of overall changes in Australian society in the 1990s. For an overview of demographic trends, see Khoo, S-E. & McDonald, P. (eds) 2003, *The Transformation of Australia's Population: 1970–2030*, University of New South Wales Press, Sydney. Paris, C. 1994, 'New Patterns of Urban and Regional Development in Australia: Demographic Restructuring and Economic Change', *International Journal of Urban and Regional Research*, vol. 18, no. 4, pp. 555–72; and Mullins, P. 1993, 'Decline of the Old, Rise of the New: Late Twentieth Century Australian Urbanisation', in J.M. Najman & J.S. Western (eds) *A Sociology of Australian Society*, 2nd edn, Macmillan, Melbourne, discuss the phenomena of coastal and 'sunbelt' urbanisation. Connell, J. (ed) 2000, *Sydney: the Emergence of a World City*, Oxford University Press, Melbourne, provides a comprehensive portrait of Australia's 'global city' in its Olympic year.

On the Internet, the Commonwealth Department of Immigration and Multicultural Affairs home page at <http://www.immi.gov.au> provides a range of up-to-date information on government immigration programs, migrant intakes, and policy issues.

Chapter 3 Employment and Urban Structure

For an excellent collection of papers on economic development and employment in Australian cities today, see the special edition of *Australian Geographer*, vol. 33, no. 3, 2002, entitled '*A Contemporary Geography of Prosperity Along Australia's Eastern Seaboard*'. Probert, B. 1993, 'The Overworked and the Out-of-Work: Redistributing Paid Work, Unpaid Work and Free Time', *Policy Issues Forum*, Autumn, pp. 31–6, covers the increasing diversity of labour force participation. Newton, P.W. & Wulff, M.G. 1999, 'Working at Home: Emerging Trends and Spatial Implications', in *Houses and Jobs in Cities and Regions: Research in Honour of Chris Maher*, ed. K. O'Connor, University of Queensland Press, Brisbane, pp. 237–46, critically examine the 'working at home' question. The 'new urban structure' and the journey to work are discussed by Brotchie, J. 1992, 'The Changing Structure of Cities', *Urban Futures*, Special Issue No. 5, pp. 13–26; Hall, P. 1992, 'Cities in the Informational Economy', *Urban Futures*, Special Issue No. 5, pp. 1–12; Forster, C.A. 1999, 'Sustainability and the Journey to Work' in *Houses and Jobs in Cities and Regions: Research in Honour of Chris Maher*, ed. K. O'Connor, University of Queensland Press, Brisbane, pp. 213–22; and in Brotchie, J., Batty, M., Blakely, E., Hall, P. & Newton, P. (eds) 1995, *Cities in Competition: Productive and Sustainable Cities for the 21st Century*, Longman Australia, Melbourne. Freestone, R. & Murphy, P. 1998, 'Metropolitan Restructuring and Suburban Employment Centers: Cross-Cultural Perspectives on the Australian Experience', *Journal of the American Planning Association*, vol. 64, no. 3, pp. 286–97, provide an incisive and sceptical examination of the relevance to Australia of the ideas put forward in Garreau, J. 1991, *Edge City: Life on the New Frontier*, Doubleday, New York.

On the Internet, the Western Sydney Regional Organisation of Councils website <http://www.wsroc.com.au> provides useful local perspectives on the issues covered in this chapter, and the Australian Bureau of Statistics home page: <http://www.abs.gov.au> provides access to a wealth of up-to-date statistical data.

Chapter 4 Housing Questions

Badcock, B.A. & Beer, A. 2000, *Home Truths: Residential Property and Home Ownership in Australia*, Melbourne University Press, Melbourne, provides a comprehensive overview of housing affordability in Australia and the future of the Great Australian Dream. For a concise, critical review of overall changes in housing policy in the 1990s, see Yates, J. 1997, 'Changing Directions in Australian Housing Policies: The End of Muddling Through?', *Housing Studies*, vol. 12, no. 2, pp. 265–77. For a discussion of the future of public housing see Badcock, B.A. 1999, 'Doing More With Less: Public Housing in the 1990s', in *Houses and Jobs in Cities and Regions: Research in Honour of Chris Maher*, ed. K. O'Connor, University of Queensland Press, Brisbane, pp. 81–95. Issues arising from the redevelopment of public housing estates are examined in Hoatson, L. & Grace, M. 2002, 'Public Housing Redevelopment: Opportunity for Community Regeneration', *Urban Policy and Research*, vol. 20, no. 4, pp. 429–41; Arthurson, K. 1998, 'Redevelopment of Public Housing Estates: the Australian Experience', *Urban Policy and Research*, vol. 16, no. 1, pp. 33–46; and Randolph, B. & Judd, B. 2000, 'Community Renewal and Large Public Housing Estates', *Urban Policy and Research*, vol. 18, no. 1, pp. 77–104.

The classic paper on the family life cycle and its weaknesses is Stapleton, C.M. 1980, 'Reformulation of the Family Life-Cycle Concept: Implications for Residential Mobility', *Environment and Planning A*, vol. 12, no. 10, pp. 1103–18. See Watson, S. 1988, *Accommodating Inequality*, Allen & Unwin, Sydney, for a feminist perspective on housing issues. Maher, C.A. 1995, 'Housing Need and Residential Mobility: The Mismatch Debate in Perspective', *Urban Policy and Research*, vol. 13, no. 1, pp. 7–19, critically evaluates the assertion that there is a mismatch between housing needs and the Australian housing stock. Paris, C. 1997, 'Reflections on Community Housing in Australia', *Urban Policy and Research*, vol. 15, no. 1, pp. 7–18, reviews the growth of the community housing sector. The 2001 census social atlases produced by the ABS for each major city should be consulted for detailed pictures of spatial variation in the character of households and housing.

An indispensable starting point for Internet research is the Australian Housing and Urban Research Institute home page: <http://www.ahuri.edu.au>, which gives access to current research findings on a wide range of housing issues. See also the National Community Housing Forum: <http://www.nchf.org.au>.

Chapter 5 The Residential Mosaic

Stimson, R.J. 1982, *The Australian City: a Welfare Geography*, Longman Cheshire, Melbourne, provides a detailed summary of research on residential differentiation in Australian cities in the 1970s. Stilwell, F.J.B. 1989, 'Structural Change and Spatial Equity in Sydney', *Urban Policy and Research*, vol. 7, no. 1, pp. 3–14 and Forster, C.A.

1991, 'Restructuring and Residential Differentiation: Has Adelaide Become a More Unequal City?', *South Australian Geographical Journal*, vol. 91, pp. 46–60, discuss changes in socioeconomic patterns in the 1980s. Badcock, B.A. 1997, 'Recently Observed Polarising Tendencies and Australian Cities', *Australian Geographical Studies*, vol. 35, no. 3, pp. 243–59; and Baum, S. 1997, 'Sydney, Australia: A Global City? Testing the Social Polarisation Thesis', *Urban Studies*, vol. 34, no. 11, pp. 1881–901, expand on recent debates concerning globalisation and social polarisation. For a useful set of papers exploring gender-related aspects of polarisation, see Gibson, K., Huxley, M., Cameron, J., Costello, L., Fincher, R., Jacobs, J., Jamieson, N., Johnson, L. & Pulvirenti, M. 1996, *Restructuring Difference: Social Polarisation and the City*, Working Paper 6, Australian Housing and Urban Research Institute, Melbourne. Latham, M. 2003, *From the Suburbs: Building a Nation From Our Neighbourhoods*, Pluto Press, Annandale, provides an optimistic view about the changing nature of differentiation in our suburbs. For a less sanguine perspective, see Gleeson, B. 2003. 'What's Driving Suburban Australia?' *Griffith Review*, Summer 2003–4, pp. 55–71.

For contrasting views about the extent and significance of inner-city revitalisation in Australia, see Reynolds, J. & Porter, L. 1998, 'Melbourne's Inner City Revival', *Urban Policy and Research*, vol. 16, no. 2, pp. 63–8 and O'Connor, K. 1998, 'Understanding Metropolitan Melbourne…Without Being Confused by Coffee and Doughnuts', *Urban Policy and Research*, vol. 16, no. 1, pp. 139–45.

Burnley, I. H. 2001, *The Impact of Immigration on Australia: a Demographic Approach*, Oxford University Press, Melbourne, provides a comprehensive overview of immigration and ethnicity in Australian cities. Dunn, K.M. 1998, 'Rethinking Ethnic Concentration: The Case of Cabramatta, Sydney', *Urban Studies*, vol. 35, no. 3, pp. 503–27, is an informative case study employing new cultural perspectives on ethnic segregation. For a controversial view on recent trends in Sydney, see Healy, E. & Birrell, B. 2003, 'Metropolis Divided: the Political Dynamic of Spatial Inequality and Migrant Settlement in Sydney', *People and Place*, vol. 11, no. 2, pp. 65–87.

The various ABS 2001 census social atlases are again indispensable sources of basic information on patterns of residential differentiation in individual cities. The individual state volumes of the *Atlas of the Australian People* contain comprehensive discussions of patterns of ethnic segregation based on the 1996 census.

Chapter 6 Governing the Cities

For a useful collection of papers relevant to the government of Australian cities see Dollery, B. & Marshall, N. (eds) 1997, *Australian Local Government: Reform and Renewal*, Macmillan Education Australia, Melbourne. For a thorough discussion of theoretical issues in public service provision see Pinch, S. 1997, *Worlds of Welfare*, Routledge, London. Hayward, D. 1993, 'Dual Politics in a Three Tiered State', *Urban Policy and Research*, vol. 11, no. 3, pp. 166–81, provides a specifically Australian perspective.

Jones, M.A. 1993, *Transforming Australian Local Government*, George Allen & Unwin, Sydney, provides a detailed analysis of local government in Australia, and argues against policies of rationalisation and amalgamation. The case for local government amalgamations is also questioned in Byrnes, J. & Dollery, B. 2002, 'Do Economies of Scale Exist in Australian Local Government? A Review of the Research Evidence', *Urban Policy and Research*, vol. 20, no. 4, pp. 391–414. Mowbray, M. 1997, 'Intellectuals and the Local State: The Australian Local Government Literature', *Urban Policy and Research*, vol. 15, no. 4, pp. 247–58, reviews a range of recent writing on local government. See *Urban Policy and Research*, vol. 15, no. 1, 1997, pp. 55–64 for a useful series of short papers on recent privatisation trends under the title *The Privatised City*.

The merits of local employment policies are assessed in Fagan, R.H. 1987, 'Local Employment Initiatives: Long Term Strategy for Localities or "Flavour of the Month?"' *Australian Geographer*, vol. 18, no. 1, pp. 51–6.

See Lewis, M. 1999, *Suburban Backlash: The Battle for the World's Most Liveable City*, Bloomings Books, Hawthorn, for the background to the emergence of the Save Our Suburbs groups. Costello, L.N. & Dunn, K.M. 1994, 'Resident Action Groups in Sydney: People Power or Rat-Bags?', *Australian Geographer*, vol. 25, pp. 61–76, discusses local activism in general.

For a list of available Internet links to individual local government councils, see <http://www.alga.asn.au/links/>. The Save our Suburbs home page is at <http://www.sos.org.au/>.

Chapter 7 Sustainable Cities?

The early sections of this chapter have drawn extensively from four official reports: Australian Bureau of Statistics 1996, *Australians and the Environment*, AGPS, Canberra, Cat. no. 4601.0; Australian Urban and Regional Development Review 1995, *Green Cities*, Strategy paper #3, Department of Housing and Regional Development, Canberra; Australia, Department of the Environment, Sport and Territories 1996, *Australia: State of the Environment*, CSIRO, Melbourne; and Australian State of the Environment Committee 2001, *Australia State of the Environment*, CSIRO Publishing on behalf of the Department of the Environment and Heritage, Canberra (see particularly the theme report *Human Settlements*).

See also Aplin, G., Mitchell, P., Cleugh, H., Pitman, A. & Rich, D. 1995, *Global Environmental Crises: an Australian Perspective*, Oxford University Press, Melbourne, and Smith, D.I. 1998, *Water in Australia: Resources and Management*, Oxford University Press, Melbourne, particularly chapter 3. For an extended discussion of urban sustainability from an international perspective, see Haughton, G. & Hunter, G. 1994, *Sustainable Cities*, Regional Studies Association, London.

The urban form debate has generated a large—and at times heated—literature. The best known statement of the case in favour of denser, less car-dependent cities is Newman, P. & Kenworthy, J. 1989, *Cities and Automobile Dependence: an International Sourcebook*, Gower, Aldershot. The arguments are presented in more concise form in Newman, P. & Kenworthy, J. 1991, 'Sustainable Settlements: Restoring the Commons', *Habitat Australia*, vol. 19, no. 4, pp. 18–21. Troy has been the most outspoken critic of consolidation in recent years. His views are summarised in Troy, P.N. 1996, *The Perils of Urban Consolidation*, Federation Press, Annandale. See also Kirwan, R. 1992, 'Urban Form, Energy and Transport: A Note on the Newman-Kenworthy Thesis', *Urban Policy and Research*, vol. 10, no. 1, pp. 6–23, and Newton, P.W. (ed.) 1997, *Re-shaping Cities for a More Sustainable Future*, Research Monograph 6, Australian Housing and Urban Research Institute, Melbourne. Brotchie, J., Batty, M., Blakely, E., Hall, P. & Newton, P. (eds) 1995, *Cities in Competition: Productive and Sustainable Cities for the 21st Century*, Longman Australia, Melbourne, parts 4 and 5, contains a range of relevant papers. Attempts to plan for a polynuclear structure in Melbourne are assessed in Logan, A. 1986, 'A Critical Examination of Melbourne's District Centre Policy', *Urban Policy and Research*, vol. 4, no. 2, pp. 2–14. Mees, P. 2000, *A Very Public Solution: Transport in the Dispersed City*, Melbourne University Press, Melbourne, argues for the viability of public transport in Australian cities.

For a discussion of immigration and environmental issues, see Burnley, I., Murphy, P & Fagan, R. 1997, *Immigration and Australian Cities*, Federation Press, Annandale, chapter 6. Kupke, V. 1996, 'Local Agenda 21: Local Councils Managing for the Future', *Urban Policy and Research*, vol. 14, no. 3, pp. 183–98 provides an assessment of progress on Local Agenda 21.

For information on environmentally sustainable housing, see Ballinger, J.A., Prasad, D.K. & Rudder, J.A. 1992, *Energy Efficient Australian Housing*, Australian Government Publishing Service, Canberra; Gow, S. 1994, 'Energy-Efficient Housing', *Australian Planner*, vol. 31, no. 4, pp. 228–35; Mills, D., Stock, E. & Lowe, I. 1998, 'Local Government, Energy Efficiency and Greenhouse Policies', *Australian Planner*, vol. 35, no. 4, pp. 12–19; and Troy, P.N., Holloway, D., Pullen, S., & Bunker, R. 2003, 'Embodied and Operational Energy Consumption in the City', *Urban Policy and Research*, vol. 21, no. 1, pp. 9–44.

The Internet contains an immense range of good—and not so good!—material on environmental sustainability. The following home pages are sound starting points: The Commonwealth Department of the Environment and Heritage: <http://www.deh.gov.au>; The Institute for Sustainable Futures: <http://www.isf.uts.edu.au>; Urban Ecology Australia: <http://www.urbanecology.org.au/index.html>. Many local government authorities are also now on the Internet, and provide details of their Local Agenda 21 programs and other environmental activities. For a list of available links to individual councils, see <http://www.alga.asn.au/links/>. For international material see the United Nations Human Settlements Programme Urban Environment Forum: <http://hq.unhabitat.org/programmes/uef/>.

Chapter 8 Urban Futures

For a comprehensive discussion of metropolitan planning and neoliberalism in Australia, see Gleeson, B. & Low, N. 2000, *Australian Urban Planning: New Challenges, New Agendas*, Allen & Unwin, Sydney; The House of Representatives Standing Committee for Long Term Strategies 1992, *Patterns of Urban Settlement:*

Consolidating the Future, AGPS, Canberra; the National Housing Strategy 1992, *National Housing Strategy: Agenda for Action*, AGPS, Canberra, and the various publications of the Australian Urban and Regional Development Review provide 'official' federal overviews of urban and housing issues under the Labor administration. The major policy debates are also summarised in non-technical language in Collins, T. 1993, *Living For The City*, ABC Books, Sydney. State planning strategies can be accessed from the web sites of the relevant state government departments. Departmental names and structures change on a regular basis but at the time of writing the following links lead to the current planning documents: New South Wales: <http://www.dipnr.nsw.gov.au/>; Victoria: <http://www.dse.vic.gov.au/dse/index.htm>; Queensland: <http://www.dlgp.qld.gov.au/>; Western Australia: <http://www.wapc.wa.gov.au/>; South Australia: <http://www.planning.sa.gov.au.>.

For a critical discussion of globalisation and urban policy see Stilwell, F.J.B. 1997, *Globalisation and Cities: an Australian Political-Economic Perspective*, Urban Research Program Working paper 59, Australian National University, Canberra. For the urban consolidation debate see the relevant section of further reading for chapter 6, plus McLoughlin, J.B. 1991, 'Urban Consolidation and Urban Sprawl: A Question of Density', *Urban Policy and Research*, vol. 9, no. 3, pp. 148–156; Troy, P.N. 1992, 'Let's Look at That Again', *Urban Policy and Research*, vol. 10, no. 1, pp. 41–9 and Troy, P.N. 1992, 'The New Feudalism,' *Urban Futures*, vol. 2, no. 2, pp. 36–44.

For a comprehensive discussion of disadvantage in Australia see Fincher, R. & Saunders, P. 2001, *Creating Unequal Futures: Rethinking Poverty, Inequality and Disadvantage*, Allen & Unwin, Crows Nest, NSW. The debate about locational disadvantage is summarised in a collection of short papers in *Urban Policy and Research*, 12, no. 3, 1994, pp. 180–99 entitled *Locational Disadvantage and Spatial Inequality: New Perspectives on an Old Debate*. The following papers provide a useful introduction to social exclusion/inclusion and social capital concepts and policies: Cox, E. 1999, 'Can Social Capital Make Societies More Civil?', *Australian Planner*, vol. 36, no. 2, pp. 75–87; Hague, E, Thomas, C & Williams, S. 1999, 'Left Out? Observations on the RGS-IBG Conference on Social Exclusion and the City', *Area*, vol. 31, no. 3, pp. 293–6; Taylor, M. 1998, 'Combating the Social Exclusion of Housing Estates', *Housing Studies*, vol. 13, no. 6, pp. 819–32; Winter, I.(ed) 2000, *Social Capital and Public Policy in Australia*, Australian Institute of Family Studies, Melbourne. See also the UK Social Exclusion Unit website at <http://www.socialexclusionunit.gov.uk/>, and the South Australian Social Inclusion Initiative website at <http://www.socialinclusion.sa.gov.au/>

Troy, P.N. (ed.) 1995, *Australian Cities: Issues, Strategies and Policies for Urban Australia in the 1990s*, Cambridge University Press, Melbourne, provides a useful collection of papers dealing with a range of urban policy debates. Finally, some comparative perspectives on Australian urban trends and issues can be gained from sampling Pacione, M. (ed.) 1997, *Britain's Cities: Geographies of Division in Urban Britain*, Routledge, London; and Bourne, L.S. & Ley, D.F. (eds) 1993, *The Changing Social Geography of Canadian Cities*, McGill-Queen's University Press, Montreal & Kingston.

Bibliography

ABS. *See* Australian Bureau of Statistics

Alexander, I. & Houghton, S. 1995, 'New Investment in Public Transport II: Evaluation of the Northern Suburbs Railway in Perth', *Australian Planner*, vol. 32, no. 2, pp. 82–7.

Aplin, G., Mitchell, P., Cleugh, H., Pitman, A., & Rich, D. 1995, *Global Environmental Crises: an Australian Perspective*, Oxford University Press, Melbourne.

Arthurson, K. 1998, 'Redevelopment of Public Housing Estates: The Australian Experience', *Urban Policy and Research*, vol. 16, no. 1, pp. 33–46.

——2002, 'Creating Inclusive Communities Through Balancing Social Mix: A Critical Relationship or Tenuous Link?', *Urban Policy and Research*, vol. 20, no. 3, pp. 245–61.

Australia, Department of the Environment, Sport and Territories 1996, *Australia: State of the Environment*, CSIRO, Melbourne.

Australia, Department of Immigration and Multicultural and Indigenous Affairs 2003, *Statistical Tables* <http://www.immi.gov.au/statistics/statistics/statistics_menu_main.htm>, 24 February 2004.

Australian Bureau of Statistics 1999, *Environmental Issues: People's Views and Practices*, AGPS, Canberra, Cat. no. 4602.0.

——2001, *Building Approvals, Australia*, AGPS, Canberra, Cat. no. 8731.0.

——2002, *Wage and Salary Earners, Australia*, December Quarter 2001, AGPS Canberra, Cat. no. 6248.0.

——2003a, *Building Approvals: September 2003* (various states), AGPS, Canberra, Cat. no. 8731.1–5.

——2003b, Government Finance Statistics, Australia 2001–02, AGPS Canberra, Cat. no. 5512.0.

——2003c, *Australian Demographic Statistics* (time series spreadsheet) Cat. no. 3101.0.

——2003d, *Year Book Australia*, 2003, AGPS Canberra, Cat. no. 1301.0.

Australian State of the Environment Committee 2001, *Australia State of the Environment*, CSIRO Publishing on behalf of the Department of the Environment and Heritage, Canberra.

Australian Urban and Regional Development Review 1995, *Green Cities*, Strategy paper #3, Department of Housing and Regional Development, Canberra.

Badcock, B.A. 1984, *Unfairly Structured Cities*, Blackwell, Oxford.

——1994, 'Stressed-Out Communities: Out-of-Sight, Out-of-Mind', *Urban Policy and Research*, vol. 12, no. 2, pp. 191–7.

——1997, 'Recently Observed Polarising Tendencies and Australian Cities', *Australian Geographical Studies*, vol. 35, no. 3, pp. 243–59.

Badcock, B.A. & Beer, A. 2000, *Home Truths: Residential Property and Home Ownership in Australia*, Melbourne University Press, Melbourne.

Beer, A. 1993, '"A Dream Won, a Crisis Born?" Home Ownership and the Housing Market', in C. Paris, *Housing Australia*, Macmillan, Melbourne.

Bell, D. 1973, *The Coming of Post-Industrial Society*, Basic Books, New York.

Berry, M. 1984, 'The Political Economy of Australian Urbanisation', *Progress in Planning*, vol. 22, pp. 63–147.

——2003, 'Why it is Important to Boost the Supply of Affordable Housing in Australia—And How Can We Do it?', *Urban Policy and Research*, vol. 21, no. 4, pp. 413–35.

Bickl, M. 1997, Young People and Accessibility in Suburbia, BA thesis, Flinders University.

Bourne, L.S. 1993, 'The Demise of Gentrification? A Commentary and Prospective View', *Urban Geography*, vol. 14, no. 1, pp. 95–107.

Bray, J.R. & Mudd, W. 1998, *The Contribution of DSS Payments to Regional Income*, Department of Social Security Technical Paper No. 2, Canberra.

Brotchie, J. 1992, 'The Changing Structure of Cities', *Urban Futures*, Special Issue no. 5, pp. 13–26.

Brotchie, J., Batty, M., Blakely, E., Hall, P. & Newton, P. (eds) 1995, *Cities in Competition: Productive and Sustainable Cities for the 21st Century*, Longman Australia, Melbourne.

Bunker, R. 1986, 'Heroic Measures: Urban Consolidation in Australia', in J.B. McLoughlin & M. Huxley (eds), *Urban Planning in Australia: Critical Readings*, Longman Cheshire, Melbourne.

Burnley, I., Murphy, P & Fagan, R. 1997, *Immigration and Australian Cities*, Federation Press, Annandale.

Burnley, I.H. 1974, 'The Urbanisation of the Australian Population 1947–1971', in I.H. Burnley (ed.), *Urbanisation in Australia: The Post-War Experience*, Cambridge University Press, London.

Burnley, I.H. 1980, *The Australian Urban System: Growth, Change and Differentiation*, Longman Cheshire, Melbourne.

Campbell, S. 1996, 'Green Cities, Growing Cities, Just Cities? Urban Planning and the Contradictions of Sustainable Development', *Journal of the American Planning Association*, vol. 62, no. 3, pp. 296–312.

Cannon, M. 1975, *Life in the Cities: Australia in the Victorian Age: 3*, Nelson, Melbourne.

Castells, M. 1989, *The Informational City*, Blackwell, Oxford.

Collins, T. 1993, *Living for the City*, ABC Books, Sydney.

Connell, J. (ed) 2000, *Sydney: the Emergence of a World City*, Oxford University Press, Melbourne.

Daly, M.T. 1988, 'Australian Cities: The Challenge of the 1980s', *Australian Geographer*, vol.19, no. 1, pp. 149–61.

Daly, M.T., O'Connor, K. & Stimson, R.J. 1993, 'The Restructuring of Space Economies in Australian States and Metropolitan Cities', *Conference Papers, 13th Meeting of the Pacific Regional Science Conference Organisation*, Whistler, B.C., Canada.

Davidson, J. (ed.) 1986, *The Sydney–Melbourne Book*, George Allen & Unwin, Sydney.

Dowling, R., Gollner, A. & O'Dwyer, B. 1999, 'A Gender Perspective on Urban Car Use: A Qualitative Case Study', *Urban Policy and Research*, vol. 17, no. 2, pp. 101–10.

Dunn, K.M. 1993, 'The Vietnamese Concentration in Cabramatta: Site of Avoidance and Deprivation or Island of Adjustment and Participation?', *Australian Geographical Studies*, vol. 31, no. 2, pp. 228–45.

Engels, F. 1962, *The Condition of the Working Class in England in 1844*, George Allen & Unwin, London.

Fagan, R.H. & Webber, M. 1994, *Global Restructuring: the Australian Experience*, Oxford University Press, Melbourne.

Fincher, R. 1989, 'Class and Gender Relations in the Local Labor Market and the Local State', in J. Wolch & M. Dear (eds), *The Power of Geography: How Territory Shapes Social Life*, Unwin Hyman, Boston.

——1991, 'Locational Disadvantage: An Appropriate Policy Response to Urban Inequities?', *Australian Geographer*, vol. 22, no. 2, pp. 132–5.

Forster, C.A. 1991, 'Restructuring and Residential Differentiation: Has Adelaide Become a More Unequal City?', *South Australian Geographical Journal*, vol. 91, pp. 46–60.

Freestone, R. 1982, 'The Garden City Idea in Australia', *Australian Geographical Studies*, vol. 20, no. 1, pp. 24–48.

——1993, 'Heritage, Urban Planning, and the Postmodern City', *Australian Geographer*, vol. 24, no. 1, pp. 17–23.

——1996, 'The making of an Australian Technoburb', *Australian Geographical Studies*, vol. 34, no. 1, pp. 18–31.

Freestone, R. & Murphy, P. 1993, 'Review of a Debate: *Edge City*', *Urban Policy and Research*, vol. 11, no. 3, pp.184–9.

——1998, 'Metropolitan Restructuring and Suburban Employment Centers: Cross-Cultural Perspectives on the Australian Experience', *American Planning Association Journal*, vol. 64, no. 3, pp. 286–97.

Frost, L. 1990, *Australian Cities in Comparative View*, McPhee Gribble, Ringwood.

Garreau, J. 1991, *Edge City: Life on the New Frontier*, Doubleday, New York.

Giradet, H. 2003, *Creating a Sustainable Adelaide*, Department of the Premier and Cabinet, Adelaide.

Gleeson, B. 2003. 'What's Driving Suburban Australia?', *Griffith Review*, Summer 2003–4, pp. 55–71.

Gleeson, B. & Low, N. 2000, *Australian Urban Planning: New Challenges, New Agendas*, Allen & Unwin, Sydney.

Gordon, P., Richardson, H.W. & Jun, M-J. 1991, 'The Commuting Paradox: Evidence From the Top Twenty', *American Planning Association Journal*, vol. 57, no. 4, pp. 416–20.

Government of South Australia 2003, *South Australia's Draft Transport Plan*, Government of South Australia, Adelaide.

Gray, F. 1975, 'Non-Explanation in Urban Geography', *Area*, vol. 7, no. 4, pp. 228–35.

Gregory, R.G. & Hunter, B. 1996, 'The Macro Economy and the Growth of Income and Employment Inequality in Australian Cities', Second Meeting of the Project Group on Distressed Areas, 25–26 January, OECD, Paris.

Gunn, M. 1998, 'A Tale of our Cities: Urban Australia, A Special Report', *The Australian*, 18 April.

Gwyther, G. 2003, 'Paradise Planned: Socio-Economic Differentiation and the Master Planned Community on Sydney's Urban Fringe', paper presented to the State of Australian Cities National Conference, Parramatta, December 2003.

Hall, P. 1992, 'Cities in the Informational Economy', *Urban Futures*, Special Issue No. 5, pp. 1–12.

——1999, 'How Cities Can be Expected to Change', *Australian Planner*, vol. 36, no. 2, pp. 66–71.

Harman, E.J. 1983, 'Capitalism, Patriarchy and the City', in C. Baldock & B. Cass (eds), *Women, Social Welfare and the State in Australia*, George Allen & Unwin, Sydney, pp. 104–29.

Hart, J. F. (ed.) 1991, *Our Changing Cities*, The Johns Hopkins University Press, Baltimore.

Hayward, D. 1997, 'The Privatised City: Urban Infrastructure Planning and Service Provision in the Era of Privatisation', *Urban Policy and Research*, vol. 15, no. 1, pp. 55–6.

Healy, E. & Birrell, B. 2003, 'Metropolis Divided: the Political Dynamic of Spatial Inequality and Migrant Settlement in Sydney', *People and Place*, vol. 11, no. 2, pp. 65–87.

Hoatson, L. & Grace, M. 2002, 'Public Housing Redevelopment: Opportunity for Community Regeneration?', *Urban Policy and Research*, vol. 20, no. 4, pp. 429–41.

Hugo, G.J. 1986, *Australia's Changing Population*, Oxford University Press, Melbourne.

——1989, *Atlas of the Australian People: South Australia*, AGPS, Canberra.

——2003, 'Changing Patterns of Population Distribution', in S-E. Khoo & P.McDonald (eds), *The Transformation of Australia's Population: 1970–2030*, University of New South Wales Press, Sydney.

Industry Commission 1993, *Taxation and Financial Policy Impacts on Urban Settlement*, Report, vol. 1, AGPS, Canberra.

Jackson, R.V. 1977, *Australian Economic Development in the Nineteenth Century*, Australian National University Press, Canberra.

Johnson, L.C. 1993, 'Text-Ured Brick: Speculations on the Cultural Production of Domestic Space', *Australian Geographical Studies*, vol. 31, no. 2, pp. 201–13.

Jones, M.A. 1989, *Managing Local Government: Leadership for the 21st Century*, Hargreen, Melbourne.

Kendig, H. & Paris, C. 1987, *Towards Fair Shares in Australian Housing*, IYSH National Committee of Non-Government Organisations, Canberra.

Kling, R., Olin, S. & Poster, M., (eds), 1991, *Postsuburban California: The Transformation of Orange County Since World War II*, University of California Press, Berkeley.

Kupke, V. 1996, 'Local Agenda 21: Local Councils Managing for the Future', *Urban Policy and Research*, vol. 14, no. 3, pp. 183–98.

Lang, J. 1992, 'Women and Transport', *Urban Policy and Research*, vol. 10, no, 4, pp. 14–25.

Latham, M. 1992, 'Liverpool in the 1990s', *Australian Planner*, vol. 30, no. 1, pp. 29–32.

——2003, *From the Suburbs: Building a Nation From Our Neighbourhoods*, Pluto Press, Annandale.

Ley, D. 1986, 'Urban Structure and Urban Restructuring', *Urban Geography*, vol. 7 no. 6, 530–5.

Lewis, M. 1999, *Suburban Backlash: The Battle for the World's Most Liveable City*, Bloomings Books, Hawthorn.

Logan, M.I. 1968, 'Work-Residence Relationships in the City', *Australian Geographical Studies*, vol. 6, no. 2, pp. 151–66.

Logan, M.I., Whitelaw, J.S. & McKay, J. 1981, *Urbanisation: The Australian Experience*, Shillington House, Melbourne.

Mackay, H. 1993, *Reinventing Australia: The Mind and Mood of Australia in the 90s*, Angus & Robertson, Sydney.

Maher, C., Whitelaw, J., McAllister, A., Francis, R., with Palmer, J., Chee, E. & Taylor, P. 1992, *Mobility and Locational Disadvantage Within Australian Cities*, Social Justice Research Project into Locational Disadvantage Report 2, AGPS, Canberra.

Maher, C.A. 1982, *Australian Cities in Transition*, Shillington House, Melbourne.

Maher, C.A. 1993, 'Recent Trends in Australian Urban Development: Locational Change and the Policy Quandary', *Urban Studies*, vol. 30, nos. 4/5, pp. 797–825.

Marcuse, P. 1993, 'What's so New About Divided Cities?', *International Journal of Urban and Regional Research*, vol. 17, no. 3, pp. 355–65.

McCarty, J.W. 1970, 'Australian Cities in the Nineteenth Century', *Australian Economic History Review*, vol. 10, no. 2, pp. 107–37.

McDonald, P. & Kippen, R. 2002, 'Scenarios for the Future Population of Sydney', *Australian Geographer*, vol. 33, no. 3, pp. 281–99.

McLoughlin, J.B. 1991, 'Urban Consolidation and Urban Sprawl: A Question of Density', *Urban Policy and Research*, vol. 9, no. 3, pp. 148–56.

McNeill, J. 1997, 'Local Government in the Australian Federal System', in *Australian Local Government: Reform and Renewal,* ed. B. Dollery & N. Marshall, Macmillan Education Australia, Melbourne, pp. 17–39.

Mees, P. 1994a, 'Too Good to be True: Are Journeys to Work Really Becoming Shorter?', *Australian Planner,* vol. 32, no. 1, pp. 4–6.

——1994b, 'Continuity and Change in Marvellous Melbourne', *Urban Futures,* vol. 3, no. 4, pp. 1–11.

——2000, *A Very Public Solution: Transport in the Dispersed City,* Melbourne University Press, Melbourne.

——2003, 'Public Transport Privatisation in Melbourne: What Went Wrong?', paper presented to the State of Australian Cities National Conference, Parramatta, December 2003.

Moriarty, P. 2002, 'Environmental Sustainability of Large Australian Cities', *Urban Policy and Research,* vol. 20, no. 3, pp. 233–44.

Mullins, P. 1993, 'Decline of the Old, Rise of the New: Late Twentieth Century Australian Urbanisation', in J.M. Najman & J.S. Western (eds), *A Sociology of Australian Society,* 2nd edn, Macmillan, Melbourne.

Murdie, R.A. 1969, *Factorial Ecology of Metropolitan Toronto 1951–61,* University of Chicago Dept. of Geography, Research Paper 116.

National Population Inquiry 1975, *Population and Australia: A Demographic Analysis and Projection, Volume One,* AGPS, Canberra.

New South Wales Department of Planning 1993, *Sydney's Future,* NSW Government, Sydney.

New South Wales Department of Planning 1995, *Cities for the 21st Century,* NSW Government, Sydney.

Newman, P. & Kenworthy, J. 1989, *Cities and Automobile Dependence: an International Sourcebook,* Gower, Aldershot.

——1992, *Winning Back the Cities,* Australian Consumers', Association and Pluto Press, Leichhardt.

Newton, P.W. (ed.) 1997, *Re-shaping Cities for a More Sustainable Future,* Research Monograph 6, Australian Housing and Urban Research Institute, Melbourne.

Newton, P.W. & Wulff, M.G. 1999, 'Working at Home: Emerging Trends and Spatial Implications', in *Houses and Jobs in Cities and Regions: Research in Honour of Chris Maher,* ed. K. O'Connor, University of Queensland Press, Brisbane, pp. 237–46.

Newton, P.W., Baum, S., Bhatia, K., Brown, S.K., Cameron, A.S., Foran, B., Grant, T., Mak, S.L., Memmott, P.C., Mitchell, V.G., Neate, K.L., Pears, A., Smith, N., Stimson, R.J., Tucker, S.N. and Yencken, D., 2001, *Human Settlements, Australia State of the Environment Report 2001 (Theme Report),* CSIRO Publishing on behalf of the Department of the Environment and Heritage, Canberra.

O'Connor, K. 1992, 'Economic Activity in Australian Cities: National and Local Trends and Policy', *Urban Futures,* Special Issue No. 5, pp. 86–95.

——1993, *The Australian Capital City Report 1993,* Centre for Population and Urban Research, Monash University, Melbourne.

——2003, 'Melbourne 2030: A Response', *Urban Policy and Research*, vol. 21, no. 2, pp. 211–15.

O'Connor, K., Stimson, R. & Daly, M. 2001, *Australia's Changing Economic Geography: a Society Dividing?*, Oxford University Press, Melbourne.

O'Connor, K & Rapson, V. 2003, 'Employment in City and Suburban Melbourne: the Changing Relationship', *People and Place*, vol. 11, no. 4, pp. 41–52.

O'Neill, P. & McGuirk, P. 2002, 'Prosperity Along Australia's Eastern Seaboard: Sydney and the Geopolitics of Urban and Economic Change', *Australian Geographer*, vol. 33, no. 3, pp. 241–61.

Paris, C. 1993, *Housing Australia*, Macmillan, Melbourne.

Parolin, B & Kamara, S. 2003, 'Spatial Patterns and Functions of Employment Centres in Metropolitan Sydney, 1981 to 1996', paper presented to the State of Australian Cities National Conference, Parramatta, December 2003.

Peel, M. 1995, 'The Urban Debate: From "Los Angeles" to the Urban Village', in P.N. Troy (ed.) *Australian Cities: Issues, Strategies and Policies for Urban Australia in the 1990s*, Cambridge University Press, Melbourne.

Pigram, J.J. 1986, *Issues in the Management of Australia's Water Resources*, Longman Cheshire, Melbourne.

Pinch, S. 1989, 'The Restructuring Thesis and the Study of Public Services', *Environment and Planning A*, vol. 21, no. 7, pp. 905–26.

Powell, D. 1993, *Out West: Perceptions of Sydney's Western Suburbs*, George Allen & Unwin, Sydney.

Rabin, J. 1974, *Soft City*, Fontana Collins, London.

Randolph, B. & Judd, B. 1999, 'Social Exclusion, Neighbourhood Renewal and Large Public Housing Estates', paper presented to the Social Policy Research Centre Conference 'Social Policy for the 21st Century: Justice and Responsibility', University of New South Wales, 21–23 July 1999.

Randolph, B. & Judd, B. 2000, 'Community Renewal and Large Public Housing Estates', *Urban Policy and Research*, vol. 18, no. 1, pp. 77–104.

Reynolds, J. 2003, personal communication, November 24.

SA Water 1997, *Annual Report 1997*, SA Water, Adelaide.

Searle, G. 1993, 'The Spatial Restructuring of Sydney's Economy, 1981–1991: Case Studies of 12 Industries/Activities', *Regional Science Association (ANZ Section), Conference Papers*, Armidale.

——1996, *Sydney as a Global City*, NSW Department of Urban Affairs and Planning, Sydney.

Short, J. 1989, 'Yuppies, Yuffies and the New Urban Order', *Transactions, Institute of British Geographers, New Series*, vol. 14, no. 2, pp.173–188.

Smith, N. & Williams, P. (eds) 1986, *Gentrification of the City*, Allen & Unwin, London.

Soja, E., Morales, R. & Wolff, G. 1983, 'Urban Restructuring: an Analysis of Social and Spatial Change in Los Angeles', *Economic Geography*, vol. 59, no. 2, pp. 195–230.

Soja, E.W. 1989, *Postmodern Geographies*, Verso, New York.

South Australia Environment Protection Authority 2003, *State of the Environment Report for South Australia 2003,* Environment Protection Authority, Adelaide.

South Australian Housing Trust 2002, *Trust in Focus 2001/2001*, South Australian Housing Trust, Adelaide.

Spearritt, P. 1978, *Sydney Since the Twenties*, Hale & Iremonger, Sydney.

Stilwell, F.J.B. 1989, 'Structural Change and Spatial Equity in Sydney', *Urban Policy and Research,* vol. 7, no. 1, pp. 3–14.

——1993, *Reshaping Australia: Urban Problems and Policies*, Pluto Press, Leichhardt.

——1997, *Globalisation and Cities: an Australian Political–Economic Perspective*, Urban Research Program Working Paper 59, Australian National University, Canberra.

Stockwell, S. 1995, 'The Brisbane Model: Considering a Unique Experiment', *Urban Policy and Research*, vol. 13, no. 2, pp. 89–96.

Stretton, H. 1989, *Ideas for Australian Cities*, (3rd edn), Transit Australia, Sydney.

——1994, 'Transport and the Structure of Australian Cities', *Australian Planner*, vol. 31, no. 3, pp. 131–6.

Troy, P.N. 1992, 'Let's Look at That Again', *Urban Policy and Research,* vol. 10, no. 1, pp. 41–9.

——1996, *The Perils of Urban Consolidation*, Federation Press, Annandale.

Troy, P.N., Holloway, D., Pullen, S., & Bunker, R. 2003, 'Embodied and Operational Energy Consumption in the City', *Urban Policy and Research*, vol. 21, no. 1, pp. 9–44.

Twopeny, R.E.N. 1883, *Town Life in Australia*, Elliot Stock, London.

United Nations Commission on Environment and Development 1987, *Our Common Future*, Oxford University Press, New York.

UK Social Exclusion Unit 2000, *National Strategy for Neighbourhood Renewal: A Framework for Consultation*, Cabinet Office, London.

Victoria, Department of Infrastructure 1998, *From Doughnut City to Cafe Society*, Department of Infrastructure, Melbourne.

——2002, *Melbourne 2030: Planning for Sustainable Growth*, Department of Infrastructure, Melbourne.

Victoria, Department of Planning and Development 1994, *Melbourne Metropolitan Strategy: A Discussion Paper*, Department of Planning and Development, Melbourne.

Victoria, Ministry for Planning 1993, *Planning a Better Future for Victorians*, Minister for Planning, Melbourne.

Walker, R.A. 1981, 'A Theory of Suburbanisation: Capitalism and the Construction of Space in the United States', in M. Dear & A.J. Scott (eds), *Urbanisation and Urban Planning in Capitalist Society*, Methuen, London.

Weber, A.F. 1963, *The Growth of Cities in the Nineteenth Century*, Cornell University Press, Ithica.

Winter, I. (ed) 2000, *Social Capital and Public Policy in Australia*, Australian Institute of Family Studies, Melbourne.

Wirth, L. 1938, 'Urbanism as a Way of Life', *American Journal of Sociology*, vol. 44, no. 1, pp. 3–24.

Wulff, M. 1997, 'Private Renter Households; Who are the Long Term Renters?', *Urban Policy and Research*, vol. 15, no. 3, pp. 203–10.

Yates, J. 1997, 'Changing Directions in Australian Housing Policies: The End of Muddling Through?', *Housing Studies*, vol. 12, no. 2, pp. 265–77.

——2000, 'Is Australia's Home Ownership Rate Really Stable? An Examination of Change Between 1975 and 1994', *Urban Studies*, vol. 37, no. 2, pp. 319–42.

Index